BEN JONSON

Macmillan Literary Lives
General Editor: Richard Dutton, Professc
University of Lancaster

This series offers stimulating accounts of the literary careers of the most admired and influential English-language authors. Volumes follow the outline of writers' working lives, not in the spirit of traditional biography, but aiming to trace the professional, publishing and social contexts which shaped their writing. The role and status of 'the author' as the creator of literary texts is a vexed issue in current critical theory, where a variety of social, linguistic and psychological approaches have challenged the old concentration on writers as specially gifted individuals. Yet reports of 'the death of the author' in literary studies are (as Mark Twain said of a premature obituary) an exaggeration. This series aims to demonstrate how an understanding of writers' careers can promote, for students and general readers alike, a more informed historical reading of their works.

A list of the titles in the series follows overleaf

Published titles

Morris Beja
JAMES JOYCE

Cedric C. Brown
JOHN MILTON

Richard Dutton
WILLIAM SHAKESPEARE

Jan Fergus
JANE AUSTEN

Kenneth Graham
HENRY JAMES

Paul Hammond
JOHN DRYDEN

W. David Kay
BEN JONSON

Mary Lago
E. M. FORSTER

Alasdair D. F. Macrae
W. B. YEATS

Joseph McMinn
JONATHAN SWIFT

Kerry McSweeney
GEORGE ELIOT (MARIAN EVANS)

John Mepham
VIRGINIA WOOLF

Michael O'Neill
PERCY BYSSHE SHELLEY

Leonée Ormond
ALFRED TENNYSON

George Parfitt
JOHN DONNE

Gerald Roberts
GERARD MANLEY HOPKINS

Felicity Rosslyn
ALEXANDER POPE

Tony Sharpe
T. S. ELIOT

Gary Waller
EDMUND SPENSER

Cedric Watts
JOSEPH CONRAD

Tom Winnifrith and Edward Chitham
CHARLOTTE AND EMILY BRONTË

John Worthen
D. H. LAWRENCE

Forthcoming titles

Ronald Ayling
SEAN O'CASEY

Deirdre Coleman
SAMUEL TAYLOR COLERIDGE

Peter Davison
GEORGE ORWELL

James Gibson
THOMAS HARDY

Philip Mallett
RUDYARD KIPLING

Ira Nadel
EZRA POUND

Angela Smith
KATHERINE MANSFIELD

Grahame Smith
CHARLES DICKENS

Janice Thaddeus
FANNY BURNEY

John Williams
WILLIAM WORDSWORTH

Barry Windeatt
GEOFFREY CHAUCER

David Wykes
EVELYN WAUGH

Ben Jonson

A Literary Life

W. David Kay

Associate Professor of English
University of Illinois at Urbana-Champaign

MACMILLAN

First published 1995 by
MACMILLAN PRESS LTD
Houndmills, Basingstoke, Hampshire RG21 2XS
and London
Companies and representatives
throughout the world

ISBN 0–333–46446–X hardcover
ISBN 0–333–46447–8 paperback

A catalogue record for this book is available
from the British Library.

10   9   8   7   6   5   4   3   2   1
04 03 02 01 00 99 98 97 96 95

Copy-edited and typeset by Povey–Edmondson
Okehampton and Rochdale, England

Printed in Great Britain by
Antony Rowe Ltd., Chippenham, Wiltshire, England

Series Standing Order (Macmillan Literary Lives)

If you would like to receive future titles in this series as they are published, you can make use of our standing order facility. To place a standing order please contact your bookseller or, in case of difficulty, write to us at the address below with your name and address and the name of the series. Please state with which title you wish to begin your standing order. (If you live outside the UK we may not have the rights for your area, in which case we will forward your order to the publisher concerned).

**Standing Order Service, Macmillan Distribution Ltd,
Houndmills, Basingstoke, Hampshire, RG21 2XS, England**

To Marilyn

Contents

Preface

Although modern estimates of Ben Jonson's art rank him decidedly below his rival and contemporary William Shakespeare, at his death in 1637 many readers considered him to be the pre-eminent English poet and playwright. The magnificent folio edition of his *Works* in 1616 had given dramatic poetry a new dignity and set a precedent followed in the Shakespeare folio of 1623. His comedies, though lacking the romantic interest of Shakespeare's or Beaumont and Fletcher's, seemed through their comical satire to fulfil the Horatian office of poetry – to instruct and to delight – more thoroughly than those of his great peers. His tragedies *Sejanus* and *Catiline* were admired for their presentation of Roman history as a mirror of Jacobean politics. His graceful lyrics provided a pattern for the next generation of Cavalier poets, and his imitation of Latin models in his poetry of praise and blame helped to shape the neo-classic poetics of Dryden and Pope.

The eminence and influence which Jonson attained in the world of seventeenth-century letters are the result not only of his artistic gifts, but also of his powerful personality and his ability to exploit the medium of print. The impulse toward rivalry was a fundamental motivation for Jonson; when we look closely at his literary milieu we discover that he was often reacting very particularly to works by his competitors or seeking to surpass them in some way. Yet by suppressing many of his plays and publishing others with dedications and commendatory poems in a format more customary for serious non-dramatic verse, he created an illusory sense of himself as a writer who swam against the dramatic currents of his age, defying popular taste and championing classical principles. Moreover, his public persona was a paradoxical mixture of the prophetic and the familiar. On the one hand, he was a poetic high priest, nobly celebrating virtue and satirising vice while exalting the role of letters in the ideal commonwealth. On the other hand, he was the waggish 'Ben' – the irrepressible character whose known idiosyncrasies helped to excuse his unbridled ridicule, egotism, and irreverent familiarity with the great.

Jonson's skill at manipulating his image poses special problems for the biographer. As Alexander Leggatt has shrewdly observed, his mask, like Shaw's, 'could be a way not of embodying but of concealing the essential man'.[1] We must continually probe behind the public figure for what can be deduced about his personal behaviour and compare the actual facts of his literary development with the shape imposed on his career by print. Much of his biographical record has been lost to time, but the survival of some records, letters, and manuscript poems gives us a fuller picture of his relationships with his contemporaries and supplements the 'authorised' version of his career suggested by the arrangement of the 1616 Folio. Most revealing, though not without its biases and interpretive challenges, is the manuscript 'Informations by Ben Jonson to W[illiam] D[rummond] when he came to Scotland upon foot, 1619', a transcript of remarks made by Jonson to his host, the Laird of Hawthornden, during Jonson's two or three week visit in the Christmas season of 1618/19. Now generally known as the *Conversations with William Drummond*, it provides a first-person account of Jonson's life as he cared to tell it in 1619 and frank judgments about his poetic rivals and patrons. Even here, Jonson is partly on stage – boasting of his intimacy with English poets and courtiers and reciting his poems or criticising those of others to impress his provincial host, whose private opinion of his guest's character is reserved for a final blistering summation.

The Jonson who emerges from a full reading of the record is therefore much more complex than the figure he would like us to see, a Jonson often troubling in his contradictions, but always fascinating. Dependent on the theatre in his early years and grounded in its conventions as an actor-playwright, he adopted an air of lofty scorn for popular taste even as he exploited popular dramatic formulas in new ways. Given to espousing norms that were opposed to his own deep-seated tendencies, he denied behaviour that contradicted his principles. Gifted (or cursed) with an irreverent wit and a stubbornly assertive character, he chose to write in forms such as the court masque and the poetry of praise that invited flattery. Alienated from the corruption and extravagance of the Jacobean court, he was gradually drawn into its life and became dependent on its rewards. Yet even though he did not perfectly conform to his own ideals, Jonson's life is an instructive example of the challenges faced by a Renaissance humanist committed to a programme of moral and artistic reform. More-

over, the very contradictions of his personality are expressed in the
varied qualities of his art: social tact, ethical seriousness, learned
inventiveness, lyric grace, playful self-criticism, comic irony, satiric
wit, vivid realism – the list is impressive in its range.

Every biographer of Jonson stands greatly indebted to the
monumental edition of his works by C. H. Herford and Percy and
Evelyn Simpson. Their *Ben Jonson*, 11 vols. (Oxford, 1925-52), brings
together, in addition to the texts, most of his life records, early
commentary on his works, stage and publication history, and a mass
of helpful annotation on literary sources, contemporary allusions
and the persons he addresses. Serious students of his work should
become thoroughly acquainted with its resources. Herford's brief
biographical sketch has recently been updated by two studies:
Rosalind Miles' *Ben Jonson: His Life and Work* (London, 1986), offers a
lively survey of the biographical record, while David Riggs' *Ben
Jonson: A Life* (Cambridge, Mass., 1989) synthesises much recent
critical and historical scholarship into an intricate psychoanalytic
interpretation of Jonson's life and work. In accordance with the
focus of this series, the present volume aims at a *literary* life which
emphasises Jonson's efforts to maintain his independence from the
conditions of theatrical production and court patronage and
considers how his works are influenced by and yet positioned
against those of his competitors.

Since I have written with a student audience in mind, I have
chosen modernised texts of Jonson's works. Quotations from his
*Epigrams, The Forest, Underwoods, Miscellaneous Poems, Timber: or
Discoveries* and *Conversations with Drummond* (abbreviated respec-
tively in citations and notes as *Epig., For., Und., M.P., Disc.* and
Conv.) are from George Parfitt (ed.), *Ben Jonson: The Complete Poems*
(Harmondsworth, 1988), which retains Jonson's expressive punc-
tuation. Quotations from the plays and masques are from G. A.
Wilkes (ed.), *The Complete Plays of Ben Jonson*, 4 vols. (Oxford, 1981)
and Stephen Orgel (ed.), *Ben Jonson: The Complete Masques* (New
Haven, 1969), abbreviated as *Plays* and *Masques* respectively. In the
interests of consistency, I have modernised the spelling and
orthography of all other texts and titles, even when I have quoted
from old-spelling texts. I have, however, retained the spelling
humourous to indicate the Jonsonian sense of 'affected or
temperamental behaviour like that understood to be caused by an
imbalance of the four bodily fluids or humours' (see Chapter 2).
Latin titles are given in English translation with the original Latin in

parentheses after the first reference when the title is not an obvious cognate. All dates have also been adjusted to New Style usage, which begins the new year on 1 January rather than 25 March as in Jonson's day.

W. David Kay

Acknowledgements

I am grateful to Richard Dutton for inviting me to write this volume and for being a most alert General Editor, tactfully sharing his own extensive knowledge of Jonson and the period. My researches on Jonson's career were begun under the rigorous but friendly mentoring of G. E. Bentley. Members of the faculty Renaissance Seminar at the University of Illinois at Urbana-Champaign have been a helpful sounding board as I have developed my ideas, and Achsah Guibbory, Carol Neely, Jan Hinely and Richard Wheeler have provided special assistance. From start to finish Michael Shapiro has been a loyal and frank Jonsonian friend, patiently reading the whole manuscript and making detailed suggestions. David Riggs, James Shapiro and Martin Butler have kindly made available copies of forthcoming work. Malcolm Smuts, Linda Levy Peck and Caroline Hibbard offered useful suggestions about historical backgrounds. Blair Worden's stimulating lecture on *Sejanus* at the first Reading conference on 'Politics, Patronage, and Literature' did much to develop my thinking about the play's political connections. Elizabeth Heale, Cedric Brown, Andrew Gurr, Blair Worden, David Norbrook, Trevor Howard-Hill, Arthur Kinney, Eugene Waith and Thomas M. Greene have been gracious hosts to a visiting scholar, and Jonas Barish, Lester Beaurline and George E. Rowe have provided encouraging aid. The Research Board of the University of Illinois at Urbana-Champaign has funded research assistance and released time. Librarians at the University of Illinois, the Guildhall Library, the British Library, the Bodleian Library and Cambridge University have been unfailingly considerate and helpful. To all, my thanks.

W. D. K.

1
Fathers

It is probable that Ben Jonson (as he preferred to spell his name) was born on 11 June 1572.[1] Like that of so many Elizabethan writers, his family background and childhood circumstances are obscured by the gaps in surviving records. He told William Drummond that

> his grandfather came from Carlisle, and he thought from Annandale to it, he served Henry VIII, and was a gentleman. His father lost all his estate under Queen Mary, having been cast in prison and forfeited, at last turned minister: so he was a minister's son. He himself was posthumous born, a month after his father's decease, brought up poorly, put to school by a friend (his master Camden), after taken from it, and put to another craft (I think was to be a wright or bricklayer). (*Conv.*, ll. 227–35)

His father's Christian name is not recorded, and scholars have been unable to single him out from among the myriad Johnsons who lived in Tudor England or to trace his earlier ancestry. To Jonson, however, his family history was primarily a tale of gentility denied. Although, as a posthumous child, he never knew his father, he clearly identified with his standing as an educated gentleman and resented the poverty which kept him from achieving the same status. Much of the motivating power behind his ambitious literary career was the desire to regain the social position which he believed to be his birthright. His narrative to Drummond indicates that this goal was not achieved without extraordinary struggle – struggle in which two surrogate father-figures played conflicting roles.

The blocking figure in this family drama seems to have been Jonson's step-father, whom he never directly mentions. His existence is first suggested by the seventeenth-century biographer Thomas Fuller, who records of Jonson that 'when a little child he lived in Hartshorn Lane near Charing-cross, where his mother married a bricklayer for her second husband'.[2] Fuller's account has been made credible by the discovery of one Robert Brett, a

1

bricklayer linked in a deed of 1586 to Hartshorn Lane and also to construction at Lincoln's Inn, where Jonson himself is later said by Fuller to have worked.[3] An enterprising tradesman capable of handling large contracts, Brett erected buildings at Lincoln's Inn worth 606*l*. 13*s*. 4*d*. and 1260*l*. respectively in 1600/01 and 1607–1609, and he eventually served as both Warden and Master of the Tylers and Bricklayers Company.

About Jonson's mother little is known except for an anecdote recording her courage and affection toward him on the occasion of his imprisonment over *Eastward Ho* in 1605. She may possibly be the Rebecca Brett who was buried at St. Martin's on 9 September 1609, just eleven days after the death of Robert Brett.[4] If so, much of her attention during Jonson's childhood must have been directed to Brett and his children, of whom there were at least two. The parish register at St. Martin-in-the-Fields records the baptism of two sons who were later to succeed to Brett's bricklaying business: John, on 1 January 1582; and Robert, on 22 March 1584. Two other Bretts listed in the baptismal register, Margareta (b. 16 June 1585) and Anthony Brett (b. 31 October 1591), may also have been Jonson's siblings or relatives, as may the Sarah, Alice and Rebecca Bretts buried on 15 July 1581, 25 September 1589 and 24 April 1595 respectively.

Whether the Brett household was a harmonious one we can only speculate. Jonson's plays contain several conflict-ridden marriages between tradesmen husbands and genteel wives with higher social aspirations, but there is no evidence that he based these portraits on personal experience. Disagreement about his education, however, would not have been unlikely. Robert Brett's signature in the Court Minute Book of the Tylers and Bricklayers Company for 8 March 1608 shows that he was more literate than many of his fellows, who signed company documents only with their marks.[5] However, he seems to have viewed his own sons as recruits for the family business, and it would not be surprising if he expected Jonson to take the same path. Jonson's mother, on the other hand, may have envisioned a different future for the child of her first marriage.

At any rate, Jonson was given some schooling, though it was probably less than might be predicted for the writer who was to become the age's leading neo-classicist. According to Fuller, Jonson went first to a private school in St. Martin's church, where he would have learned to read and write in English and acquired the rudiments of Latin grammar. Through the aid of a family friend, he was then enrolled in the College of St. Peter at Westminster as one of the *oppidans* or town-boys who, as day students, joined the forty Queen's Scholars from 6 a.m. to 6 p.m. each school day.[6] As refounded by Queen Elizabeth, Westminster School was among the more rigorous grammar schools in England and, with Edward Grant as Headmaster and William Camden as Second Master, was acquiring a reputation for the study of Greek as well as Latin.[7] The education Jonson received there and his contact with William Camden in particular were to make a life-long impact on his art.

The curriculum at Westminster was designed according to the humanist principles encouraged by Desiderius Erasmus and Juan Luis Vives, the continental educational reformers who helped to reshape Tudor education in the reign of Henry VIII.[8] Its aims were to develop piety and morality and to encourage the speaking and writing of Latin and Greek through imitation of the best authors, moving progressively from simple texts adapted to schoolboy capabilities to a more challenging selection of classical oratory, poetry, history and moral philosophy. Although there is no guarantee that their directives were followed to the letter, the statutes issued on the school's reorganisation in 1560 are quite explicit about the texts to be studied.[9] The youngest boys in the first and second forms began with the moral distichs of Cato, the colloquies about schoolboy life by Vives and Corderius, selections from *Aesop's Fables* and from the Roman dramatist Terence, the *Sacred Dialogues* of Sebastian Castalio and the *Familiar Colloquies* of Erasmus. In the third and fourth forms, they continued their reading of Terence and added the Roman historian Sallust, the epistles of Cicero as edited by Johannes Sturm, Cicero's *On Moral Duty* (*De Officiis*), Ovid's *Laments* (*Tristia*), and selections from Martial, Catullus and Erasmus' *Apophthegms*. In the fourth form, they also learned Greek grammar and began reading the *Dialogues* of Lucian. In the fifth form they read in Latin: the universal history of Justin, Cicero's *On Friendship* (*De Amicitia*), Ovid's *Metamorphoses* and Horace; in Greek: selections from Plutarch and the orations of Isocrates. In the sixth and seventh forms, they studied Virgil and Roman history (Caesar's *Commentaries*, Livy, Lucan, Silius Italicus) in Latin; and Homer, the orations of Demosthenes and the Psalms in Greek. In the seventh form, they began the study of Hebrew. From their readings, the boys were expected to gather in their notebooks 'the flowers, phrases or idioms, also antitheses, epithets, synonyms, proverbs, similes, comparisons, stories, descriptions of seasons, places, persons, fables, sayings, figures of speech, apophthegms'.[10]

Their prescribed exercises also fostered skill at composition, starting
with simple translation from English to Latin, and moving on to the
writing of themes, first in Latin and then in Greek prose and verse.

Since Jonson told Drummond that he was 'taken from' school, it is
not certain how far he progressed through the Westminster
curriculum. Later testimony established that as Second Master
Camden was in charge of the third and fourth forms, while an usher
taught the most elementary students, and for this reason it is
sometimes assumed that Jonson would have gone no further than
the fourth form.[11] This assumption is consistent with the wording of
his epigram to his old teacher: 'Camden, most reverend head, to
whom I owe / *All* that I am in arts, *all* that I know' (*Epig.* XIV, italics
mine). On the other hand, his praise of Camden may involve some
poetic license. Even if he had been subjected to a formal
apprenticeship (an eight-year term in the Tylers and Bricklayers
company) he could have continued much longer, for an apprenticeship ending at the statutory age of twenty-four would not need to
begin until age sixteen, while Westminster schoolboys began their
seven-year curriculum at age seven or eight.[12] It is perhaps worth
noting in this regard that Jonson's *English Grammar* does imply some
familiarity with Hebrew, a seventh-form subject at Westminster.[13]
His statement to Drummond, therefore, may mean no more than
that his education was terminated at or near the end of grammar
school by parental insistence.[14]

Regardless of how long he stayed at Westminster, however, he
was profoundly affected by his studies there. The desire to mine the
'ore' of classical literature and to refine it into his own English
compositions was to become a life-long impulse, one aided
considerably by the Tudor practice of memorising all one's school
lessons. Years later Jonson boasted of his memory in his *Discoveries*,
'I can repeat whole books that I have read, and poems, of some
selected friends, which I have liked to charge my memory with. . . .
Whatsoever I pawned with it, while I was young, and a boy, it offers
me readily, and without stops' (ll. 601–11). Jonson's contention is
borne out by the many passages from his grammar school textbooks
which were later incorporated into his poetry and plays.

Of course, the Westminster curriculum was not intended to train
poets or playwrights, but to produce graduates whose knowledge of
the Biblical languages and Latin eloquence prepared them to serve
God and the Queen. Nevertheless, there was much in the prescribed
reading that might stimulate the fancy of an imaginative schoolboy.

One of Jonson's favourite works, for example, would seem to have been Erasmus' *Familiar Colloquies*, which were written to inculcate practical morality and piety while stretching the pupil's Latin vocabulary and his knowledge of speech formulas. Yet these educational goals were realised through delightful dialogues that often contain good-humoured banter, sly irony, and tales of trickery or deception. Precisely which colloquies were read at Westminster we cannot tell for sure, but Jonson was to return again and again to the volume for inspiration for his own satire on affectation and superstitious folly. He borrows directly from 'The Ignoble Knight, or Faked Nobility' for Carlo Buffone's ironic advice to the upstart Sogliardo in *Every Man out of His Humour*; he adapts the self-deluded sighting of a non-existent spirit from 'Exorcism, or the Spectre' for his satire on the greedy legacy-hunters in the final courtroom scene of *Volpone*; and in *The Alchemist* he combines incidents from 'Alchemy' and 'Beggar Talk' into the deception of Sir Epicure Mammon. Equally appealing to Jonson were the dialogues of Lucian, which Erasmus had translated into Latin but which pupils at Westminster read in Greek. They were to suggest Jonson's playfully irreverent characterisation of Mercury and Cupid in *Cynthia's Revels*, his amusing purgation of Crispinus' bloated vocabulary in *Poetaster*, and – most notably – the ironic deceptions of the legacy hunters in *Volpone*.

The most immediate stimuli to Jonson's dramatic sensibilities, however, must have been the prominence given to Roman drama at Westminster. Because their dialogue was comprehensible to younger students and was viewed as both morally sound and a model of colloquial Latinity, the plays of Terence figured heavily in the early stages of the Westminster curriculum, as they did in many other Tudor grammar schools. The Westminster statutes also required the performance of two school plays at Christmas – an English play to be staged by the cathedral choirboys and a Latin one by the Queen's Scholars. Somewhat surprisingly, in light of their omission from the offical syllabus, works by Plautus seem to have been frequently chosen for the Christmas Latin play and therefore may have been given some attention in class as well. Surviving records from the 1560s show that Terence's *The Self-Tormentor* (*Heautontimorumenos*) and Plautus' *The Braggart Warrior* (*Miles Gloriosus*) were performed in 1564, *The Wisdom of Solomon* (*Sapientia Solomonis*) by the humanist Sixt Birck and Plautus' *The Twin Menaechmi* in 1565/6 when Queen Elizabeth attended, Plautus'

The Rope (Rudens) in 1566/7, and his *The Haunted House (Mostellaria)* in 1569.[15] As a town boy, Jonson probably had no direct role in the Latin plays, but he would certainly have been present at them, and they would have reinforced the interest in theatre gained from speaking Terence in the classroom. In the third intermean to *The Staple of News*, he refers humorously to the potentially subversive role of drama in grammar-school education, playing on Gossip Censure's ignorance about the true nature of Terence's works: 'I would have ne'er a cunning schoolmaster in England. . . . They make all their scholars play-boys! Is't not a fine sight, to see all our children made interluders? Do we pay our money for this? We send them to learn their grammar, and their Terence, and they learn their play-books?'.[16]

These are doubly ironic words from a dramatist whose play-books are full of Plautine and Terentian echoes. Whether he was remembering his school lessons and the Westminster Latin plays or whether his early acquaintance with Roman drama had inspired him to read further, Jonson repeatedly draws on some half-dozen works by the Roman comic writers, imitating bits of dialogue, varying their plots, and addressing his audience as Plautus and Terence had done. His first recorded success, *The Case Is Altered*, is an artful combination of Plautus' *The Pot of Gold (Aulularia)* and *The Captives*; and the tricks played on Old Knowell by Brainworm in *Every Man in His Humour* are very much in the spirit of Terence's *The Brothers (Adelphoi)*, where the clever slave Syrus sends the over-anxious Demea on exhausting wild-goose chases in search of his son Ctesipho, whose prodigality Demea fears. Yet Jonson's reworking of Plautus and Terence is not confined to the early phase of his writing, as is sometimes asserted, but continues into the great comedies of his middle years. Both *Volpone* and *The Alchemist* are prefaced by an acrostic poem summarising the plot, like those printed in Renaissance editions of Roman drama, and both contain intrigue patterned after Roman models. Mosca, the 'parasite' in *Volpone* is actually a variation on the Roman clever servant – like the slave Chrysalus in Act III, Scene ii of Plautus' *The Two Bacchides* he boasts of his ability to 'change a visor swifter than a thought', and he ridicules the deaf Corbaccio much as Tranio in Act IV, Scene iv of Plautus' *The Haunted House* teases the uncomprehending Theopropides. In *The Alchemist* the roguish Face's attempt to scare off his returned master Lovewit by claiming that his house is plague-infested is modelled on Tranio's pretence that Theopropides' house is haunted, while Surly's assumption of a Spanish disguise in order to expose Face's trickery conflates two separate episodes from Plautus' *The Carthaginian* (*Poenulus*). The epilogues to both *Volpone* and *The Alchemist* are also inspired by *The Carthaginian*, the source for Volpone's claim that 'the seasoning of a play is the applause' and for Face's metaphor of the audience as a jury. A major basis of Jonson's appeal to the educated members of the Elizabethan theatre audience, then, would have been the fact that his plays are recognisable reworkings of familiar grammar-school texts, cleverly 'Englished' by him.

In addition to encouraging his taste for irony and intrigue comedy, Jonson's Westminster training affected his art in other ways. Three of the poets read in the middle forms – Martial, Catullus and Horace – were to become important models for his poetic imitation: epigrams in the manner of Martial, Catullan love lyrics, and Horatian epistles comprise most of the poetry he published in the 1616 Folio. His readings in Cicero's epistles would also have played an important role in developing his repertory of rhetorical strategies. Erasmus' *On Letter Writing* (*De Conscribendis Epistolis*), a commonly-used guide to the study of composition in Tudor schools, employs Cicero's epistles to illustrate various modes of argument – advice, rebuke, encouragement, persuasion, dissuasion and consolation – modes which Jonson himself practises frequently in his poetry and drama. For example, his poem 'On My First Son' (*Epig.* XLV) imitates Cicero's consolatory letter to Titius (the last selection in the edition by Sturm used at Westminster), arguing that our sense of personal loss should be moderated by the recognition that young men or boys who die have been 'rescued by the immortal gods from all these miseries and merciless conditions of life'.[17] In his birthday ode 'To Sir William Sidney' (*For.* XIV), he also follows the general Ciceronian strategy, endorsed by Erasmus, of encouraging a young man to noble action by reminding him of his father's or his ancestors' achievements.[18] In such cases, his mature poetry may be an extension or application of the schoolboy themes he was asked to compose at Westminster.

Finally, the sententiousness of his verse and the neo-Stoic character of his thought, which was later to be fixed decisively by his independent readings in Seneca, were undoubtedly encouraged by the apophthegms he learned in the earliest forms.[19] The very first text studied by Westminster scholars, the *Moral Distichs* of Cato (edited for school use by Erasmus), is essentially a collection of memorable short sayings encapsulating classical wisdom. While struggling over its word-forms and syntax, students were also expected to absorb its precepts for right living – precepts which instructed them to love their parents, fear the schoolmaster, respect superiors, restrain the tongue, be temperate in drinking wine, moderate their anger, bear poverty patiently, contemn riches, think of adversity even during prosperity, live according to nature and not fear death.[20] The Stoic bias of these lessons would have been further reinforced in the third form by readings in Cicero's *On Moral Duty*. The Roman statesman's discussion of the four cardinal virtues (wisdom, justice, fortitude, and temperance) and his examination of the conflict between what is expedient (*utile*) and morally right (*honestus*) follows that of the Stoic Panaetius, stressing the need to control the appetites and passions with reason and arguing that only that which is morally right can be truly expedient. Jonson's remark to Drummond that 'of all styles he loved most to be named honest' (*Conv.*, l. 658) perhaps reflects the impact of Cicero on him, and many of Cicero's specific points, such as his condemnation of the Roman worship of wealth or his distinction between true wisdom and the self-interested deceit that passes for wisdom, were later to be echoed indirectly in Jonson's poems and plays.

The greatest single influence on Jonson's intellectual and artistic development, however, came not from the books he read at Westminster, but from the teacher under whom he read them. In William Camden he found a mentor extraordinary for his wide-ranging knowledge and for his gentleness. All too many Tudor schoolmasters depended on the birch rod as a motivator: Edward Grant, the Westminster headmaster, was a notorious whipper whose lashings left Richard Neile, later to be Archbishop of York, with a distaste for Latin studies.[21] Camden, however, seems to have inspired his charges by the example of his own scholarship. In the early 1580s, when Jonson most likely was his pupil, he was completing his ambitious work, the *Britannia* (published 1586). A 'chorographical' description of the British isles, it recounted the history of Britain through descriptions of its various regions, and traced the successive waves of invaders – Britons, Romans, Saxons, Danes, and Normans – who contended for control of the islands. The learning Camden brought to his task is impressive. He had mastered Celtic and Anglo-Saxon, using the word-roots in place-names as evidence for the migration and settlement of the different peoples, and he had carefully compared the various accounts of ancient Britain, attempting to locate places mentioned in the Roman itineraries through archaeological investigations carried on during school vacations. His rigorous evaluation of evidence led him to reject Geoffrey of Monmouth's chauvinistic myth of London's founding by Brutus, but his work is no less a celebration of his country. Camden emphasises the identification of Britain with 'the Fortunate Isles', stressing the mildness of its climate and its fertility. Moreover, his interest in heraldry and genealogy led him to think of the British landscape as dotted not only with historically significant places, but also with the seats of nobility exemplary for their virtue. As Richard Peterson puts it, 'In his record of his investigations . . . individuals and families stand out amid other features of the land, like living landmarks – indeed, like outcroppings of the Golden Age or the Roman past vigorously reemerging to improve national life'.[22]

Camden's enthusiasm for his researches seems to have been shared with his pupils and former pupils, some of whom went along on his various field trips. For him the classical world was not distant and alien, but a living presence waiting to be rediscovered just under the surface of modern Britain. The antique coins and Roman artefacts illustrated in the *Britannia* must have aroused the curiosity of his pupils, and even the unused matter omitted from that volume but published later in his *Remains . . . concerning Britain* (1605) – a miscellany of information about 'the inhabitants thereof, their languages, names, surnames, empresas, wise speeches, poesies, and epitaphs' – would have provided a remarkable fund of anecdote and illustration for classroom use. Jonson's epigram to Camden (*Epig.* XIV) expresses his awe at his comprehensive knowledge:

> What name, what skill, what faith hast thou in things!
> What sight in searching the most antique springs!
> What weight, and what authority in thy speech!
> Man scarce can make that doubt, but thou canst teach.
>   (ll. 7–10).

Though adapted from Pliny, Jonson's praise is both a fitting tribute to Camden and the statement of an ideal he himself had internalised, as can be seen from his own wide reading and his citation of classical authorities in the notes to his tragedies and masques.

Camden's example was also to shape many of Jonson's poetic practices and themes. He told Drummond in 1619 'that he wrote all his [verses] first in prose, for so his master Camden, had learned him' (*Conv.*, ll. 382–3) – an intriguing remark, for it suggests that Camden had encouraged the making of English poetry as part of his classroom exercises. Moreover, many of the minor forms of poetic wit practised by Jonson, such as anagrams, impresas (a combination of motto and pictorial symbol) and epitaphs, are collected by Camden in his *Remains*. Jonson was later to speak scornfully of acrostics, shape-verses, and anagrams and to repeat a Latin verse condemning the love of difficult trifles as shameful and worthy of fools (*Conv.*, ll. 442–7), but in fact his cleverness at devising appropriate anagrams and impresas for his symbolic characters was to be one of the bases of his success as a masque writer – witness his anagram of 'IUNO' (the Roman goddess of marriage) and 'UNIO' (the union of married couples and kingdoms) in *Hymenaei*.

It was, however, Camden's conception of an imperial Britain linked to a Roman past and his stress on noble names that were to have the most profound effect on his young pupil. Jonson's *Epigrams*, in which the Earl of Pembroke has 'the honour of leading forth so many good, and great names . . . to their remembrance with posterity' ('Dedication', ll. 16–18), is the poetical counterpart of Camden's roll-call of the great county families, and Jonson's poetry of praise could claim the same justification that Camden offers for naming living persons: 'to praise good men is but to show a light of direction as out of a watch tower to posterity. True is that saying of Symmachus: *Imitation is encouraged with the seemly praises of the good, and imitating virtue is cherished by the example of others' honour*.'[23] Jonson's emphasis on the moral qualities suggested by the names of those he praises also owes something to Camden, whose extensive discussion of naming in the *Remains* rejects as superstitious any suggestion that names are predictive, but does insist on their value as standards for conduct: 'Withal we may make this fruit by consideration of our names which have good, hopeful and lucky significations, that accordingly we do carry and conform our selves so that we fail not to be answerable to them, but be "men of our names"' (p. 37). Encouraging his contemporaries to be 'men of their names' was to be one of Jonson's major occupations throughout his poetical career, as was his celebration of Jacobean Britain as a revival of the glories of a Roman past. In both enterprises he was following the lead of his learned teacher.

Camden, in fact, became not only an influential mentor, but a surrogate parent of sorts, one whom Ben was proud to acknowledge. Jonson is often accused of being an envious and ungrateful friend, but with Camden he was generous in his praise. Quintilian had recommended that schoolboys 'should love their masters not less than their studies, and should regard them as the parents not indeed of their bodies but of their minds' (II.ix.1).[24] Jonson's tributes to his teacher take those words to heart. In the close of his epigram to him he apologises for his own inadequacy, but asks him to accept his 'piety' (the Roman *pietas* or devotion of which Quintilian speaks), and in a specially printed presentation copy of *Cynthia's Revels* (1601) he included a touching tribute to the man he called 'the best parent of his muses,' signing himself 'a former pupil, a friend forever'.[25]

Jonson's gratitude to Camden was no doubt intensified by Camden's continuing interest in him after he was forced to leave Westminster. Either by economic necessity or by his stepfather's insistence, he was 'taken from school' and set to work at bricklaying. In the long run, this change may have benefited English letters, for Jonson's inability to continue his schooling or to proceed to Oxford or Cambridge may have saved him from the higher forms of pedantry, while supplying a powerful impetus for compensatory self-education and creative activity. In the short run, however, it must have occasioned considerable turmoil in the aspiring poet and made his continuing intellectual and artistic development very difficult indeed.

2

The Actor-Playwright

The youth who left Westminster School for his step-father's trade of bricklaying had been given a solid grounding in the classical languages and inspired with a love of literature, but how or when he decided to become a dramatic poet is difficult to determine. Unlike Shakespeare, whose 'lost years' are completely undocumented, many of Jonson's activities in his later youth and early manhood are known, but the surviving records are incomplete. However, when one combines the evidence from official documents with Jonson's own statements and those of others, one can sketch in a rough outline of his early life. His initial work as a bricklayer was apparently followed by brief service as a soldier in the Low Countries, an early marriage, entry into the Tylers and Bricklayers Company, a dramatic apprenticeship as an actor-playwright with the theatrical troupe known as Pembroke's Men and as a collaborative playmaker for the Lord Admiral's Men. By 1598, when he wrote his first piece for Shakespeare's company, the Lord Chamberlain's Men, he had begun to develop the comedy of humours into a vehicle for dramatic satire, but he had established neither an exclusive claim to the form nor a secure economic base for his poetic career.

Jonson himself was not proud of his trade or his early theatrical associations, and he passed over them lightly in the biographical sketch he gave to William Drummond. Of the period after his schooling Drummond says only that he was 'put to another craft (I think was to be a wright or bricklayer), which he could not endure, then went he to the Low Countries, but returning soon he betook himself to his wonted studies' (*Conv.*, ll. 234–8). His bricklaying, which was to become the object of taunts from critics and enemies throughout his career, is here dismissed as if it were the briefest of interludes, when in fact, as we shall see below, it almost certainly continued intermittently for some years. Contemporary biographers, following Jonson's lead, also minimise his craft connections. Thomas Fuller places his apprenticeship after an abortive term at Cambridge and reports that it was bought out by some friendly patrons:

12

He was statutably admitted into Saint John's College in Cambridge . . . where he continued but few weeks for want of further maintenance, being fain to return to the trade of his father-in-law [that is, 'step-father'] . . . . He helped in the building of the new structure of Lincoln's Inn, when having a trowel in his hand, he had a book in his pocket.

Some gentlemen, pitying that his parts should be buried under the rubbish of so mean a calling, did by their bounty manumise him freely to follow his own ingenious inclinations.[1]

Fuller's gossipy contemporary John Aubrey also retails the rumour that Jonson had worked with his step-father 'on the garden-wall of Lincoln's Inn next to Chancery Lane', adding the detail 'that a knight, a bencher, walking through and hearing him repeat some Greek verses out of Homer, discoursing with him and finding him to have a wit extraordinary, gave him some exhibition to maintain him at Trinity College in Cambridge'.[2] No record survives of any residency at Cambridge, whether at St. John's or Trinity, and it surely did not last long, if it took place at all. Jonson's work at Lincoln's Inn could have been in 1588, when a Thomas Brett was paid for construction of a wall near Holborn, or in 1590 or 1591, when Robert Brett was also paid for repair work on the walls, or (since Fuller mentions the 'new structure') as late as 1600–1 or 1607–9, when Brett erected more substantial buildings.[3] Aubrey's story of Jonson's recitation from Homer has the ring of truth in so far as it captures the streak of exhibitionism that enabled him to promote himself effectively, even in adverse circumstances.

Jonson's brief military service in the Netherlands probably occurred before the autumn of 1594, when records indicating his presence in London become more continuous. England controlled three 'Cautionary Towns' (Brill, Flushing and the fort of Rammekens), so-called because they were held as collateral until repayment of the loans made by Queen Elizabeth to the Protestant states for their war against Spain, and Jonson probably joined the garrison at one of them. In his account to Drummond, he boasted of a single combat in which he was victorious: 'In his service in the Low Countries, he had, in the face of both the camps, killed an enemy and taken *opima spolia* from him' (*Conv.*, ll. 238–40). His use of the phrase '*opima spolia*' or 'rich spoils' – a Latinism used to describe the battle honours won by a general in killing the enemy commander, suggests that he was acting out fantasies of military glory stimulated by his schoolboy reading of Virgil and Roman history. Some commentators have attributed the praise of peace in Jonson's masques to his early disillusionment with the war in Holland, but he could never have been a true pacifist.[4] He remained proud of his service, and although he often satirises braggart soldiers who claim credit for non-existent exploits, he also repeatedly praises military valour in his poetry, as in Epigram CVIII, 'To True Soldiers':

> Strength of my country, whilst I bring to view
> Such as are miscalled captains, and wrong you;
> And your high names: I do desire, that thence
> Be nor put on you, nor you take offence.
> I swear by your true friend, my muse, I love
> Your great profession; which I once did prove:
> And did not shame it with my actions, then,
> No more, than I dare now do, with my pen.
>
> (ll.1-8)

The life of a garrison soldier, however, was generally an unheroic affair. The letters of Sir Robert Sidney, the governor of Flushing, reveal that the English companies were ill-fed, ill-clothed, and often ravaged by disease.[5] Little wonder, then, that Jonson, whose literary interests pointed him in other directions, went home quickly.

If Jonson did return to his accustomed studies, as he told Drummond, he must have found himself contending with many distractions. Fuller's picture of the poet labouring with a trowel in his hand and a book in his pocket suggests that his reading was often conducted in odd moments stolen from other work. And if he is the Benjamin Johnson listed in the parish register of St. Magnus the Martyr as marrying Anne Lewis on 14 November 1594, he must have been even harder pressed thereafter to find time for poetry.[6] His marriage at twenty-two, well below the early seventeenth-century average age for Londoners of twenty-eight, is perhaps to be explained by his revelation in the *Conversations* that he was 'in his youth given to venery' (l. 285).[7] Of Anne Lewis nothing is known except his statement that she 'was a shrew yet honest' (*Conv.*, l. 249). Jonson's remark probably reveals as much about the stresses on his early marriage as it does about Anne's character, for his roving eye and the financial difficulties attendant on his unsettled condition would have given Anne much to complain about. Their marriage was soon blessed (or burdened) with children. Jonson's first son, Benjamin, who was seven when he died in the late spring or summer of 1603 must have been conceived in the summer or autumn of 1595. It is not certain whether Mary, 'the daughter of their youth' memorialised in Epigram XXII, was born before or after him.[8]

It was perhaps the need for a financial base of support for his young family that led Jonson to join the Tylers and Bricklayers Company in June of 1595, thereafter making periodic payments of his accumulated quarterly fees in June and October 1596, April 1599, July 1601, November 1602, and May 1611.[9] Since a normal apprenticeship would have been terminated by his marriage and service in the Netherlands, he probably joined, as Fuller suggests, by 'redemption' (that is, by purchasing his freedom). Membership in the guild would have established his eligibility for citizenship in London and allowed him to work for wages as a journeyman.[10] His repeated appearance in the company's quarterage book suggests that he spent much more time in guild circles than he was willing to admit to Drummond. The Tylers and Bricklayers' regulations required, on pain of fine, attendance at company meetings at Bricklayers' Hall in Aldgate Street, at the annual election dinners cooked by Hugh Halton and held on the feast of St. Bartholomew the Apostle (24 August), at the funerals of members, and at the annual procession of the Lord Mayor of London to Westminster, when each livery company paraded as a group.[11] Jonson's derision of Anthony Munday as Antonio Balladino, '*Pageant* Poet to the City of *Milan*', in *The Case is Altered* (published 1609) is thus the product of his first-hand observation of Munday's Lord Mayor's pageants.[12] His reaction against the citizen ethos may also be seen in the burlesque treatment of virtuous and prodigal apprentices in *Eastward Ho* (written jointly with George Chapman and John Marston). For the most part, however, he merely repressed his connections with London guild life, neither idealising it after the fashion of Thomas Dekker's *The Shoemakers' Holiday* nor drawing on it as a continuous source of satiric material in the manner of Thomas Middleton's 'City' comedies.

Of Jonson's earliest theatrical connections, little is known. John Aubrey reports that after his return from the Netherlands, he 'acted and wrote, but both ill, at the Green Curtain' in the London suburb of Shoreditch.[13] The Lord Chamberlain's Men did produce Jonson's

Every Man in His Humour at the Curtain Theatre in 1598, but there is
no record of his having acted there. If Dekker's jibes in *Satiromastix*
(1601) are to be believed, his first acting experience was gained on
the road. In *Poetaster*, Jonson had made the double mistake of
lampooning the common players and ridiculing Dekker through the
figure of Demetrius. Dekker fought back in speeches by the
colourful Captain Tucca, who taunted Horace-Jonson about his
own past:

> *Tuc.* Thou hast been at Paris Garden hast not?
> *Hor.* Yes, Captain, I ha'played Zulziman there.
> *Sir Vaugh.* Then, Master *Horace*, you played the part of an honest
> man.
> *Tuc.* Death of Hercules! he could never play that part well in's life
> – no, Fulkes, you could not! Thou call'st *Demetrius* 'journeyman
> poet', but thou put'st up a supplication to be a poor journeyman
> player, and had'st been still so, but that thou could'st not set a
> good face upon't. Thou hast forgot how thou amblest (in leather
> pilch) by a play-wagon, in the highway, and took'st mad
> Jeronimo's part, to get service among the mimics; and when the
> Stagerites banish'd thee into the Isle of Dogs, thou turn'dst ban-
> dog (villainous Guy) and ever since bitest. Therefore I ask if th'ast
> been at Paris Garden, because thou hast such a good mouth, thou
> bait'st well.
>
> (IV.i.121-35)[14]

Personal satire is not always the most trustworthy source of
biographical information, but Tucca's speech makes four points
emphatically: (1) Jonson had been an unsuccessful actor; (2) he had
acted the part of Hieronymo in Kyd's *The Spanish Tragedy* with a
travelling company; (3) he had played the role of Zulziman (now
completely unidentifiable) in Paris Garden; (4) he was thought of as
a 'biting' satirist after his association with the suppressed play *The
Isle of Dogs.*

Dekker's satire confirms what we know from other sources, that
Jonson was a member of Pembroke's Men, which did act at the
Swan Theatre in Paris Garden.[15] Originally formed from a branch of
the Queen's Men along with personnel from the amalgamated Lord
Admiral's and Strange's Men in 1592, Pembroke's Men illustrate the
unstable history of Elizabethan acting troupes and the financial
difficulties under which they laboured. Despite a good beginning

with court performances in the Christmas season of 1592/3, they were driven into the country by the plague and returned in late September 1593 so impoverished that they had to pawn their costumes. After some years of obscurity in which our only record of them is from provincial performances in 1595–6, a company of that name reappears in late February 1597, when Robert Shaw, Richard Jones, Gabriel Spencer, William Bird, and Thomas Downton entered into an agreement with Francis Langley to play for twelve months at the Swan, not too far from Philip Henslowe's Rose Theatre on the south bank of the Thames. Possibly Jonson had travelled with this troupe in its 1595–6 tour, when there is a gap in his quarterage payments to the Tylers and Bricklayers Company, but he certainly seems to have been one of the 'accomplices and associates' of the five main sharers who agreed with Langley to rent the Swan early in 1597.

In hiring Jonson, the five sharers of Pembroke's Men may have hoped that they were acquiring the services of an actor-playwright like Shakespeare who could assure their success through his contributions to their repertory. It is possible that the earliest version of his comedy *The Case Is Altered*, later produced by the Children of the Chapel, was written for them. Thomas Nashe's allusion to it in his pamphlet *Lenten Stuff* (written in the spring of 1598 and published in 1599) is evidence that it was in existence long before its production by the boy actors. If Jonson had written it when he was an actor with Pembroke's Men, he could have retained ownership of it when the company dissolved later in the year.[16] That dissolution was directly due to his penchant for satire. Sometime in the spring or early summer, he collaborated with Nashe on a play entitled *The Isle of Dogs*, perhaps based on a conceit first used in Nashe's entertainment *Summer's Last Will and Testament* (1592). There Autumn condemns the 'dog-days' of summer as bringers of plague, and Orion the Hunter replies with a paradoxical encomium on dogs, whom he compares to humans:

> Cynics they are, for they will snarl and bite;
> Right courtiers to flatter and to fawn;
> Valiant to set upon the enemies,
> Most faithful and most constant to their friends.[17]

Orion's defence of dogs and dog-days brings an ironic retort from the fool Will Summers, who comments 'If I had thought the Ship of

Fools would have stayed to take in fresh water at the Isle of Dogs, I would have furnished it with a whole kennel of collections to the purpose.'[18] The Isle of Dogs to which Summers refers was a spit of land projecting into the Thames across from the Queen's palace at Greenwich. Then primarily a refuse dump and haven for debtors and criminals, it acquires in Summer's usage a metaphorical identity as a paradise of fools whose vices suggest analogies to canine traits.[19]

Presumably Nashe and Jonson furnished their play with 'a whole kennel' of such vices to be satirised, but in doing so they overstepped the bounds of dramatic licence. Their work was in some way responsible for the general complaint about stage plays made by the Lord Mayor and the aldermen of London to the Privy Council on 28 July, which resulted in the closing of the theatres. *The Isle of Dogs* was the specific subject of a directive from the Privy Council to Richard Topcliffe, Thomas Fowler, Richard Skevington, Dr. Giles Fletcher and Roger Wilbraham on 15 August, informing them that 'upon information given us of a lewd play that was played in one of the playhouses on the Bankside, containing very seditious and slanderous matter, we caused some of the players to be apprehended and committed to prison, whereof one of them was not only an actor but a maker of part of the said play'. Topcliffe and his associates were directed to interrogate the prisoners, as well as to 'peruse such papers as were found in Nashe's lodgings'. The identity of the imprisoned actors is revealed in the Privy Council's warrant of 8 October for the release of Gabriel Spencer and Robert Shaw, 'stage-players', and 'the like warrant for the releasing of Benjamin Johnson'.[20] His imprisonment was his first experience of the repressive authority by which the Elizabethan government managed political and religious dissent. He revealed to Drummond that 'in the time of his close imprisonment, under Queen Elizabeth, his judges could get nothing of him to all their demands but 'aye' and 'no'. They placed two damned villains to catch advantage of him, with him [in his cell], but he was advertised by his keeper' (*Conv.*, ll. 252–6).[21] His collaborator Nashe fled to the Norfolk town of Yarmouth and, in his *Lenten Stuff*, disclaimed responsibility for the offensive material in *The Isle of Dogs*: 'I having begun but the induction and the first act of it, the other four acts without my consent, or the least guess of my drift or scope, by the players were supplied, which bred both their trouble and mine too'.[22]

Nashe's denial of responsibility for *The Isle of Dogs* was, of course, very much in his self-interest, but whether or not the play was the product of a true collaboration, he and Jonson were in many ways kindred spirits. Four years older than Jonson and already established – along with John Lyly, Robert Greene, Christopher Marlowe and George Peele – as one of the 'University Wits', Nashe was known primarily for the colourful invective and the clever inventiveness of his prose pamphlets. Like Jonson's, Nashe's works betray a tension between allegiance to 'the hierarchical community of Tudor ideology' and 'a cynical perception of injustice and exploitation', and like Jonson, Nashe promoted the 'humanistic conception of the exalted social role of the poet'.[23] Nashe's preface to Greene's *Menaphon*, where he promises to 'persecute those idiots and their heirs unto the third generation, that have made Art bankrupt of her ornaments' may well have served as the pattern for Jonson's dedication to *Volpone*, where Jonson pledges to 'raise the despised head of Poetry again, and stripping her out of those rotten and base rags, wherewith the times have adulterated her form, restore her to her primitive habit, feature, and majesty'.[24] Nashe's 'arraignment' of the pedantical scholar Gabriel Harvey in his *Strange News* (1592) and his parody of Harvey's 'inkhorn' vocabulary in his *Have with You to Saffron-Walden* (1596) may also have inspired Jonson's purge of John Marston's language in his *Poetaster, or His Arraignment* (1601). Nashe had also helped develop the satirical character sketch which Jonson translated to the stage in his 'humour' plays, and like Jonson he ridiculed alchemists and cunning-men and criticised Puritans for their claims to private inspiration, their rejection of holiday customs, and their gluttony and hypocrisy.

Lacking a text, we can only speculate about what may have led *The Isle of Dogs* to be labelled 'lewd' and 'seditious'. It is likely, however, that Nashe and Jonson had angered particular persons with their satire. Nashe had a history of offending in this fashion, and as Charles Nicholl has pointed out, the language of Jonson's letter to the Earl of Salisbury during his imprisonment for *Eastward Ho* (1605) clearly implies that personal satire was the issue in the earlier case:

I protest to your Honor, and call God to testimony (since my first error, which, yet, is punished in me more with my shame, than it was then with my bondage), I have so attempered my stile, that I have given no cause to any good man of grief; and, if to any ill, by touching at any general vice, it hath always been with a regard, and sparing of particular persons.[25]

Drawing the line between libellous attacks on individuals (a Star Chamber offence when directed at the great) and generalised moral satire with possible topical applications was to be a recurrent problem for Jonson throughout his career. In *The Isle of Dogs* affair, he paid for his indiscretion with seven weeks' imprisonment, an experience that led him to 'temper' his style thereafter so that his targets were more ambiguous. This is not to say that he ceased to ridicule individuals; only that he did so by blending allusions to them into composite portraits that could not be identified exclusively with specific victims.

The closing of the theatres in late July effectively broke up Pembroke's Men. While some of the company continued to act at the Swan after the ban on playing was lifted, others moved to Philip Henslowe's Rose Theatre and were gradually absorbed into the Lord Admiral's Men. Jonson, too, seems to have intended to join Henslowe's company, for on 28 July he took out a loan of four pounds from Henslowe, reimbursing him 3s.9d. as the down payment toward an unspecified 'share'. No further payments were made, and after his imprisonment, he seems to have been involved primarily in playwriting.[26] Henslowe's *Diary* records a payment to Jonson on 3 December 1597 of one pound toward 'a book which he was to write for us before Christmas next' and for which 'he showed the plot unto the company', and also a further loan of five shillings on 5 January 1598. On 18 August 1598 Henslowe loaned the Lord Admiral's Men six pounds to buy a play called *Hot Anger Soon Cold* from Henry Porter, Henry Chettle and Jonson, and on 23 October he recorded a payment to George Chapman 'on his playbook and two acts of a tragedy of Benjamin's plot'. In the meantime, Jonson had also completed *Every Man in His Humour* for the Lord Chamberlain's Men, which was performed as a 'new' play on 20 September, when a foreign visitor lost three hundred crowns to a pickpocket at the Curtain. It was followed during the late autumn of 1599 by its sequel, *Every Man out of His Humour*, produced at the recently opened Globe Theatre by the Lord Chamberlain's Men, but Jonson had apparently been working on two plays for the Lord Admiral's Men at the same time. Henslowe's *Diary* lists payments on 10 August 1599 to Jonson and Thomas Dekker in earnest of a book called *Page of Plymouth* (apparently a domestic tragedy) and to

Jonson, Dekker, Henry Chettle, and '[an]other gentleman' on 3 September for *Robert the Second, the King of Scot's Tragedy*, for which Jonson alone was given a further advance of twenty shillings on 27 September. No final payment is recorded for either, but there is no reason to assume they were not finished.[27]

These records show that Jonson was not an 'attached' dramatist, as were many playwrights who signed exclusive contracts with a single acting company, but worked as a free-lance writer for both of the leading theatrical troupes.[28] They also tantalise us with the realisation that his early artistic development can never be fully traced because he left unpublished his collaborative works and those he did not consider worthy to be included in his canon. In 1619, he told William Drummond that 'the half of his comedies were not in print' (*Conv.*, l. 398), and all of his early tragedies and domestic dramas are missing. Apparently the latter were not bad by the standards of the time, for in his *Palladis Tamia*, registered for publication in September 1598, Francis Meres lists Jonson as among 'our best for Tragedy'. Likewise, John Weever, in his *Epigrams in the Oldest Cut and Newest Fashion* (1599), praises 'embuskin'd Johnson' (that is, Jonson the tragic author) for his rich style and 'wondrous gallant spirit'.[29] Jonson's hack-work, however, remained the property of the dramatic companies for which it was written, while many plays of which he was the sole author seem to have been produced under an agreement that gave him publication rights a year or two after their first performance.

It is important to remember Jonson's extensive theatrical apprenticeship because it corrects the myth that he began as an 'experimental' dramatist at odds with the theatre for which he wrote. This impression is due largely to his arrangement of the 1616 Folio, in which the first work is a carefully revised version of *Every Man in His Humour*, prefaced by a dedication to William Camden which identifies it, incorrectly, as the 'first fruits' of Jonson's muse and by a prologue which criticises the 'ill customs' of Elizabethan dramaturgy.[30] In fact, as we have seen, Jonson was thoroughly immersed in the popular theatre of the 1590s and only gradually found his distinctive voice. Although he repeatedly ridiculed the bombastic speech and the disregard of the unities in popular tragedy and romance, he knew the popular repertory well and drew on those parts of it that were adaptable to his purposes. True, he generally scorned romantic comedy like Shakespeare's that showed 'a duke to be in love with a countess, and that countess to be in love with the duke's son, and the son to love the lady's waiting-maid: some such cross wooing, with a clown to their serving-man'; nevertheless, his own satiric mode of comedy was deeply indebted to elements of the morality play, trickster comedy, the disguise play, and citizen and domestic comedy.[31] Eventually, he became skilled at amusing sophisticated theatre-goers with witty inversions of Elizabethan dramatic conventions, but in his earliest works he is content to imitate established comic sub-genres, sharpening normative judgements and satiric detail while down-playing romantic sentiment.[32]

This is especially true of the two comedies usually assigned to his early 'Roman' phase – *The Case Is Altered* and *Every Man in His Humour*. In both, New Comedy elements, modified in accordance with Elizabethan tastes, provide the framework of the plot, but the real basis of dramatic organisation is the exhibition of humourous behaviour. In *The Case Is Altered*, as in Shakespeare's *The Comedy of Errors*, two Plautine originals are combined into an elaborate multiple plot: the action of the *Captivi*, in which a father unknowingly persecutes his long-lost son when the latter, now a slave, changes identities with his captured master, is joined with the more purely comic material of the *Aulularia*, in which a miser fears that the courtship of his daughter is really a ruse to gain his gold. The resulting compound is typically Elizabethan in its profusion. Count Ferneze's reunion with his son Camillo is mirrored by the discovery that Rachel de Prie, the supposed daughter of the miserly Jaques, is really the stolen sister of Lord Chamont, whom Camillo had served; Rachel is courted not only by Paulo Ferneze, but (in a manner reminiscent of *The Two Gentlemen of Verona*) by his false friend Angelo, who first tries to seduce and then to rape her, and by the steward Christophero and the clown Peter Onion. A number of theatrical types add to the play's dramatic interest. Jaques de Prie is a comic miser whose nervous fears about his house are reminiscent of Shylock as well as of Plautus' Euclio. The daughters of Count Ferneze, Aurelia and Phoenixella, answer their suitors with witty couplets after the fashion of the ladies in *Love's Labours Lost*. And as in Shakespeare's 'great feast of language', Jonson's verbal humour is further enriched by the banter of the Lylyesque pages Finio and Pacue, by punning jokes on Onion's nature and by the comic malapropisms and exuberant diction of his companion, Juniper, the 'merry cobbler' who won Thomas Nashe's admiration.

Unfortunately, an over-emphasis on Jonson's Shakespearean models can make *The Case Is Altered* seem merely like romantic comedy that does not reach its full potential. Although Paulo Ferneze's perfunctory forgiveness of the unfaithful Angelo in V.viii is more credible when compared with Valentine's reconciliation to Proteus in the *Two Gentlemen of Verona*, the resolution of Jonson's plot lacks the moral depth and emotional resonance of Shakespeare's endings, and Rachel de Prie is wooden and undeveloped in comparison to her Shakespearean counterparts.[33] Jonson's true interests lie elsewhere. Many of his characters are identified with a dominant mood or 'humour', and he constructs his plot so that their humours bring them into conflict with each other. Strictly speaking, an imbalance of the four humours or bodily fluids (blood, phlegm, black bile and yellow bile) was held to produce a dominant temperament (the sanguine or mirthful, the phlegmatic or stolid, the melancholy, or the choleric). However, Jonson and his contemporaries also used the term to apply to various kinds of temperamental predispositions, to a wide range of passions and to specific social affectations. In *The Case Is Altered*, the varied humours include Juniper's 'sprightly humour' of exalted speech (I.iv.9), the temperamental mirth and melancholy of Aurelia and Phoenixella respectively, Count Ferneze's 'wayward humour' of grief and impatience (see I.vi.83–7) and Jaques de Prie's obsessive anxiety about his gold. No consistent effort is made to change the characters, but the play's focus is on their exaggerated emotion. The real dramatic climax is not the reunion of Rachel and Paulo, but the meeting of Count Ferneze (lamenting the loss of his son), Christophero (lamenting the loss of Rachel de Prie's love), and Jaques (lamenting the loss of his gold).[34] Their unanswered appeals to each other for help are wryly observed by Maximilian and by Francisco Colonnia, who invite Aurelia and Phoenixella to laugh with them at the trio's 'constant passions' (V.xi.29).

The Case Is Altered thus belongs with a sub-class of Elizabethan 'humour' comedies in which irrational behaviour is held up for ridicule. The dramatic seasons of 1597 and 1598 saw a sudden vogue for comedy of this sort, often combined with the presentation of distinctive verbal affectations. The fashion was begun by George Chapman's *An Humourous Day's Mirth*, performed by the Lord Admiral's Men to record-setting audiences between March and November 1597.[35] Chapman depicts a number of passionate or temperamental humours, including jealousy, hypocritical lust, and melancholy. His humour characters are either subjected to comical frustrations or driven completely out of their humours by the plots of the witty gallant Lemot, who doubles as a satiric 'presenter' exhibiting the affected speech and predictable behaviour of a group of gallants. Fashionable foolery is also ridiculed in the figure of the gull Labesha, Seigneur de Foolasa. To soften the play's derisive laughter, Chapman provides a conventionally festive ending occasioned by two marriages. His successful formula was copied by Shakespeare in *The Merry Wives of Windsor*, probably written for the Garter Feast in April 1597, where Ford's jealousy, Dr. Caius' choler, Falstaff's lust, and Page's 'impatience' are all purged or frustrated in the course of the action, which is resolved by the most understated romantic union in Shakespeare's comedies, the marriage of Anne Page to young Fenton. Like Chapman, Shakespeare includes a gull – Master Slender – and various forms of colourful language, from the Host's 'mad' jollity, through Pistol's Marlovian bombast, to Nym's obsession with the term 'humour' itself. A third play in the same sub-genre is Henry Porter's *The Two Angry Women of Abington*, probably produced sometime in 1598, which also depicts the comical punishment of jealousy and choler and features the 'humourous mirth' of Nick Proverbs, whose name indicates his distinctive manner of speech.

When Jonson wrote *Every Man in His Humour* for the Lord Chamberlain's Men in the summer of 1598, then, he was following a dramatic trail blazed by Chapman and Shakespeare and partially explored in his own *The Case Is Altered*. Like *An Humourous Day's Mirth* and *The Merry Wives of Windsor*, *Every Man in His Humour* features a loose construction in which the various humour characters are manipulated in a series of separate actions that gradually become interwoven.[36] The misguided 'cares' of Lorenzo Senior (Old Knowell) about his son's imagined prodigality, the unfounded jealousy of Thorello (Kitely), the 'heady rashness or devouring choler' of Giuliano (Downright), the affected gentility of the country gull Stephano and the city gull Matheo and the affected bravery of the braggart soldier Bobadilla – all these become the target of intrigues conducted by Lorenzo Junior (Edward Knowell), his servant Musco (Brainworm), and his friend Prospero (Wellbred). The Terentian motif of tormenting the prying father is thus only one of several linked intrigues, and the concluding marriage between young Lorenzo and Hesperida (Bridget), like its counterparts in

Chapman and Shakespeare, is treated in a fairly perfunctory fashion, serving primarily to assure a festive conclusion.

Yet while the essential features of *Every Man in His Humour* are largely derivative, Jonson does make several distinctive contributions to the form of humour comedy. First, his ridicule of affected humours is expanded and intensified, drawing on the traditions of non-dramatic satire. The fashionable posturing of Stephano, Matheo, and Bobadilla brings to the stage the same type of false pretence satirised in the epigrams of Sir John Davies and Sir John Harington, in the verse satires of Joseph Hall, John Marston, Everard Guilpin and John Donne, and in such satiric prose pamphlets as Thomas Nashe's *Pierce Penniless his Supplication to the Devil* or Thomas Lodge's *Wits Misery and the World's Madness: Discovering the Devils Incarnate of This Age*.[37] Bobadilla's Italianate fencing terms, affected oaths and tobacco-taking and Matheo's sonneteering and affected melancholy are conventional targets of satiric portraiture, but Jonson's skill lies in the way he selects, combines, and gives dramatic vitality to the traits ridiculed by his predecessors. His satire seems so lively because his fools are not limited to a single trait, but exhibit some new affectation each time they appear on stage. Moreover, in their eagerness for self-display they illustrate what Alvin Kernan has called the 'energy of dullness', aggressively seeking to impress others with their superficial accomplishments.[38] For example, Shakespeare's gull, Slender, is characterised primarily by his shy indifference to Anne Page's charms and can bring himself to make only a few timid boasts about his fencing and his courage at bear-baiting in order to impress her. By contrast, the country gull Stephano, the lowest in Jonson's hierarchy of fools, is hypersensitive to imagined slights to his gentility, eagerly shows off the cheap sword he has been tricked into buying by Musco, is quick to copy the absurd oaths ('by the foot of Pharaoh') employed by Bobadilla and swaggers boldly in Giuliano's lost cloak.[39]

The dramatic vitality of Jonson's affected humour characters has led some recent interpreters to argue that Jonson is secretly celebrating the tenacity of their self-delusion, but the second quality that distinguishes *Every Man in His Humour* from other humour comedies of the period is the greater clarity of Jonson's satiric norms and his more rigorous exposure and punishment of affectation. His pretenders are judged against the standard of neo-Stoic and neo-Platonic ideals, which condemn the substitution of

'superficial forms' for 'a perfect real substance' (I.i.74–5) and oppose
'true election' – rational choice – to the sway of mere 'opinion' (see
I.i.181–5 and I.iv.33–40).[40] Moreover, Matheo's plagiarism and
Bobadilla's cowardice are contrasted with the poetic idealism of
Lorenzo Jr. and the courage of Prospero, who stands up to the
choleric Giuliano. In the end, the lack of self-knowledge shown by
Bobadilla and Matheo is punished through Doctor Clement's
ironically appropriate sentence (a night-long penance in sackcloth
and the ashes of Matheo's plagiarised poems), which later struck
Jonson as too harsh and was eliminated in the Folio version. The
folly of passionate humour is also condemned more explicitly than
in Chapman and Shakespeare, where irrationality seems to be
accepted as an amusing fact of the human condition; Lorenzo Sr.'s
long soliloquy on the proper dominance of reason over the passions
(II.ii.1–26) and Thorello's description of the corruption of judgement
by imagination (I.iv.200–17) are both ironic in that their speakers
accurately describe failings they cannot overcome, but they establish
the satiric norms against which irrationality is judged. Jonson thus
fulfils the instructive purpose that Sir Philip Sidney ascribes to the
satiric poet, who 'sportingly never leaveth until he make a man
laugh at folly and, at length ashamed, to laugh at himself' and who
'giveth us to feel how many headaches a passionate life bringeth us
to'.[41]

Even at this early stage, then, the primary goal of Jonsonian
comedy is neither romance nor reconciliation, but ridicule – though
ridicule that is tempered by mirth and a delight in innocent wit.
Already, too, one can see the characteristic concentration of comic
effect caused by combining in new and more ironic ways effects
used less imaginatively by his predecessors. *Every Man in His
Humour* seems to have been a moderately successful play (the title
page of the 1601 Quarto says that it was acted 'sundry times'), but
perhaps because it followed current dramatic fashion so closely, it
attracted no special notice when it was first produced. It does,
however, anticipate the direction that Jonsonian drama was
increasingly to take and so justifies its position at the head of the
1616 Folio.

3

The Emerging Classicist

If *Every Man in His Humour* created any stir at all on its opening day, Jonson had little time to enjoy it. Only two days later he fought a fatal duel in the fields at Shoreditch near the Curtain Theatre with his old colleague from Pembroke's Men, Gabriel Spencer (then acting with the Lord Admiral's Men), and was indicted for his murder.[1] Philip Henslowe reported the news to his son-in-law, the actor Edward Alleyn, with distress: 'It is for me hard and heavy since you were with me. I have lost one of my company, which hurteth me greatly – that is, Gabriel, for he is slain in Hogsden Fields by the hands of Benjamin Jonson, bricklayer'.[2] Although he was only twenty-two years old at his death, Spencer had already won fame for his acting, for he was later praised (under the name of 'Gabriel') by Thomas Heywood in his *Apology for Actors*.[3] No stranger to quarrels, Spencer had previously killed a companion who threatened him with a candlestick by running him through the eye.[4] Jonson's account of their duel makes Spencer the aggressor and emphasises his own disadvantage: 'being appealed to the fields, he had killed his adversary, which had hurt him in the arm, and whose sword was ten inches longer than his: for the which he was imprisoned, and almost at the gallows' (*Conv.*, ll. 241–4). In his own eyes, apparently, he played the role of a Prospero/Wellbred standing up courageously to a choleric Giuliano/Downright, but in the court's eyes his violence was willful. Jonson was found guilty but was saved from hanging by 'benefit of clergy' (a medieval concession to educated persons who could escape capital punishment once by demonstrating that they could read and translate a verse from the Latin Bible). He was, however, branded in the thumb and his goods were confiscated.

Jonson's brush with the gallows precipitated several crises. The first was spiritual and resulted in Jonson's conversion to Catholicism. Although Jonson may have excused his killing of

Spencer as an act of courage, he was also a highly emotional man with a deep sense of guilt about his failings. The Stoic humanism to which he subscribed endorsed an ideal of rational self-control and passionless calm, but Jonson's strong aggressive and libidinous drives could not be checked easily, and he was consequently given to periods of depression and to flamboyant expressions of remorse. In his poem 'To Heaven', published in the 1616 Folio, he counters the accusation that his moments of penitence are merely the result of melancholy 'disease' or are only 'for show', asking God to judge him if he dares pretend 'To aught but grace, or aim[s] at other end' (*For.* XV, l. 8). His appeals to God, he contends, spring from his awareness of his nature:

> I know my state, both full of shame, and scorn,
> Conceived in sin, and unto labour born,
> Standing with fear, and must with horror fall,
> And destined unto judgement, after all.[superscript]
>
> (ll. 17–20)

Some such mood of penitence verging on melancholy must have overtaken him during his imprisonment in 1598, and it apparently opened him to persuasion that the Catholic Church offered a surer way to salvation than the Anglican confession. He told William Drummond that during his imprisonment, which lasted until his trial in October, he took 'his religion by trust, of a priest who visited him in prison. Thereafter he was twelve years a papist' (*Conv.*, ll. 244–6). Considering that his father had suffered for his Protestantism under Queen Mary and that his old teacher William Camden had prided himself on his conversion of several Irish students to Anglicanism, Jonson's embrace of Catholicism is surprising, but it is by no means unique. As a compromise solution, the Anglican settlement opened Englishmen who accepted an ecclesiastical hierarchy and high-church ritual to continuing persuasion that Catholicism was the true and original faith, and the spectacle of laymen and missionary priests willing to risk persecution for their beliefs must have heightened Catholicism's appeal. Moreover, two of Jonson's intellectual heroes, Erasmus and Justus Lipsius, the neo-Stoic scholar, had remained faithful to the Roman church despite their disagreements with it.[5]

It has been suggested, without firm evidence, that the priest who converted Jonson was Father Thomas Wright, a Jesuit whose treatise on *The Passions of the Mind in General* was published in a second edition with commendatory poems by Jonson and his friend Hugh Holland in 1604.[6] Wright was imprisoned in the Clink in the summer of 1598, but seems to have been given more freedom to come and go during late September and October. Although he was one of the Jesuit missionary priests who risked death to win England back to Rome, he broke with his order in insisting that the Oath of Allegiance was compatible with Catholic faith. His skill in argument is certified by his conversion of the Anglican clergyman William Alabaster during debates held at the Dean of Westminster's residence in 1597. In *The Passions of the Mind* he also reveals a keen sensitivity to the psychology of conversion, as when he notes that in order to induce anyone 'to pensiveness, sorrow for his sins, the fear of God, or any sad passion' one should 'take him at such times as melancholy most oppresseth him'.[7] Wright's interest in the relationship between the passions and humours, treated at length in the first two books of his work, would no doubt have made him a welcome visitor to a dramatist who had just written a comedy of humours. On the other hand, Jonson may have met Wright in Catholic circles at a later date and been invited to contribute his prefatory poem to Wright's treatise because of his reputation as the age's leading 'humourist'.

Jonson's second crisis was monetary. He was never thrifty – Drummond later described him as 'careless either to gain or keep' (*Conv.*, l. 690), and his financial situation following the confiscation of his goods must have been very pressing indeed. At this time the going rate for a completed play was only six pounds, regardless of the number of authors. Despite payments for his share of *Hot Anger Soon Cold* and for completing *Every Man in His Humour*, his income from playwriting was not sufficient to meet his needs. On 2 April 1599, he borrowed ten pounds from the actor Robert Browne, promising its return on Whitsunday (27 May); his subsequent payment of his back quarterage fees to the Tylers and Bricklayers Company in April 1599 may indicate that he reverted to bricklaying out of necessity. His collaboration with Thomas Dekker and Henry Chettle on *Page of Plymouth* and *Robert the Second, the King of Scot's Tragedy* in August and September no doubt also reflects his need for cash. The birth of a second son, Joseph, christened at St. Giles, Cripplegate, on 9 December 1599, must have further strained his resources despite his recent income from *Every Man out of His Humour*.[8] Browne's money had not been repaid, and when he could get no satisfaction, he had Jonson imprisoned for debt; late in January 1600 he was awarded a judgment of eleven pounds, which Jonson must have raised somehow in order to be released from the Marshalsea Prison.[9]

Had Jonson taken a different approach to playwriting, he might have resolved his difficulties more easily. The Elizabethan theatre had a voracious appetite for scripts. Employing a repertory system in which a number of different plays were performed in any given period, with less popular ones dropped as their drawing power diminished, theatrical companies required a constant supply of new plays, for which they paid between six and ten pounds a piece. Playwrights who were able to compose rapidly and were willing to collaborate with others on a production-line basis could make substantial sums in comparison to non-dramatic poets. For his 'copious industry' in producing all or part of some forty-five plays for Philip Henslowe's companies between 1598 and 1604 Dekker earned one hundred and ten pounds; Chettle was paid one hundred and twenty-three pounds for his share in fifty plays over a five-year period. Even learned poets who wrote primarily for patronage sometimes turned to the theatre in periods of need. George Chapman, who ventured into playwriting periodically to support his translation of Homer, worked on seven plays (including the 'tragedy of Benjamin's plot') over fourteen months in 1598 and 1599; Michael Drayton collaborated on sixteen plays in the same period. Although the records of Jonson's collaborations indicate that he was occasionally willing to write under such conditions, he preferred to produce what John Webster was to call his 'laboured and understanding works' more deliberately.[10] In *Satiromastix* Dekker taunted him (unfairly) for the slowness of his composition: 'You nasty tortoise, you and your itchy poetry break out like Christmas, but once a year' (V.ii.201–3). Jonson responded in the 'Apologetical Dialogue' affixed to *Poetaster* with contempt for such 'scribes', who reduced writing for 'the abused theatres' to a mere 'trade' (ll. 196–8).

Jonson had already dissociated himself from inferior artists in the Quarto version of *Every Man in His Humour*, where Lorenzo Junior laments the condition of Poetry

> As she appears in many, poor and lame,
> Patch'd up in remnants and old worn rags,
> Half-starv'd for want of her peculiar food,
> Sacred invention

and exclaims against poetasters like Matheo, who stands for all poets pandering to popular taste:

> That such lean, ignorant, and blasted wits,
> Such brainless gulls, should utter their stol'n wares
> With such applauses in our vulgar ears;
> Or that their slubber'd lines have current pass
> From the fat judgements of the multitude.
> (V.iii. 301–4, 317–21)

Auditors familiar with the Elizabethan literary scene would have found nothing new in such attacks, nor in Lorenzo Junior's celebration of poetry as 'blessed, eternal, and most true divine' when it was 'attired in the majesty of art' and 'set high in spirit with the precious taste / Of sweet philosophy' (ll. 299, 307–9). Similar assertions of poetry's value and complaints about its popular abuses were to be found in Nashe's preface to Greene's *Menaphon* (1589), in Sidney's *An Apology for Poetry* (published 1595), and in the prefatory letter 'To the Honourable Gentlemen of England, True Favourers of Poesy' in Drayton's *Matilda* (1594). What was unusual about Jonson's pronouncements was that they were made in the theatre – the very home of popular taste. Instead of accepting the theatre's function as an entertainment industry and serving it anonymously as did other dramatists, Jonson sought to dignify playwriting by holding up a new standard for dramatic poetry. In the process, he not only created controversy and gained personal notoriety, but he succeeded in elevating the status of drama itself.[11]

Jonson also differed from the average playwright of his time in that he engaged in systematic study and sought a wider circle of learned company. Unlike the dramatists attached by contract to particular theatrical troupes, he was not so much concerned to find suitable narrative materials that he could turn into plots as to broaden and deepen his Westminster education. In 'An Execration upon Vulcan', written in 1623 after his library was ravaged by fire, he laments the loss of various works in progress and of 'twice twelve years stored up humanity' (l. 101), a term which suggests that he had begun regular reading and note-taking by 1599 or 1600. Apparently an avid book-buyer from his early years onward, Jonson eventually assembled a substantial collection, though he told Drummond that 'sundry times he hath devoured his books, i.[e.] sold them all for necessity' (*Conv.*, ll. 328–9), as he may well have done when arrested for debt in 1599. Some idea of his wide-ranging reading may be obtained from the catalogue of existing volumes containing his signature or his motto, 'Tanquam explorator' ('ever the scout/spy'), the younger Seneca's phrase for his habit of finding material for reflection in the works of philosophers who did not belong to his own Stoic school of thought.[12] Many of Jonson's books have been lost to the 1623 fire or to the indifference of later times, but the two hundred surviving titles indicate that his library was strongest in Greek and Latin authors, including texts of the major poets and playwrights, historians and philosophers, and in contemporary scholarship on ancient language, literature and customs. He also collected neo-Latin poetry and the works of such noted humanists as Petrarch, Erasmus and Vives; major English poets such as Chaucer, Spenser, Daniel, Drayton, Chapman and Marston; rhetorical or educational treatises such as George Puttenham's *The Art of English Poesy* and Richard Mulcaster's *Positions*; works by such continental authors as Montaigne and Guicciardini, usually in translation; and theological or devotional works. He had minor interests in Roman military history, geometry, the occult (witchcraft, alchemy, and astrology) and, surprisingly – given his scorn of romantic comedy – Greek and continental romances.

Jonson's continuing studies show how thoroughly he had internalised the aims of his Westminster education and how powerful was his drive to learn all he could about classical, and particularly Roman, culture. Despite his historical interest in the details of Roman life, however, he approached the classics not as products of a distant civilisation, but as continuing sources of wisdom, critical guidance and artistic inspiration. According to William Drummond, Jonson listed Pindar, Martial, Horace, Juvenal and Persius as authors to be read 'for delight', praised Petronius, Pliny the younger and Tacitus as those he thought 'spoke best Latin', and declared that 'Quintilian's 6, 7, 8 books were not only to be read, but altogether digested' (*Conv.*, ll. 123–6). His emphasis on Quintilian is significant, for it was largely from the Roman rhetorician's *The Education of an Orator* (*Institutio Oratoria*) and from Horace's *The Art of Poetry* which he had translated by 1605 and on which he later wrote a commentary, that he derived his views on poets and poetry.

In fact, his recommendation that parts of Quintilian were to be 'altogether digested' is itself an illustration of his thorough absorption of classical ideals, for at X.i.19 Quintilian himself had drawn out the analogy between reading and digestion, urging that 'just as we do not swallow our food till we have chewed it . . . so what we read must not be committed to the memory for subsequent imitation while it is still in a crude state, but must be . . . reduced to a pulp by frequent re-perusal'. Jonson's practice of assimilating what he read is exemplified by his *Timber: or Discoveries*, 'made upon men and matter: as they have flowed out of his daily readings; or had their reflux to his peculiar notion of the times'. These 'explorata' (as they are called in the heading of the posthumous 1640 Folio edition, where they were published for the first time) are notes taken by the poet-'explorator' while spying out passages from other men's works with which he particularly agreed. From the publication dates of his sources and from occasional allusions, it is apparent that many passages in *Discoveries* were composed in the late 1620s or the 1630s, but some could have been written at any time in his career, and there is no reason to believe them to be substantially different in character from the 'twice twelve years stored up humanity' that Jonson lost in the 1623 fire. The entries vary in length from aphoristic sayings to substantial essays; in most cases they have been translated from Latin sources, condensed and reworded in Jonson's own curt style, and – where appropriate – given a personal or a contemporary reference. In his comments on wit, for example, Jonson adapts Quintilian's comparison (II.v.11–12) between the exaggerated qualities of Roman style and the Romans' use of depilatories, curling irons, and cosmetics in personal adornment:

> But now . . . right and natural language seems to have least of the wit in it; . . . as if no face were fair, that were not powdered, or painted! No beauty to be had, but in wresting, and writhing our own tongue! . . . All must be as affected, and preposterous as our gallants' clothes, sweet bags, and night-dressings: in which you would think our men lay in, like ladies: it is so curious.
>
> (*Disc.*, ll. 714–27)

The passage as a whole is an accurate paraphrase of its source, but Jonson's additions transform it into a criticism of Jacobean taste and the effeminacy of male fashion in the early seventeenth century. Moreover, since the views expressed are consistent with his repeated satire on linguistic and sartorial affectation, they have the force of a personal statement even though they are not original.

The process of appropriation illustrated here is typical of Jonson's method in general; his poems, plays, and masques are full of passages from classical literature that have been 'Englished' in such a way that they speak directly to the conditions of his time. Modern readers who think of poets as spinning poetry out of their own insights tend to discount Jonson's art when they discover that much of his matter is adapted from Roman or Greek authors. Elizabethan and Jacobean writers, however, were less concerned with originality than with the skilful reworking of age-old themes. They agreed with Horace that it is harder 'to treat in your own way what is common' than to give the world 'a theme unknown and unsung'.[13] The 'sacred invention' about which Lorenzo Junior rhapsodises in *Every Man in His Humour* is the power of finding material – from whatever source – that is appropriate to the occasion for which one writes and of arranging it in artful or ingenious ways. Moreover, although Jonson was concerned with the integrity and the consistency of his voice, he did not see himself, like the Romantics, as a unique sensibility, but as the spokesman for the best values of his culture. As George Parfitt has observed, for Jonson 'aesthetics is finally at the service of ethics; the poet's task, as good man, is to make himself virtuous by self-examination and by learning from others, and to place this virtue and wisdom at the service of society'.[14] By incorporating the thought of the Roman moralists into his own writing and by identifying contemporary examples of the behaviour which they praised or ridiculed, he was fulfilling the elevated office that he envisioned for poetry.

Quintilian had assumed that his young orator would imitate not only the matter, but also the manner of experienced speakers. In the Renaissance, poetic theorists blended his views with those of Horace and the two Senecas into a doctrine of poetic imitation, which Jonson summarises clearly in the *Discoveries* in a passage adapted from the Latin of Joannes Buchler's *Poetical Institute* (1635):

> The third requisite in our poet, or maker, is imitation, to be able to convert the substance, or riches of another poet, to his own use. To make choice of one excellent man above the rest, and so to follow him, till he grow very he, or so like him as the copy may be mistaken for the principal. . . . Not, to imitate servilely, as Horace saith, and catch at vices, for virtue: but, to draw forth out of the best, and choicest flowers, with the bee, and turn all into honey, work it into one relish, and savour: make our imitation sweet:

observe how the best writers have imitated, and follow them. How Virgil, and Statius have imitated Homer; how Horace, Archilochus . . . and so of the rest.

(*Disc.*, ll. 3057–76)

Although Jonson must have written this passage not too long before his death, it expresses principles he had followed since his earliest days. The metaphor of the imitator as a bee is derived from Seneca's Epistle LXXXIV, but Buchler and Jonson are essentially following Quintilian, who twice recommends that the advanced student pick one speaker for special imitation, though he cautions against too exclusive devotion to a single model. In pointing to Virgil's imitation of Homer and Horace's of Archilochus, Jonson in effect advocates selecting a different guide for each poetic genre, as he himself had followed Horace in his verse epistles, Martial in his epigrams, and Pindar in his odes.

The concept of imitation was to hold a special appeal for writers in seventeenth-century England because it reflected a parallel between their own artistic situation and that of Romans in the early empire. Republican Rome, grown to imperial strength, had conquered the east but had in turn been conquered by Greek culture. Just as English grammar-school and university students were educated in Latin, the Romans studied Greek and found in Greek literature possibilities lacking in their own poetry. Either by writing Latin plays based on Greek models, as Plautus and Terence revised and combined the plots of Menander, or by introducing Greek verse forms into Latin, as Horace imitated the iambics of Archilochus in his *Epodes*, or by bringing greater artistic skill and discrimination to forms pioneered by earlier Roman writers, as Horace improved upon the verse satires of Lucilius, Roman poets in the time of Augustus and his immediate successors saw themselves as raising Latin literature to a new level of achievement. Little wonder, then, that late Elizabethan writers, confronted at once by the seeming linguistic and metrical crudity of medieval and early Tudor poetry, by the respect for classical literature instilled by Tudor education and by the example of classically inspired French and Italian poets, found that the doctrine of imitation spoke to their own cultural condition. The belief that English poets should rival the achievement of their classical predecessors by imitating the genres in which they wrote is evident in Francis Meres' 'A Comparative Discourse of our English Poets with the Greek, Latin, and Italian Poets', included in his *Palladis Tamia, Wits Treasury* (1598). Meres' comparison of Shakespeare's comedies and tragedies to the works of Plautus and Seneca is often quoted, but it is only one example from among many parallels that he draws between English and classical authors. His remarks about Spenser's pastorals are typical of his stress on imitation and invention:

> As Theocritus is famous for his *Idylls* in Greek, and Virgil for his *Eclogues* in Latin: so Spenser their imitator in his *Shepherds' Calendar* is renowned for the like argument, and honoured for fine poetical invention and most exquisite wit.[15]

Jonson's desire to present himself as the English Horace, Martial, Pindar, or Aristophanes is perfectly in accord with the spirit of the age.

The tension between following one's literary models so 'as the copy may be mistaken for the principal' and avoiding servile devotion is, of course, difficult to maintain. Yet as Richard S. Peterson notes, the doctrine of imitation promoted by the ancient poets and rhetoricians involved 'a paradoxical combination of affectionate respect for authority and vigorous independence that had a powerful appeal for the loyal yet headstrong young Jonson'.[16] It was paradoxical, first of all, because Quintilian, Horace and Seneca had themselves championed the cause of modern letters; the debate between ancients and moderns which was to preoccupy much English criticism in the seventeenth century had its inspiration in the ancients' own responses to their literary past and in the echoes of their views by such Renaissance humanists as Vives, whose lead Jonson follows in *Discoveries*:

> To all the observations of the ancients, we have our own experience: which, if we will use, and apply, we have better means to pronounce. It is true they opened the gates, and made the way, that went before us; but as guides, not commanders: . . . . Truth lies open to all; it is no man's several.
>
> (ll. 166–73)

The last two sentences in this passage are a quotation from Seneca's Epistle XXXIII, where he argues against filling his works with maxims by earlier Stoics. Jonson – like Dryden after him – is actually faithful to the spirit of classical literary theory in asserting the potential merit of modern writing.

Jonson's relation to his literary predecessors was paradoxical in a second sense because it combined imitation and rivalry. Quintilian had countered the dangers of uninspired copying by urging the orator to strive to outdo his predecessors: 'for the man whose aim is to prove himself better than another, even if he does not surpass him, may hope to equal him. But . . . the mere follower must ever lag behind' (X.ii.10). Horace, too, had fostered a spirit of independence, at once acknowledging his indebtedness to the early Roman satirist Lucilius and criticising him for mixing Latin and Greek phrases and for his hasty, unpolished compositions. Their competitive spirit attracted the combative Jonson, sanctioning his drive to outstrip the authors whose initiative he followed. To be sure, it would have seemed presumptuous to claim superiority to a classical writer like Horace or Martial. Jonson was generally content with the recognition that he was their English equivalent, though in private he may have boasted, as he did to William Drummond, of his skill in assimilating the work of so many different classical writers at once: 'He was better versed, and knew more in Greek and Latin, than all the poets in England, and quintessenceth their [Greek and Latin writers'] brains' (*Conv.*, ll. 645–7). In his great middle comedies, as we shall see, he aspired to surpass ancients and moderns alike by recombining motifs from earlier comedy and satire into more intricate and more richly ironic plots.

For the most part, however, his rivalry was directed at his fellow Elizabethans, with whom he was often at odds.[17] His strategy, in fact, often was to distinguish himself from his contemporaries by claiming to have realised a more authentic classicism or a higher standard of art even when working with forms that had been introduced by others. For example, in Epigram XVIII, 'To My Mere English Censurer', he answers critics who complain that his epigrams are different from those of most English epigrammatists:

> To thee, my way in epigrams seems new,
> When both it is the old way, and the true.
> Thou say'st, that cannot be: for thou hast seen
> Davies, and Weever, and the best have been,
> And mine come nothing like. I hope so.
>
> (ll. 1–5)

Whereas he disparaged the epigrams of Sir John Harington and John Owen as 'bare narrations' because they lacked 'point' (the witty turn by which Martial makes his ironic implications clear), he sought to set his own epigrams off from those of his English rivals in the genre by capturing the essence of Martial's manner.[18] His bold use of direct address, his habit of dismissing his victims with a curt phrase, his subtle innuendo and his play on the moral implications of closely related terms (a device also used in his epistles) are all stylistic traits adapted from Martial.

Jonson's impulse to outdo his fellow poets by imitating classical forms more authentically is first manifested in his works of 1599 and 1600. The earliest statement of his neo-classical creed is the Induction and 'Grex' (or chorus) of *Every Man out of His Humour*, initially performed sometime in the late autumn or early winter of 1599 and entered for publication on 8 April 1600.[19] There Jonson rejects strict adherence to neo-classical 'laws' of comic construction, reserving for modern playwrights 'the same licence, or free power, to illustrate and heighten our invention' as was enjoyed by the ancients, yet he describes his play as 'strange, and of a particular kind by itself, somewhat like *Vetus Comoedia* [that is, Greek Old Comedy]' (Ind., ll. 228–9, 258–9). In fact, *Every Man out of His Humour* is not entirely strange in form, being merely a conventional comedy of humours without the reconciliation and marriage that ensure a festive ending, and its induction and 'Grex', though more critically self-conscious, functions essentially the same way as Will Summers' commentary in Nashe's *Summers' Last Will and Testament*. Yet Jonson apparently saw his exclusive concentration on driving the affected characters out of their humours as a translation of the aggressive spirit of Aristophanic comedy to the Elizabethan stage, and he signalled his innovation by choosing for part of his title-page motto Horace's boast that he had introduced the biting iambics of Archilochus to Latin poetry.[20]

A second, and almost contemporaneous, claim of innovation was made in his 'Epistle to Elizabeth, Countess of Rutland' (*For.*, XII), where he speaks proudly of 'my strange poems, which, as yet, / Had not their form touched by an English wit' (ll. 81–2). Written for delivery on New Year's Day 1600, the 'Epistle to Rutland' does not specify which poems Jonson had in mind. Possibly he was thinking of the epistolary form itself, which – like the epigram of praise – proved ideal for soliciting patronage from Jonson's noble acquaintances.[21] Despite such earlier antecedents as Wyatt's 'Mine Own John Poins', poems modelled on Horace's two books of verse epistles were relatively new to English poetry in the 1590s. Thomas Lodge had included eight epistles, composed in iambic pentameter couplets, in his *A Fig for Momus* (1595), advertising them in his address 'To the Gentlemen Readers Whatsoever' as being 'in that kind, wherein no Englishman of our time hath publically written'; in fact, however, many of them are merely versified proverbs or treatises.[22] By 1600 John Donne had written a number of verse letters, ranging from short poems on friendship and absence to several longer pieces addressed to Rowland Woodward and Sir Henry Wotton which glance satirically at court, country and city while repeating the Stoic advice to cultivate the inner self. Their high sententiousness is shared by the six epistles included in Samuel Daniel's *A Panegyric Congratulatory* (1603), addressed to various nobles on such appropriate themes as justice, honour, contempt of Fortune, and virtuous self-knowledge. Jonson had earlier ridiculed Daniel as an old-fashioned Petrarchan in *Every Man in His Humour* by having Matheo plagiarise from the first sonnet in Daniel's *Delia*; Daniel's verse epistles, which are generally considered to be among his best poems, mark his rivalry with Jonson for the taste of a new generation. Jonson's self-consciousness about their competition is evident from his reference in the 'Epistle to Rutland' to the Countess of Bedford's having 'a better verser got, / (Or poet, in the court account) than I', one who 'doth me (though I not him) envy' (ll. 68–70), an allusion that Drummond of Hawthornden, on Jonson's own authority, related to Daniel.[23]

Whether the 'Epistle to Rutland' antedates Daniel's efforts in the genre is uncertain, but it already exhibits the qualities that were to make Jonson the pre-eminent writer of the form in the early seventeenth century. Like those of Donne and Daniel, his verse epistles draw on the Stoic wisdom of the Roman moralists in ways appropriate to the character of his addressees, but they blend the personal and the public, joining to his satiric criticism of the age's vices and his philosophical commentary a self-consciousness about his own role as poet or friend, and they are written in a plain style that is at once familiar and dignified. The 'Epistle to Rutland' begins with observations on the corrupting effects of gold that are appropriate to its presentation on New Year's Day, when clients gave gifts to patrons in hope of greater reward, and evolves into an encomium on the value of poetry calculated to appeal to Lady Rutland, the daughter of Sir Philip Sidney. It is at once a moral commentary contrasting the virtues of the classical Golden Age with contemporary greed and a tactful claim to patronage. Jonson's assumption that his 'offering will find grace' with the Countess makes it impossible for her to refuse him a reward without denying that she shares her father's 'love unto the muses' (ll. 30, 33), while his mention of her friend Lucy Russell, the Countess of Bedford, implies that the social coterie to which she belongs is deservedly celebrated for virtue and beauty.[24] At the same time, the theme of poetry as the source of fame allows him to introduce his own aspirations for recognition.

Stylistically, Jonson effectively captures the speaking tone of voice, approximating Horace's ideal of 'poetry, so moulded from the familiar that anybody may hope for the same success, may sweat much and yet toil in vain when attempting the same'.[25] As D.J. Palmer has noted, 'the classical temper' of his epistles' springs from a plain style that is 'informal but without slackness or superfluity, incisive and penetrating in judgement, and eschewing eccentricity to achieve that authoritative "antiquity of voice" '.[26] Although his verse is rarely rough, his frequent use of caesura, enjambment and extra stress creates a powerful tension between verse form and syntax. The tautness of his verse does much to eliminate the tedium that sometimes besets Lodge's or Daniel's epistles, and it sustains his own pose as a judicious, plain-spoken commentator on the human scene.

In boasting of his 'strange poems' Jonson may also have been thinking of such early works as the 'Epode' (*For.* XI) and the Pindaric 'Ode to James, Earl of Desmond' (*Und.* XXV), both of which were quoted in Robert Allot's *England's Parnassus, or The Choicest Flowers of Our Modern Poets* (1600), or the 'Ode Enthusiastic' (*M. P.* XXXI) that is labelled in one contemporary manuscript collection as a poem to Lady Bedford.[27] The 'Epode', at least, was a genuine innovation, its alternating five-foot and three-foot iambic lines forming a rough equivalent to the iambic couplets of Horace's *Epodes*. Michael Drayton was to include a section of odes, primarily of Horatian inspiration, in his *Poems Lyric and Pastoral* (1606), and on that basis he has been called 'the first proper ode writer in English' by one historian of the form.[28] However, Jonson's 'Ode to Desmond' was written before August 1600 and may well precede Drayton's odes. Addressed to an Irish earl imprisoned in the Tower of London, it employs the elevated style and elaborate stanza form of Pindar:

> Where art thou, genius? I should use
> Thy present aid: arise invention,
> Wake, and put on the wings of Pindar's muse,
>> To tower with my intention
>> High, as his mind, that doth advance
> Her upright head, above the reach of chance,
>> Or the times' envy:
>> Cynthius, I apply
> My bolder numbers to thy golden lyre:
>> O, then inspire
> Thy priest in this strange rapture; heat my brain
>> With Delphic fire:
> That I may sing my thoughts, in some unvulgar strain.
>
> (ll. 1–13)

Jonson's mention of poetic rapture may sound strange coming from someone who reported that 'he wrote all his [verses] first in prose' (*Conv.*, l. 382), but reference to inspired invention is a consistent feature of his comments about the poetic process. Jonson's imitation of Pindar here produces a mannered and bombastic style that is not his best medium. The 'Ode Enthusiastic', a celebration of Lady Bedford's graces written in six four-line stanzas consisting of two trimeter couplets, is closer to the Horatian model and is more typical of Jonson's short, polished lyrics.

As an innovator in lyric form, Jonson did not make so public a claim to recognition as he did for his dramatic work, but he apparently boasted enough about his 'strange poems' to stir up some reaction. The 'Epode' and the 'Ode Enthusiastic' were published in 1601 in Robert Chester's *Love's Martyr* as part of 'The Turtle and the Phoenix' poems dedicated to Sir John Salusbury; the 'Ode to Desmond' was not published in its entirety until after Jonson's death but must have been widely enough circulated in manuscript for Thomas Dekker's parody of it in *Satiromastix* (1601) to be effective (see Chapter 4). Jonson's vaunted classicism also seems to be alluded to in Drayton's 'To Himself and the Harp', the introductory ode in his *Poems Lyric and Pastoral*, which defends Drayton's right to compete in the form:

And why not I, as he
That's greatest, if as free,
(In sundry strains that strive,
Since there so many be)
Th'old lyric kind revive?

I will, yea, and I may;
Who shall oppose my way?
For what is he alone,
That of himself can say,
He's heir of Helicon?
(ll. 1-10)[29]

Drayton's vaguely-worded resentment at those who would promote themselves as the exclusive heirs to Greek and Latin poetry is yet another indication of the intense rivalry among the leading professional poets, a rivalry directed in this case toward Lady Bedford's favour in particular.[30] In the competition for patronage in the early seventeenth century, the claim to an authentic classicism was an obvious advantage which Jonson exploited, stimulating Drayton, like Daniel, to attempt new forms rather than be left behind.

4
Comical Satire and the War of the Theatres

At the same time that Jonson was competing with Daniel and Drayton for patronage for his lyric poetry, he was also redirecting his theatrical energies toward the more literate and sophisticated members of the Elizabethan public. In *Every Man out of His Humour* (1599) and *Cynthia's Revels* (1600) he extended the comedy of humours into a distinctive form of 'comical satire' orientated toward the taste of the London gallants and wits with whom he increasingly associated. Yet while his poetic skill and classical learning gained him entry into elite social and intellectual circles, his poverty and low status made his position tenuous, and his ridicule of fashionable folly risked offending the very groups from whom he sought patronage. His self-consciousness about his marginal position in society underlies his characterisation of the poet-figures Macilente in *Every Man out of His Humour* and Crites in *Cynthia's Revels*, but these fantasies of social vindication only provoked the theatrical quarrel with John Marston and Thomas Dekker that is now known hyperbolically as 'The War of the Theatres'. Although this incident is sometimes dismissed impatiently by critics who deny that topical satire has artistic significance, it reveals much about the tensions in the Elizabethan literary system, and it marks an important stage in Jonson's emergence as a 'laureate dramatist'.[1]

One striking anomaly in Jonson's situation was that the bricklayer-turned-playmaker kept extraordinary company for someone of his rank. No doubt this was partly due to continuing contacts with his old schoolmaster William Camden, to whom he continued to pay affectionate tribute, and with some of his Westminster schoolfellows. Though apparently never a member of the Society of Antiquaries which Camden and his former pupil Sir Robert Cotton founded in 1587, he was on close terms with Cotton and with Hugh Holland, a fellow-Catholic and former Westminster boy for whose poem *Pancharis* he contributed commendatory verses in 1603. Holland described Cotton's lodging at Lord Hunsdon's house in

43

the late 1590s as 'the rendezvous of all good and honest spirits so
[that] it seemed a kind of university', and a letter of his to Cotton
includes greetings to Jonson, to Camden and to Richard Martin, the
lawyer and wit to whom Jonson dedicated *Poetaster* in the 1616
Folio.[2] Other literary men who were friends of Cotton and Camden
(though not equally close to Jonson) were Michael Drayton and the
epigrammatist John Davies.[3]

Perhaps through Martin or Cotton, both members of the Middle
Temple, Jonson also made acquaintances in the four London legal
societies known collectively as the Inns of Court (Gray's Inn,
Lincoln's Inn, the Middle and Inner Temple). In the sixteenth
century, these institutions not only provided chambers for barristers
and legal education for aspiring lawyers, but they also served as the
residence of many young gentlemen who participated in London
society for a few years while acquiring a smattering of law. Jonson's
ties with the Inns of Court are advertised in the Folio dedication of
Every Man out of His Humour, where he addresses them as 'the
noblest nurseries of humanity and liberty in the kingdom': 'I
understand you, gentlemen, not your houses. . . . When I wrote this
poem, I had friendship with divers in your societies; who, as they
were great names in learning, so they were no less examples of
living' (ll. 6–10). These 'great names' cannot be definitely identified,
but many of Jonson's known acquaintances were younger lawyers
and gentlemen with a literary bent.[4] The majority were members of
the Middle Temple, particularly those associated with the *Prince
d'Amour* revels of 1597/8, in which Richard Martin played the
leading role as the Prince of Love. Other members of this group
were Benjamin Rudyerd, the addressee of three of Jonson's
epigrams, and John Hoskyns, a lawyer and member of parliament
whose manuscript treatise *Directions for Speech and Style* is excerpted
in Jonson's *Discoveries*.[5] Hoskyns, who was somewhat older than the
others, was noted for his learning, for in addition to his rhetorical
treatise he is reported to have begun work on a Greek lexicon, and
he was a poet of some facility. His emphasis on brevity, perspicuity,
and plainness in letter writing may have helped to shape Jonson's
style. According to John Aubrey, when Hoskyns' son Sir Bennet
desired Jonson to admit him to the company of his 'sons' Jonson
replied, 'I dare not; 'tis honour enough for me to be your brother: I
was your father's son and 'twas he that polished me'.[6] Among
Jonson's other Middle Temple acquaintances were the character
writer Thomas Overbury; the future diplomat Henry Wotton; the

poet John Marston; and Sir John Salusbury, to whom Marston, Jonson, Chapman, and Shakespeare dedicated *The Turtle and the Phoenix* in 1601. The Inns of Court author with whom Jonson was to have the closest association was John Donne. From 1591 to 1594 Donne had been a member of Lincoln's Inn, where he is reported by Sir Richard Baker to have been 'a great visitor of ladies, a great frequenter of plays, a great writer of conceited verses'.[7] When Jonson first met Donne is uncertain, though his statement to Drummond (*Conv.*, ll. 104–5) that Donne had 'written all his best pieces ere he was twenty-five years old' – that is, before 1597 – suggests an early acquaintance, and Jonson surely would have thought of him in an Inns of Court context. Donne's continuing celebrity in those circles is documented by the Middle Temple student John Manningham, a friend of Hoskyns, Martin, Rudyerd, and Overbury, whose diary for 1602–3 includes anecdotes about Donne, Jonson, and Marston and quotations from Donne's prose paradoxes and his poems.[8]

The spirit of this loosely connected fellowship – and of the Inns of Court environment as a whole – is aptly characterised by Jonson's terms 'humanity' and 'liberty'. In part the Inns were centres of 'humanity' precisely because of their 'liberty': they imposed no formal academic requirements aside from residence and attendance at the mock disputations or moots, leaving their commoners free to pursue their own studies in what Sir George Buc called 'the third university of England' – London. While less seriously inclined residents spent their time and money attending the theatre and the fencing schools or acquiring the skills that formed Buc's 'science of revelling' (music, dancing, and so on), many others, like Donne, combined their legal studies with the reading of theology, history, philosophy and literature, ancient and modern.[9] Isaac Walton reports that in 'the most unsettled days of his youth' Donne was accustomed to study from 4 a.m. to 10 a.m., 'though he took great liberty after it'.[10] At the Inns this 'liberty' meant not only the freedom to enjoy the pleasures of the city and court, but also participation in licensed misrule at holiday revels. Formally, misrule was channelled into the 'law sports' held during the holiday seasons, combining masques, mock ceremonies, and satiric shows. Informally, it overflowed into such riotous activities as 'forcibly breaking open chambers in the night and levying money as the Lord of Misrule's rent' for which Davies, Martin and others were censured in 1591 and expelled or suspended in the following year.[11] The aggressive energies vented at such periods of misrule were later to find expression in parliamentary opposition to royal policies, but in the 1590s their chief outlet was satiric wit. The literary genres favored by Inns writers – erotic elegy, satiric epigram and formal verse satire – reflected a masculine, unsentimental view of life and displayed their real or fantasised skill at sophistical seduction, witty bawdry, and satiric observation. Some of their works were circulated only in manuscript, but by the late 1590s many had found their way into print, including John Davies' *Epigrams*, Marston's *The Metamorphosis of Pygmalion's Image and Certain Satires* (1598) and *The Scourge of Villainy* (1598), and his cousin Everard Guilpin's *Skialetheia, or A Shadow of Truth in Certain Epigrams and Satires* (1598).

Some awareness of the Inns of Court as a literary milieu is important for understanding Jonson's three comical satires, for they are calculated for the sensibilities of auditors who are urbane, alert to ironies, knowledgeable about and yet somewhat detached from the fashionable world of Elizabethan London. The kind of social pretence and courtly affectation they ridicule is exactly like that targeted in the *Prince d'Amour* revels of 1597/8 and in the formal verse satires of Marston, Guilpin and Donne. In *Every Man in His Humour*, of course, Jonson had already drawn on Elizabethan prose and verse satire for his characterisation of Matheo and Bobadilla, and his chief satiric agents, Lorenzo Junior (Young Knowell) and Prospero (Wellbred), saw themselves, like the Inns of Court satirists, as 'an elite of wits in a world of gulls'.[12] *Every Man out of His Humour*, performed by the Lord Chamberlain's Men at the newly erected Globe Theatre in the autumn of 1599, mimics the form of verse satire even more directly, concentrating exclusively on affected humours and presenting itself as the work of the satirist Asper ('harsh, severe'), a scourge-bearing moralist in the mould of Marston's Kinsayder and other rough satyr-satirists of the 1590s. Some of Jonson's changes were a logical extension of his original humour formula, but he was no doubt also responding to the recent ban on formal satire. On 1 June, the Archbishop of Canterbury and the Bishop of London, apparently concerned about the proliferation of libel and personal invective, ordered many titles to be burned and prohibited the further publication of satire and epigrams.[13] In such a climate, a humour comedy presented as a 'comical satire' would have held a special box-office appeal for more sophisticated theatre-goers. That the play was produced by the Lord Chamberlain's Men may indicate their early interest in competing with the newly reopened private playhouses at St. Paul's and Blackfriars for a fashionable clientele.[14]

Jonson's appropriation of Elizabethan formal satire in *Every Man out of His Humour* is an excellent example of the way he builds on and yet maintains his independence from the works of others. Like Marston's Kinsayder, Asper is overcome by the 'fierce indignation' that inspired the Roman poet Juvenal. Bursting on stage with a whip in hand, he threatens 'to strip the ragged follies of the time / Naked, as at their birth' (ll. 17–18). Jonson's prose 'character' of Asper ('He is of an ingenious and free spirit, eager and constant in reproof, without fear controlling the world's abuses') indicates that he is not intended as a pure parody, but neither does Jonson identify himself whole-heartedly with the Juvenalian spirit of contemporary satire. Asper functions as his spokesman in explaining the concept of humours, in arguing for freedom from strict comic 'laws' and in appealing to 'attentive auditors, / Such as will join their profit with their pleasure' (Ind., ll. 201–2), but his zeal is presented as 'ridiculously intense'.[15] Moreover, Jonson offers a second version of 'our poet' when the character Carlo Buffone later toasts the audience:

This is that our poet calls Castalian liquor, when he comes abroad, now and then, once in a fortnight, and makes a good meal among players . . . : marry, at home he keeps a good philosophical diet, beans and buttermilk: an honest pure rogue, he will take you off three, four, five of these [glasses of wine], one after another, and look villainously when he has done, like a one-headed Cerberus (he do not hear me, I hope) and then, when his belly is well ballasted, and his brain rigged a little, he sails away withal, as though he would work wonders when he comes home.

(ll. 318–27)

The poet described here is not Asper but a younger, more impoverished version of the sack-drinking persona familiar from Jonson's later years. The effect is to create a double-ironic frame, making Asper's zealous assault on folly and vice a self-conscious pose adopted by 'Ben', whose own foibles are playfully delineated in the Horatian spirit of self-criticism.[16]

The amusing irony with which Jonson treats his satiric persona is carried over into the main body of the play. Although Jonson's exclusive concentration on the purgation of humours makes *Every*

Man out of His Humour seem harsh in comparison with conventional stage comedy, his choice of satiric targets confirms its status as 'comical' satire. Whereas Asper envisions 'earth cracked with the weight of sin' (Ind., l. 8) and inveighs against vice and corruption, the play's *dramatis personae* are a representative sample of the lighter follies ridiculed in Elizabethan verse satire. At the same time, the evocation of such London settings as the Mitre Tavern and the middle aisle of St. Paul's Cathedral creates a vivid sense of the fashionable urban scene in its kaleidoscopic variety, realising the dramatic potential inherent in the satiric method of Donne and Marston.

The most successful characters in *Every Man out of His Humour* are two figures openly borrowed from Marston's *Certain Satires*. Fastidious Brisk, patterned on Marston's Briscus, is the epitome of courtly superficiality, illustrated by his extensive wardrobe, for which he has mortgaged his lands to the citizen Deliro, and by his affected diction (reminiscent of John Hoskyns' strictures against 'the perfumed terms of the time').[17] Although, like Marston's Duceus of Satire III, he speaks airily of his familiarity with counts and countesses, his interview with his mistress Saviolina (III.ix) leaves him disgraced, comically unable to handle the various props by which he means to show off his vapid accomplishments. The germ of this scene comes from Marston's *Certain Satires*, I, in which the satirist takes away the viol Briscus uses to entertain his mistress, striking him 'more mute than a *Pythagoran*' (l. 26).[18] Jonson has Brisk employ a tobacco-pipe as well, masking his witlessness in a cloud of smoke and a cacophany of off-key music. Exposed to Deliro as a pretender by Macilente, he is finally left to languish in prison for debt.

Below Brisk on Jonson's ladder of fashionable pretenders is his imitator, the clothes-conscious Fungoso, an Inns of Court reveller artfully developed from Marston's sketch in Satire III of a gallant who, after 'two year's fast and earnest prayer / The fashion change not', has finally hoarded up enough 'fair gay clothes' to appear in public.[19] Whereas Marston typically satirises his youth for hiring a 'Ganymede' to further his 'riot and lewd luxury', Jonson sees the comic possibilities in the futile struggle to keep ahead of fashion on a marginal income. Fungoso's doomed efforts to match Brisk's elegant wardrobe form one of the most comical lines of action in the play, for he twice spends all his savings and then some to copy Brisk's costume, only to find with dismay that Brisk has a newer outfit on his next appearance. The very model of a modern consumer, Fungoso remains more vital today than Marston's figure because Jonson focuses on his basic impulse to be fashionable.

Although partly inspired by his literary models, Jonson's satire on Brisk's and Fungoso's obsession with their 'outsides' expresses a personal bias against extravagant dress. The testimony of John Aubrey is that 'his habit was very plain. I have heard Mr. Lacy, the player, say that he was wont to wear a coat like a coachman's coat, with slits under the arm-pits'.[20] His portrait, painted by Abraham van Blyenberch when Jonson was in his late forties, portrays him in a simple black woolen doublet and a flat linen collar: David Riggs remarks of it that Jonson 'has not been assimilated into the world of elegant gentlemen and ladies who ordinarily sat for artists like van Blyenberch'.[21] Jonson's separateness, his sense of social difference, should perhaps be stressed. Because he celebrates his friendships with wits and courtiers in poems and dedications, it is tempting to infer a greater intimacy with some of his acquaintances than may actually have existed. At the time of the 'Comical Satires' Jonson had not yet won a secure position in the genteel world he satirised. Even among the Inns of Court wits with whom he shared so much he was not on a footing of complete equality; his sense of poetic vocation, in particular, was different from theirs. For example, Donne avoided publishing his poems in his lifetime and restricted access to his manuscripts; even when writing complimentary verses in hopes of patronage, he was anxious lest he lose his dignity as a gentleman.[22] Jonson, as we have seen in Chapter 2, had already begun to campaign vigorously for the value of poetry, and in those works with which he chose to be publicly identified he would insist that his plays were not trifling entertainments but true works of art. Moreover, as Richard Helgerson has noted, his public stipulation that the good poet must first be a good man left him no easy escape from his literary persona.[23] Although in private conversations with male friends like William Drummond he shared an extensive repertory of bawdy epigrams and salty anecdotes, he publically dissociated himself from the erotic wit of the Inns of Court elegists, rejecting the elegy as 'too loose, and cap'ring' for the 'stricter vein' of his muse (*M.P.* CIX, l. 2).

So, too, the social perspective of Jonson's satire is subtly different from that of Donne or Marston, who moved more easily in the world they ridiculed and have therefore been suspected of expressing some 'self-guiltiness' in their criticism of fashionable gallantry.[24] Jonson, on the other hand, spoke as an outsider hostile to the groups he satirises, though like Marston and Donne, he 'yearned to involve [himself] more deeply in the world [he] pretended to scorn'.[25] In *Every Man out of His Humour* he attempts with remarkable self-consciousness to achieve through the figure of Macilente, Asper's dramatic persona, a catharsis of the envy he felt. His unresolved ambiguities, however, surface in the play's ending, which never successfully dispels the aggressive energies aroused. The detractor Carlo Buffone, modelled on Charles Chester, a well-known London figure, does receive poetic justice when Sir Puntarvolo, goaded by Carlo's derisive similes, seals his moustache to his beard with wax.[26] But Macilente, who engineers the dishumouring of Carlo and most of the other characters, escapes unpunished. Macilente is yet another thinly-disguised version of Jonson, a poet who 'carries oil and fire in his pen' to 'blow a man up with a jest' (I.ii.186–8). Identified as both a soldier and a scholar, he is said to be 'a man well parted' who 'falls into . . . an envious apoplexy' because he lacks 'that place in the world's account which he thinks his merit capable of' (*Plays*, I:281). Unable to endure the inequities of Fortune with Stoic patience, he employs his wit to expose or frustrate all the fools more fortunate than he. In the original conclusion Jonson distanced himself from Macilente by treating him as a humour to be purged; there Macilente returns to court with the intent of railing at vice and is reformed by the sight of Queen Elizabeth. When having an actor impersonate the queen on the public stage provoked criticism, Jonson changed the ending so that Macilente, having dishumoured the other characters, merely declares himself 'empty of all envy'. The revised ending thus seems to sanction Macilente's spite while condemning Carlo Buffone's, thereby highlighting the play's function as a vindictive fantasy directed at a society which did not, despite Jonson's wit and learning, admit him to full status.[27]

Although *Every Man out of His Humour* aroused some controversy, it established Jonson in the public eye as the age's leading 'humourist', the title under which he was later attacked in John Weever's *The Whipping of the Satire* (1601). One reason this association stuck was that the play was quickly printed in an edition of one thousand copies by William Holme in April of 1600; it received a second printing, and possibly a third, before the year was out.[28] The publication of a public-theatre play so soon after its production was itself extraordinary, for plays were normally considered the property of the dramatic company and were kept out of print as long as they had theatrical value. As a young actor-playwright Jonson had been content to serve as an anonymous script-writer; he apparently now reserved the right to print his work within a year or two of performance, seeking to build an artistic reputation by appealing directly to the literate public.[29] The *Every Man out of His Humour* Quarto is everywhere calculated to impress the buyer with its difference from ordinary play-books, which were published without the editorial apparatus that modern readers have come to expect. Contrary to custom, Jonson includes 'The Names of the Actors' (that is, characters), satiric prose 'character' descriptions in the Theophrastan manner, a Latin title-page motto boasting of the work's originality and literary merit, and careful act and scene divisions. The title-page does not mention the Lord Chamberlain's Men, but stresses that the play is printed 'as it was first composed' by the author and contains 'more than hath been publically spoken or acted'. Jonson may here be referring to parts of the Induction and Grex (or chorus), which explain his theory of satiric comedy and condemn unworthy poets and ignorant critics alike. His implication throughout is that *Every Man out of His Humour* is a serious work of art deserving *literary* status. We so readily grant that status to the works of Shakespeare that we forget how radical a claim this was in 1600.

In Jonson's revised conclusion the Epilogue had promised the Globe audience that if *Every Man out of His Humour* pleased them, 'Our lean and spent endeavours shall renew / their beauties with the Spring [of 1600] to smile on you'.[30] However, Jonson's next play, *Cynthia's Revels, or The Fountain of Self-Love*, was written for the newly reorganised Children of the Chapel Royal, acting at the private theatre fitted up in the old monastery of Blackfriars. In light of the fact that Shakespeare's company later produced Thomas Dekker's attack on Jonson in *Satiromastix*, it is possible that his move signals a disagreement with the Lord Chamberlain's Men, but we should not assume that strained relations were the only cause; writing for the children's troupes, which broke the near-monopoly enjoyed by the Lord Chamberlain's and the Lord Admiral's Men after the tightening of theatrical controls in 1597, may simply have seemed the more attractive alternative.[31] If Dekker's taunts in *Satiromastix* about Jonson's presence in the playhouse are to be believed, the private theatres offered greater authorial control over the productions, or at least greater recognition for the author. They certainly offered a more selective theatrical clientele. Conveniently situated near the Inns of Court and the fashionable residences along the Strand, the Blackfriars Theatre (like its counterpart at St. Paul's) attracted a more highly educated audience and one more orientated toward the court, whose patronage of the chorister troupes had been the original justification for their being.[32]

Cynthia's Revels has generally been viewed as an experiment in dramatic form, but in fact it was carefully designed with court performance and the repertory of the boy actors in mind. By beginning with the appearance of Echo and ending with Cynthia's reformation (aided by Arete or Virtue) of the vices who have infiltrated her court, Jonson plays against Thomas Dekker's *Old Fortunatus*, an earlier two-part play condensed for performance before the Queen in the Christmas season of 1599, which also begins with an Echo scene and ends with tributes to Virtue and to Elizabeth. Jonson's Echo has a clearer dramatic justification than Dekker's, since as the former lover of Narcissus she establishes the mythological basis of the Fountain of Self-Love that will corrupt Cynthia's courtly imposters.[33] Likewise, Jonson's allegorical masque of the courtly virtues entraps the false courtiers into appearing as their opposites and so has greater integrity than Dekker's contention between Virtue, Vice, and Fortune, which is awkwardly joined to a romantic plot involving the magical powers of Fortunatus and his two sons. As he was to do explicitly in his epigrams, Jonson is here tacitly inviting comparison between the cruder effects of his public theatre rival and his own superior art. Moreover, although he speaks slightingly in the Induction of the 'ghosts of some three or four plays, departed a dozen years since', which still haunted the stage of the Blackfriars Theatre like 'hobgoblins' (Ind., ll. 177–80), he cleverly adapts the allegorical and mythological conventions of the boy companies' earlier repertory to his satiric purposes. The figures of Mercury and Cupid are given a new sprightliness by Jonson's assimilation of witty banter from Lucian's *The Dialogues of the Gods*, and Cupid's customary role in court drama is amusingly frustrated by his discovery that the self-loving courtiers are too narcissistic to be affected by his arrows.[34]

Despite its theatrical wit, however, *Cynthia's Revels* remains the least accessible of the comical satires because of its narrow focus on courtly affectation. The masque of virtues presented to Cynthia at the conclusion is a glorification of Queen Elizabeth and her court, but most of the preceding action is given over to satire on fashionable manners. The allegorical vices who invade Cynthia's palace enact a trivialised parody of the ideal courtly world depicted in Baldassare Castiglione's *The Book of the Courtier*. Instead of debating cultural values, they engage in shallow games and meaningless social rituals, reducing Castiglione's standard of *sprezzatura* or graceful nonchalance to absurdity as they laboriously practice the complimental formulas and physical gestures of courtly address. Although Jonson distinguishes between his foolish characters and 'the better race in court / That have the true nobility, called virtue' (V.i.30–1), his claim that the gallant Hedon's pride and ignorance are 'two essential parts of the courtier' (II.ii.71–2) reveals his anti-courtly bias.[35]

Anti-court sentiment of this sort was common among (and no doubt appealing to) Inns of Court gentlemen who were dependent upon patronage yet alienated from the superficiality of aristocratic manners. Donne's Satire IV and some of the verse letters written in the Donne–Wotton circle in the late 1590s criticise the 'mimic antics' found at court and endorse an ideal of Stoic self-sufficiency.[36] Jonson personalises these themes by emphasising the hostility between Hedon and his companion Anaides (or Impudence) and the scholarly poet Crites (or Criticus, in the Quarto), but the conflict between them only serves to point the difference between his position in Elizabethan society and that of Donne and Marston. Dressed in black like the Jonson of the Blyenberch portrait, Crites first appears onstage in the company of the prodigal Asotus, yet like Jonson himself he is more an observer than a participant of the gallantry around him. Scorned repeatedly by Hedon and Anaides as 'a whoreson bookworm, a candle-waster' who 'smells all lamp-oil with studying by candlelight' (III.ii.2–3, 11), he is characterised as a Stoic sage whom 'Fortune could never break . . . nor make. . . less' (II.iii.123–4), one who 'like a circle bounded in itself, / Contains as much as man in fullness may' (V.viii.19–20). Crites' Stoicism, however, is not without its contradictions.[37] Depicted as reluctant to compose the masque by which the false courtiers are exposed and praised for being 'as distant from depraving another man's merit as proclaiming his own' (II.iii.119-20), he nevertheless intrudes on the social scene to spoil Hedon's and Anaides' witticisms (see III.ii). In the contest of courtship that occupies much of the fifth act in the Folio version he also gives Anaides 'the Dor' [that is, makes a fool of him] by parodying his manner.[38] Moreover, Jonson's very act of creating such an obvious self-idealisation is a form of self-advertisement and evidence that Jonson himself took notice of detraction, despite his endorsement of Stoic apathy.

Crites' reward by Cynthia at the play's conclusion is an equally transparent fantasy of recognition for Jonson, but how well *Cynthia's Revels* succeeded with its intended audience is uncertain. Horace-Jonson in Dekker's *Satiromastix* is asked to swear that 'When your plays are misliked at court, you shall not cry "mew" like a pussycat and say you are glad you write out of the courtier's element' (V.ii.324–6) – an allusion that seems to point to *Cynthia's Revels* in particular. On the other hand, Jonson felt confident enough of its reception to send a copy of the Quarto, published in May 1601, with a specially-printed dedicatory poem to Lucy, Countess of Bedford, whom he praises as 'Cynthia's fairest nymph' (*M.P.* III, 1. 6). That she and other members of the 'better race at court' did not find the play offensive may be inferred from Epigram XCIV, 'To Lucy, Countess of Bedford, with Mr Donne's Satires', where she is celebrated as one of the virtuous minority who dare to read and enjoy satire even though they live 'where the [subject] matter is bred' (l. 11). However, although Jonson actively sought patronage in court circles at this time, his public stance was independent, even defiant. The speaker of the Epilogue, supposedly puzzled by his instructions that he be neither 'faint, remiss, nor sorry, / Sour, serious, confident, nor peremptory', concludes ironically by quoting Jonson's own opinion: 'By [God] 'tis good, and if you like't, you may' (ll. 9–10, 20).[39]

To his fellow wit and competitor John Marston, Jonson's self-aggrandising fantasies and his tendency to 'crack rude scorn even on the very face / Of better audience' provided a tempting opportunity for ridicule.[40] Despite their collaboration on *Robert the Second* for Henslowe in September of 1599 and on *The Turtle and the Phoenix* poems later dedicated to Sir John Salusbury in 1601, relations between Jonson and Marston were uneasy. Perhaps this was because they were competing in the same mode of literature and for the same audience. Both men satirised humourous affectation and pretence from a neo-Stoic perspective, both ridiculed poets who pandered to popular taste and both moved quickly to the private theatres – Jonson at Blackfriars and Marston at Paul's. Yet Marston approached the private theatre audience, whom he viewed as his social equals, with much more tact than Jonson, who based his bid for recognition on his moral and artistic seriousness. At the same time, Jonson's affinity for the Horatian plain style led him to look with disdain on the bombastic language of Marston's verse satires. Eventually the tensions between them broke out into open theatrical warfare. Jonson told William Drummond that 'he had many quarrels with Marston, beat him, and took his pistol from him . . . the beginning of them were that Marston represented him in the stage' (*Conv.*, ll. 282–4). Encouraged by Jonson's claim in the 'Apologetical Dialogue' of *Poetaster* to have been provoked for some three years 'on every stage' by his adversaries' 'petulant styles' (ll. 95–6), Victorian theatre historians postulated an extensive exchange of personal satire between Marston, Jonson, Shakespeare, Dekker and others, but recent scholarship has been rightly sceptical of their reckless identifications.[41] Jonson may be glanced at in Marston's *Histriomastix, or The Player Whipped* in the person of the poet Chrisoganus, characterised at one point as 'a translating scholar' who can make 'a stabbing satire or an epigram' and at another point as a humanist playwright who proudly demands ten pounds per play from the acting companies. If so, however, any satire is well-disguised, for Chrisoganus often sounds more like Marston than Jonson, and Marston's opposition between Chrisoganus and the popular hack Post-haste (who seems to stand for Antony Munday) parallels Jonson's own satire on Munday as Antonio Balladino in the revised version of *The Case Is Altered*.[42] Marston's Brabant Sr., a wealthy gallant who gulls fools in *Jack Drum's Entertainment*, is also sometimes compared to Jonson, but the parallel is valid only in so far as he embodies the spirit of derisive ridicule. For his part, Jonson introduced into the acting text of *Every Man out of His Humour* a few 'fustian' speeches of learned nonsense, like those written by John Hoskyns for the *Prince d'Amour* revels, including one that burlesques the abstruse philosophical diction of Marston's verse satires.[43] Personal satire in these works, however, is limited to minor touches. The first major engagement in 'that terrible *Poetomachia* [battle of the poets]', as Dekker called it, seems to have been Marston's *What You Will*, written in response to *Cynthia's Revels*. There Marston made a clever attack on Jonson under the guise of the needy poet Lampatho Doria.

Even this identification has been resisted by some recent commentators because Lampatho, like Marston himself, is described as an academic student of philosophy who finds himself no wiser about the nature of the soul after seven years study than when he started.[44] Marston's method, however, is not pure lampoon, but a witty combination of general type-characterisation, personal satire, and literary burlesque. To his general portrait of the unsociable scholar, he adds specific details that caricature Jonson at his most unflattering: Lampatho is an impoverished poet whose foolish young admirers pay for his meals at the ordinary, who protests his 'obsequious vassalage' to every gallant he meets while satirising them behind their backs, who rails at the court because railing 'chokes the theatres' with patrons, who praises his own poetry and threatens to rhyme his critics dead if he is scorned. Marston, moreover, purposely confuses Jonson with his own characters, accusing him of the social hypocrisy of a Carlo Buffone or a Macilente and reversing the triumph of Crites. Taken to court by the epicurean Quadratus, Lampatho attracts a mistress despite his costume of 'sullen black' (IV.i.119) but is unable to keep up a stylishly careless courtship and falls into dotage, while his moral comedy 'Temperance' is rejected by the Duke with the scornful question, 'What sot elects that subject for the court?' (V.i.211). All in all, the trials of Lampatho Doria are an unmistakeable rebuff to Jonson's implicit self-glorification in *Cynthia's Revels*.

To the extent that the 'Poetomachia' was also a 'War of the Theatres', then, it seems to have begun as a quarrel among two private theatre playwrights as to which one most fitly addressed the ethos of the private theatre audience. Marston's role in defending 'fantastic' behaviour against Lampatho's railing seems rather hypocritical, for it contradicts his earlier ridicule of courtly affectation in his verse satires and tragicomedies. Presumably his personal irritation at Jonson's egotism temporarily got the better of his artistic integrity, though his work in general contains so many contrasting poses that it is often difficult to determine exactly where he stands. What began as a debate among private theatre playwrights soon broadened with Thomas Dekker's *Satiromastix, or The Untrussing of the Humourous Poet*, produced jointly by the Lord Chamberlain's Men and the Children of Paul's some time in the late spring or summer of 1601. How or why this partnership came about is not entirely clear, but both the Lord Chamberlain's Men and Dekker had reasons for lampooning Jonson: Dekker in his irritation at Jonson's open competition with *Old Fortunatus*; the Lord Chamberlain's Men in their tensions with him over *Every Man out of His Humour*.[45] Jonson, in turn, got wind of their project and, in fifteen weeks, wrote *Poetaster, or His Arraignment* as a pre-emptive strike to neutralise their planned attack.

Considering the short amount of time devoted to its composition, *Poetaster* is a clever piece of satiric imitation. Under pressure from Dekker, Jonson would later deny the parallellism between Rome and Elizabethan England, but he effectively sustains a witty interplay between the two centres of reference. His satiric re-visioning of the Augustan literary scene translates the social world of Horatian satire into Elizabethan terms and at the same time turns Marston's own strategy of mixing personal lampoon, literary burlesque, and type-characterisation back against him and Dekker. The two are identified with minor poets ridiculed by Horace, and Marston is also identified with the unnamed bore whom Horace encounters on the Sacred Way in *Satires* I.ix.[46] Dekker, whom Jonson considered 'a rogue' (*Conv.*, l. 46), is portrayed as Demetrius Fannius, a non-entity, a mere 'journeyman' playwright who writes sing-song verse and would accuse Horace of 'translating' except that he cannot understand the authors from whom he has borrowed (see V.iii.274–7). Marston–Crispinus is conceived as a typical Jonsonian gull who haunts the fringes of courtly society, eager to insinuate himself into the company of his betters but so obtuse that he gives his mistress the poetic name of Horace's witch Canidia. Self-described as 'your gentleman, parcel-poet' (IV.vi.28) and as one who has been a reveller in his time, he is distinguished by such presumably Marstonian traits as a red beard and little legs and by a coat of arms that parodies Marston's. In the concluding 'arraignment', inspired by suggestions from Nashe and Lucian, he acknowledges as his own poetry a devasting parody of *The Scourge of Villainy* and is given a purge that makes him vomit up many of Marston's distinctive terms, such as 'barmy-froth', 'puffy', and 'glibbery'. Virgil's prescription of reading Cato and Terence to improve his style in effect sends him back to grammar school.

Jonson also ridicules Marston indirectly by making Crispinus the companion of Pantilius Tucca, a braggart soldier modelled on the real-life figure of Captain Jack Hannam, who sailed with Drake in 1585. Tucca's name is derived from 'that louse Pantilius' of Horace's *Satires* I.x.78 and the Captain Tucca of Guilpin's *Skialetheia*, a close parallel to Marston's own Tubrio.[47] He is given a flair for imaginatively scurrilous epithets, but the comic effect of his speech is offset by his cowardliness, his constant wheedling of loans, his impudent familiarity, and his sudden fawning on those he has offended. His meanness of character is used to discredit the enemies of satire, for he voices both the authentic libels against Horace mentioned in *Satires* I.iv and contemporary objections to Jonsonian 'humours, revels, and satires, that gird and fart at the time' (III.iv.166–7).[48] Marston had numbered Tubrio among 'the vizarded-bifronted-Janian rout' who are not what they seem; Jonson turns his satire back upon him by making Tucca betray Crispinus. Having pretended to defend Crispinus against the charge of maligning Horace and then voted against him at the final tribunal, Tucca is revealed as one of the conspirators; Caesar's order that he be gagged and vizarded so that 'he may look bi-fronted, as he speaks' (V.iii.393) underscores the irony of having Marston–Crispinus undone by a character like those Marston had satirised.

Unfortunately for him, Jonson's satire in *Poetaster* was not limited to taunting Marston and Dekker. Tucca and his two pages also act out dramatic excerpts, ridiculing the public-theatre repertory and the Lord Chamberlain's Men. Their encounter with Histrio in III.iv mocks impoverished touring players with echoes of Marston's *Histriomastix*, parodies the bombast and rhetorical excesses of Elizabethan revenge tragedy, offers unflattering, thinly-disguised portraits of some of Shakespeare's company and, in a passage apparently cut from the 1602 Quarto by censorship, insinuates that actors serve as procurers for boys and decayed prostitutes.[49] In another passage probably omitted because it aroused complaints, Tucca and Lupus the magistrate continue Ovid Senior's ironic praise of the law by pointing out that 'a simple scholar, or none at all may be a lawyer' and that lawyers are able 'to do right or wrong, at . . . pleasure' (I.ii.107–8, 116–7). Jonson's irony would not have been lost on those Inns of Court gentlemen who had no legal aspirations and were alienated by the tedium of their studies, but his global condemnation of lawyers angered some members of the audience. Paradoxically, he may also have aroused official anxieties that he was lampooning a specific magistrate in the figure of Lupus, whose suspicion that poetry and drama are full of treasonous allegories gives rise to his accusations against Horace. In the 'Apologetical Dialogue' written in 1601 but not printed until the 1616 Folio Jonson made his customary disclaimer that he satirised no one by name, but he was interrogated by Lord Chief Justice Popham and only saved from punishment through the pleadings of Richard Martin, to whom the play is gratefully dedicated in the 1616 Folio.[50]

Yet although Jonson's aggressive wit was allowed free play in *Poetaster*, his motives were not all negative. *Poetaster* is at once a reply to his critics, a defence of satire, and a statement about the ideal relationship between poetry and the commonwealth. Jonson's depiction of the Roman literary scene sets up a hierarchy of poets based on their conception of poetry's function and so places him in relation to the literary system. By having Caesar honour Virgil in Act V he acknowledges the superiority of epic poetry to satire and yet reiterates, without embarrassing personal overtones, the partnership between poet and monarch staged in *Cynthia's Revels*. At the same time, the banishment of Ovid positions Jonson against the Inns of Court amateurs, whose libertine wit is recognised as inventive, but directed toward unworthy ends.[51] Applied strictly, Caesar's declaration that he will 'prefer for knowledge none but such / As rule their lives by it' (IV.vi.73–4) might convict Jonson, who was 'in youth given to venery', of hypocrisy, but Jonson is evaluating modes of poetry, not morals. What he is really suggesting is that 'dotage on the follies of the flesh' is not a proper subject for verse, that satire and the poetry of praise is necessarily superior to Ovidian eroticism and amorous songs. Jonson himself, of course, was ultimately to inspire a new mode of cavalier love poetry, but at this stage in his career his claim to poetic recognition was based on his identity as a public poet, here represented by Horace.

Jonson's equation with Horace is played down in the 'Apologetical Dialogue' as being merely a demonstration that even the 'great master-spirits' of the Augustan era, 'when wit and arts were at their height in Rome', did not lack for 'detractors . . . or practisers against them' (ll. 99–103). In fact the Jonson–Horace link served several important functions. It was his first public identification with the Roman poet most like him in literary tastes, and his own professional hopes were no doubt mirrored in the career of the Roman freedman's son whose literary talents elevated him to patronage by the emperor and his chief nobles.[52] Secondly, as one of the leading classical practitioners of imitation and as the chief authority for moderation in the use of new or unusual words, Horace gave authority to his own practice of 'translation' and to his image as a careful reviser. Finally, he could answer detractors of his satire by quoting Horace's denials of malicious intent and by repeating Horace's disdain for the judgement of any but the best men and poets. His identification with Horatian ideals decisively established his poetic self-image as a writer who brought broad learning, careful artistic control, and a sense of the moral function of literature to the task of writing for the theatre.

Jonson's attempted defence of his professional behaviour was less successful because it was more self-serving. His attempted refutation of the charge that he was arrogant is belied by his forcing Crispinus and Demetrius to acknowledge that Horace–Jonson transcends them in merit (V.iii.542–4). Horace–Jonson's protest that he takes 'no knowledge that they do malign me' (V.iii.156) is not credible in a play designed as a crushing retort to Marston and Dekker. His reply to Crispinus' offer of help in eliminating other rivals for Maecenas' favour (III.i.206–31) is authentically Horatian and an idealised description of patronage relationships at their best, but it glosses over Jonson's competitive rivalry with Daniel and Drayton. His denial, in the Roman poet's own words, that he would ever 'wrong, or tax a friend' (V.iii.287–303) is also dramatically persuasive, but inadequate to defend the man whom Drummond judged as 'given rather to lose a friend than a jest' (*Conv.*, l. 683).

In *Satiromastix* Dekker seizes on just such contradictions. By reversing the situation in *Poetaster*, Dekker answered Jonson 'at his own weapon', deriding him as a 'self-creating Horace' and giving Tucca a chief role in his torment. Whereas Jonson's Horace is partly authenticated by the Roman setting of the play and the Roman materials worked into it, Dekker's 'Horace' is clearly Jonson himself pretending to be Horace, and Crispinus and Demetrius are vindicated by presiding over his 'untrussing' – a savage scene in which he is led on stage bound, stripped of his satyr's suit and crowned with nettles. Jonson had stooped to jeers at Marston's shabby gentility and Dekker's poverty in *Poetaster*, but Dekker more than repays him by having Tucca mock his large nose, his pock-marked face, his bricklaying, his acting, his conviction for murder, his self-promotion and his admiration for his own work.[53] Dekker's lampoon is far more personal than *Poetaster*, and two of his chief targets are Jonson's affected classicism and his hypocrisy toward his benefactors. He deflates Jonson's pose as an enraptured 'priest of Apollo' by making him struggle laboriously to find suitable rhymes for an epithalamion like the 'Ode to Desmond'. There is much ridicule of Jonson's 'strange poems', such as his odes and the palinode to *Cynthia's Revels*, and even more of his supposed treachery to his patrons. Horace makes fun of the Welsh knight Sir Rees ap Vaughan (had he done so to Salusbury?) and, after circulating epigrams against Tucca, grovels when confronted. He also reveals to his foolish admirer Asinius Bubo that he sends form letters to impress wealthy gallants who enrol themselves as his disciples. In the oaths that end his 'untrussing' he is made to swear that after drinking with his followers at ale-houses he will not brag 'that [his] viceroys or tributary kings have done homage' to him (V.ii.313–15). As Robert Evans observes, these touches seem designed to embarass Jonson before potential patrons by depicting them as 'Maecen-asses' if they support him.[54]

Jonson responded to some of Dekker's accusations in his 'Apologetical Dialogue' to *Poetaster*, but he ignores most of the personal libels, at times feigning lofty indifference and at other moments fantasising a literary revenge so virulent it would 'make the desperate lashers hang themselves' (l. 160).[55] His dialogue was spoken at the Blackfriars only once; its proscription by the authorities, who may have intervened in other ways as well, seems to have ended the War of the Theatres. It is alluded to as past in a Cambridge academic play, the second part of *The Return from Parnassus*, acted during the Christmas season of 1601/2. There Will Kempe, the famous clown of the Lord Chamberlain's Men, tells Richard Burbage, 'O that Ben Jonson is a pestilent fellow; he brought up Horace giving the poets a pill, but our fellow Shakespeare hath given him a purge that made him bewray [that is, befoul] his credit' (lines 1770–3).[56] Much paper has been expended on speculation as to which of Shakespeare's plays contains this 'purge' of Jonson, but no convincing candidate has been put forward.[57] Who was victorious is also a matter in dispute. *Poetaster* is a far more comprehensive literary statement than *Satiromastix*, one that supports Jonson's assertion that he knew 'the strength of his own muse' (*Poet.* prologue, l. 24), but Dekker's play has more bite. Dekker himself claimed that if an inquisition were held before Apollo the poetasters would be exonerated in self-defence, but he admits that 'notwithstanding, the doctors [that is, the learned] think otherwise'.[58] He does succeed in raising some doubts about Jonson's integrity, but he also concedes Jonson's extraordinary poetic talent. Some of his hits, such as Horace's boast that he can bring 'a prepar'd troop of gallants' to 'distaste every unsalted line' in his opponents' comedies (I.ii.142–4), testify to Jonson's personal magnetism and the extensive following he had already acquired. Moreover, the War of the Theatres solidified Jonson's public image as a deliberate artist, thereby turning Dekker's ridicule of his pretensions into a sign of difference that set him off from other playwrights. In this sense he emerged the winner. Dekker's jibes may have been attended by some temporary embarrassment, but in the long run Jonson remained, as Sir Thomas Smith described him in 1605, 'the elaborate English Horace, that gives number, weight and measure to every word'.[59]

5

Matters of State

So far as one can judge by the 'Apologetical Dialogue' to *Poetaster*,
Jonson's impulse after the War of the Theatres seems to have been to
withdraw into scholarly seclusion. His decision to abandon comedy
for tragedy and his declaration that he would be satisfied to please
an audience of one, 'so he judicious be' (see ll. 220–6), indicate that
he may already have been planning his classically-inspired tragedy
of *Sejanus His Fall*. Yet it was apparently not until February 1603 that
he was relieved of anxiety about his day-to-day support. Then John
Manningham reported in his diary, on the authority of Thomas
Overbury, that 'Ben Jonson the poet now lives upon . . . [Robert]
Townshend and scorns the world'.[1] The patronage of Townshend,
and later of Esmé Stuart, Lord D'Aubigny, freed him for the
intensive classical study required for *Sejanus* and for his
'observations upon Horace his *Art of Poetry*, which (with the text
translated)' he had almost completed by the time the Quarto of
Sejanus was printed in August 1605.[2]

In the meantime, he found it necessary to supplement his finances
by writing occasionally for the Lord Admiral's Men. On 25
September 1601 Henslowe advanced him 40s. in earnest of
'additions in Geronymo', and on 22 June 1602 he paid him ten
pounds for 'new additions for Jeronymo' and in earnest of 'a book
called *Richard Crookback*'.[3] The first two entries undoubtedly refer to
Kyd's *The Spanish Tragedy*, of which there was a 'newly corrected,
amended and enlarged' edition, containing 'new additions of the
Painter's part and others', printed in 1602. Jonson's authorship of
these additions has been questioned, but since he had ridiculed
Kyd's play for its melodrama and out-dated rhetoric, he might not
have wished to acknowledge them as his own.[4]

If the 1602 additions were indeed his, they soon proved painfully
relevant to his personal life. Their subject is the grief of the
protagonist Hieronymo for his murdered son, a topic that seems to
have had a particular resonance for Jonson because of his own
experience as a father. He had also taken an interest in the boy actors
of the Children of the Chapel Royal, tutoring one of them, Nathan

Field, in Latin readings from Horace and Martial. For another, Salomon Pavy, who died in July 1602, he composed a graceful epitaph (*Epig.* CXX), claiming that Sal's skill at acting old men misled the Fates into treating him as one. Then, about a year later, his oldest son Benjamin, the child of his 'right hand', died in the plague that ravaged London in 1603 and early 1604. Jonson was visiting with Camden at the country home of Sir Robert Cotton at the time, and in his anxiety about young Ben's welfare he experienced a type of psychic phenomenon reported by others in that era. As he told Drummond, 'he saw in a vision his eldest son (then a child and at London) appear unto him with the mark of a bloody cross on his forehead, as if it had been cutted with a sword .. .. He appeared to him . . . of a manly shape, and of that growth that he thinks he shall be at the resurrection' (*Conv.*, ll. 259–69).[5]

Jonson's sorrow is expressed in one of his most powerful and effective pieces of poetic imitation, the epigram 'On My First Son' (*Epig.* XLV), which turns on the conflict between his feelings of loss and his conviction that reason and faith forbid mourning. Based on two poems by Martial and influenced by Cicero (see Chapter 1 above), it translates classical modes of consolation into Christian terms. Jonson implies that he was punished by God because his 'sin was too much hope' of his 'loved boy' (l. 2) – perhaps meaning hope not only of what young Benjamin might achieve, but also of his importance to the Jonson fortunes. He acknowledges that children are only loans from God and that, viewed objectively, his son is lucky to have escaped the 'world's, and flesh's rage' (l. 7). Though the anguished poet wishes that he could lose (or 'loose') all fatherly feeling, the poem's power derives from its assertion that his son is 'his best piece of poetry' and from its hard-won perspective on human creation in general. Jonson's final vow, that hereafter what he loves 'may never like too much' (that is, please too much), invites the reader to ponder the dangers of possessive, earth-bound affection. Nevertheless, although Jonson wrestles with the limits of human love, his poem stands as the fullest statement of paternal grief in the period.[6]

Despite his loss Jonson must quickly have been absorbed in public affairs. Queen Elizabeth's reign had come to an end on a melancholy note, its last years troubled by the rebellion and subsequent execution of her young favourite, the Earl of Essex. After a gradual decline she passed away quietly on the morning of 24 March 1603, and later that day James VI of Scotland was proclaimed James I of

England. John Manningham reported that 'the people is full of expectation and great with hope of his worthiness'.[7] Their new monarch was an experienced ruler who had curbed the factionalism of his Scottish nobles and the extremism of Presbyterian radicals in the kirk. Sternly educated by his tutor George Buchanan, he was fluent in Latin, Greek, French and Italian. He had early shown an interest in poetry, publishing *The Essays of a Prentice in the Divine Art of Poesy* in 1584 and *His Majesty's Poetical Exercises at Vacant Hours* in 1591. He was well-enough versed in Biblical studies to compose several meditations upon Scripture and to enter into theological debates, as he did to the admiration of observers at the Hampton Court conference in January 1604. He had also written two books on kingship and kingcraft: *The True Law of Free Monarchies*, setting out his theory of divine right in opposition to the Presbyterian doctrine of the Two Kingdoms, and *Basilikon Doron*, his gift of canny practical advice and moral wisdom for the young Prince Henry. He was soon to find that his manner of ruling, while effective in Scotland, provoked greater resistance in England, but in 1603 he was greeted eagerly.[8]

James' accession held out opportunities for office-seekers of all kinds, including writers. On 12 April the newswriter John Chamberlain reported that 'the very poets, with their idle pamphlets, promise themselves great part in his [the King's] favour'.[9] Once again Jonson found himself in competition with his old rivals Samuel Daniel, who composed the five-hundred line 'A Panegyric Congratulatory' for presentation to the King on his journey southward, and Thomas Dekker, who shared with Jonson and the architect Stephen Harrison the design of the seven 'Arches of Triumph' for the royal entry into London, originally planned for 25 July 1603 but postponed until the following March because of plague. In this same period, Jonson would also produce *The Entertainment at Althorp*, written for the visit of Queen Anne and Prince Henry to Sir Robert Spencer's estate on 25 June 1603, a 'Panegyre' of his own on the occasion of James' first Parliament on 19 March 1604, *The Entertainment at Highgate*, for Sir William Cornwallis' reception of the King and Queen on 1 May 1604, and the Lord Mayor's pageant, now lost, for the Haberdashers Company in October 1604.

Jonson's entertainments anticipate his later court masques in their mixture of comedy and elevated compliment. The mischievous elves, fairies, and puckish satyr who pay homage to Queen Anne in

The Entertainment at Althorp are reminiscent of *A Midsummer Night's Dream* and evidence that Jonson had neither artistic nor political reservations about reworking native traditions. His chief contribution, however, was to evoke the Roman associations of imperial Britain, peopling the landscape with classical deities and household gods and celebrating James as a new Augustus who brought peace and prosperity to his united kingdoms. Thomas Dekker, Jonson's uneasy collaborator in preparing the welcoming pageants for the King, missed the point when he sneered at 'how many pair of Latin sheets' had been 'shaken and cut into shreds' to form the attributes of Jonson's allegorical figures.[10] Jonson's Latinity both appealed to the King's scholarly tastes and reinforced the new imperial analogy. His pageant at Temple Bar began with a Roman flamen, or Priest of Mars, celebrating the rites of Anna Perenna, anciently observed on 15 March, the date of the royal entry. The Priest was interrupted by the Genius, or guardian spirit of the city, who pointed out that they were in the presence of a greater Anna (Queen Anne) and a ruler 'whose strong and potent virtues' had defaced the image of the war-god Mars. The gate of the temple, which shut at James' arrival to signal Mars' loss of power, was engraved in the Roman fashion 'Imp[erator] Iacobus Max[imus] Caesar Aug[ustus]'. The imagery in these pageants and the 'Panegyre' is drawn from Virgil's praise of Augustus as the inaugurator of a new Golden Age and from the panegyrics of Pliny the Younger and Claudian.

In his discussion of counsel in the *Discoveries* Jonson would later advise the counsellor 'to behave himself modestly, and with respect' to the prince 'yet free from flattery, or empire' (ll. 133–5). Walking this thin line between insolence and servility was to be a continuous challenge for him throughout his career as a court poet, for the conventions of poetic praise encouraged hyperbolic encomia, while his strong moral indignation and his irrepressible wit often led to ill-considered outbursts of satire. Yet for someone who has been called 'the most tactless man who ever lived', Jonson could at times demonstrate remarkable diplomatic skills.[11] Daniel had awkwardly raised the subject of Mary's execution in his long-winded panegyric and treated James' discussion of princely virtue in *Basilikon Doron* as a written contract that limited his powers, claiming that 'thy all commanding sovereignty / Stands subject to thy pen'.[12] Jonson's 'Panegyre', by contrast, diplomatically stressed the King's 'knowing arts' (l. 128) by selecting his admonitions from those James had given Prince Henry, thereby following his own precept of

counselling as if 'the prince were already furnished with the parts
he should have, especially in affairs of state' (*Disc.*, ll. 136–8). At the
same time, he was not afraid to speak out against tyranny, boldly
alluding to Henry VIII's appropriation of church lands, to his lust
and to the subversion of justice by private interests (see ll. 94–107).

In fact, despite his pursuit of the humanists' dream of an alliance
between the monarch and the scholar-poet, Jonson was deeply
uneasy about the ethos of the court and the government's policy of
repression. Although he sought court patronage, he was alienated
by the corruption, sycophancy and intrigue at court. The ageing
Queen's parsimony only increased the venality of her officers, and
the death or decline of her old advisers Walsingham and Burghley,
noted for their integrity, precipitated a power struggle between her
younger, less scrupulous favourites Sir Walter Ralegh, the Earl of
Essex and Burghley's son Sir Robert Cecil. In 1601 the Queen
remarked on the change, complaining that 'now the wit of the fox is
everywhere on foot, so as hardly a faithful or virtuous man may be
found'.[13] Cecil, her principal Secretary, proved the shrewdest,
though his ambition was disguised as service to the crown. By late
1603, he had assured himself of continuance in office under a new
sovereign and had witnessed the treason trials of his rivals Essex,
Ralegh and Lord Cobham. Ralegh was accused of plotting with
Spain on the basis of Cobham's testimony alone; his eloquent
defence against Attorney General Coke's bullying won the
admiration even of spectators predisposed to condemn him and
left the justice of his conviction in question.[14]

Improbable as the accusations against Ralegh were, threats
against the Elizabethan regime had been real, and the government
had countered them with extensive spy networks and other
repressive measures. We have seen that Jonson had experienced
its suppression of dissent at first hand. His contempt for the spies
set upon him during his *Isle of Dogs* confinement is voiced in
Epigram LIX and again in Epigram CI ('Inviting a Friend to
Supper'), where the innocent liberty of friendly sociability is
praised. As a Catholic he would have keenly appreciated such
trust in and freedom with one's associates, for communicants
frequently met in fear of arrest. One of his interrogators in 1597,
Richard Topcliffe, was noted for the savagery of his inquisitorial
methods in dealing with recusants. Jonson seems to have escaped
physical abuse, but he could hardly have been indifferent to the
torture and brutal dismemberment, often while still conscious, of

the priests who were executed for treason.[15] His indignation at the prevailing atmosphere of intrigue and fear is expressed in *Sejanus His Fall* – a nightmarish picture of Tiberian Rome, where men live in terror of informers, arbitrary justice and the executioner.

Sejanus gradually won an admiring readership in the early seventeenth century, but it was highly controversial when first performed. According to the 1616 Folio it was staged sometime in 1603 by the King's Men (formerly the Lord Chamberlain's Men) with Shakespeare in one of the major roles. Plague closed the public theatres from 19 March 1603 to March or April of 1604, but it may have been presented at court, where the company performed eight plays during the Christmas season of 1603/4. Its eventual production at the Globe provoked the audience to 'beastly rage'.[16] After some delay, perhaps because of censorship and revision, it was published in late 1605.[17] In his epistle 'To the Readers' Jonson announced that 'this book, in all numbers, is not the same with that which was acted on the public stage, wherein a second pen had good share: in place of which I have rather chosen, to put weaker (and no doubt less pleasing) [verses] of mine own' (ll. 37–40). His collaborator was most likely his fellow playwright and classicist George Chapman, whose *Bussy d'Ambois* and *The Conspiracy and Tragedy of Charles Duke of Byron* depict court intrigues based on recent French history. At some point *Sejanus* aroused official suspicions. Jonson was called before the Privy Council and 'accused both of popery and treason' by the Earl of Northampton (*Conv.*, ll. 325–7). Northampton's accusation may have been based on the published text, for Chapman's commendatory poem 'On *Sejanus*' in the 1605 volume praises James and his council (including Northampton) for their opposition to 'knowledge-hating policies' and singles out the Lord Chamberlain, the Earl of Suffolk, for defending the play against 'our herd' that came 'not to drink, but trouble / The Muses' waters' (ll. 153–4).[18]

One source of the crowd's displeasure may have been the play's astringent classicism. Avoiding the theatrical excitement character- istic of Elizabethan revenge tragedy, Jonson opts for 'truth of argument, dignity of persons, gravity and height of elocution, fullness and frequency of sentence'.[19] Sejanus, Tiberius' favourite and rival, is conceived both as an exultant Senecan villain-hero like Atreus in *Thyestes* and, like Thyestes himself, as a victim of Fortune's instability, whose horrid end warns those that 'stand upon the pinnacles of state' not to boast their 'slippery height' (Act

V, ll. 884–5). Jonson's inspiration here seems to have been the French Senecans and their English imitators Samuel Daniel and Fulke Greville, whose classically correct tragedies, complete with chorus and messengers to announce off-stage violence, are also charged with political significance. Greville burned his tragedy of *Antony and Cleopatra* for fear that it would be taken as treasonous, and Daniel's *Philotas* (produced 1604) is such an obvious parallel to the trial, confession and execution of Essex that it led to a Privy Council inquiry.[20] Since Daniel claimed to have begun *Philotas* before 1600, Jonson's choice of politicised Senecan tragedy is probably another case of his challenging a rival at his own genre.

Another influence on *Sejanus* was the contemporary vogue for Tacitus' *Annals*, Jonson's major historical source. Not rediscovered until the sixteenth century, Tacitus was immediately perceived as politically relevant because of 'the apparent similitude that is betwixt those times and ours'.[21] His works were widely read as handbooks of the arts that make for political success or failure. Jonson told Drummond that 'Tacitus . . . wrote the secrets of the council and senate, as Suetonius did those of the cabinet and court' (*Conv.*, ll. 133–4). In England, Tacitism was linked with the Senecan revival and became a vehicle for discontent in court circles, first among the followers of the Earl of Essex and later among those who opposed the Jacobean favourites, Somerset and Buckingham.[22] The prefatory epistle 'A. B. To the Reader' in Henry Savile's translation of Tacitus' *Histories* (1591), rumoured (by Jonson among others) to have been written by Essex himself, contrasts the 'happy government' of Queen Elizabeth with Roman anarchy, but in pointing maxims such as 'a good prince governed by evil ministers is as dangerous as if he were evil himself', it seems to hint at the Earl's discontent with his powerful enemies on the Privy Council.[23]

History in the Tacitean manner was even more likely than translation to be an expression of opposition. Jonson recognises this in Epigram XCV where he praises Henry Savile as the 'soul of Tacitus' and urges him to treat English subjects. 'We need his pen', he tells Savile, 'Can write the things, the causes, and the men', but most of all 'we need his faith (and all have you) / That dares nor write things false, nor hide things true' (ll. 33–6). Savile never answered Jonson's call, perhaps because he observed the fate of John Hayward, whose *First Part of the Life and Reign of King Henry IV* (1599) applied Tacitus' political maxims to the deposition of Richard II and was promptly suppressed by the government as propaganda inviting exactly the kind of rebellion conducted by Essex in 1601.[24] It was, in fact, Jonson's old master William Camden who finally wrote a Tacitean history of Elizabethan England, but Camden did so with considerable caution. His Latin 'Annals of English and Irish Affairs in the Reign of Elizabeth', translated as *The Annals or History of the Most Renowned and Victorious Princess Elizabeth* (1625), follows Tacitus' narrative method but avoids political aphorisms that might be read as oblique commentary. Although in his preface he asserts boldly, 'As for danger, I feared none, no not those who think the memory of succeeding ages may be extinguished by present power', he also confesses that 'things secret and abstruse I have not pried into'.[25] Camden issued the first part of his *Annals* in Latin in 1615, but he discreetly left the later half unpublished until after his death. Like Sir Walter Ralegh he was keenly aware 'that whosoever in writing a modern history, shall follow Truth too near the heels, it may haply strike out his teeth'.[26]

Jonson protected himself by filling the margins of the 1605 Quarto with annotations detailing his historical sources in order to show his 'integrity in the story' and to thwart 'those common torturers, that bring all wit to the rack' in their search for libellous applications.[27] In practice, he compresses or rearranges events for dramatic effect and simplifies the characterisation of his historical figures, heightening the villainy of Tiberius and Sejanus while making their victims into noble innocents, but the impression his notes create is that almost every speech or event is grounded in historical truth. He also added a moralistic conclusion to the summary of his plot in 'The Argument' of the Quarto, stating: 'this do we advance as a mark of terror to all traitors & treasons, to show how just the Heavens are in pouring and thundering down a weighty vengeance on their unnatural intents, even to the worst princes'.[28] These self-protective strategies are manifestations of what Annabel Patterson has called 'the cultural code . . . by which matters of intense social and political concern continued to be discussed in the face of extensive political censorship'.[29] Seventeenth-century readers, Patterson notes, were trained to see disclaimers of topicality as invitations to the very kind of reading they protest against and to consider how histories or translations mirrored contemporary realities. *Sejanus* evaded censorship not just because it was historically accurate, but also because it could not be reduced to a rigid allegory of recent events. Its power lies in its complex relationship to the political life of the time and its ability to dramatise the ambivalent attitudes toward politics held by Jonson and his contemporaries.

Tacitus' *Annals* was read in the early seventeenth century either as a manual of state intrigue or as a warning against tyrannical rule.[30] The two perspectives represent opposing attitudes toward morality in government, and Jonson incorporates both into *Sejanus*. He makes the audience privy to the plotting and counterplotting of Tiberius and Sejanus as they seek to destroy Roman liberty and each other, but he also gives many of Tacitus' moralisations to the followers of Prince Germanicus who are targetted for destruction. We are thus positioned both to observe the contest of expert intriguers who view power as an end in itself and to share the indignation of noble natures at Rome's enslavement.

Tiberius and Sejanus are depicted as Machiavellian strategists whose speeches are riddled with excerpts from *The Prince*.[31] Tiberius, sinister and enigmatic, uses Sejanus to eliminate those Tiberius fears while tricking him into thinking that his ambitions have been unnoticed. Sejanus himself is a skilful, but slightly cruder Machiavel, aiming at the throne through the poisoning of Prince Drusus, marriage to his wife Livia, and control of the young Nero, Drusus and Caius Caligula. Like the more cynical Renaissance Taciteans, Sejanus argues that 'reason of state' justifies Tiberius' destruction of his kin (see II.170–85), but neither he nor Tiberius is motivated by any concern for the common welfare. After Sejanus has been undone by Tiberius' serpentine letter to the Senate, Arruntius predicts – correctly – that his new agent Macro 'will become / A greater prodigy in Rome' than Sejanus was (V.741–2); readers familiar with Tacitus would be aware that Macro was later responsible for Tiberius' own death.

Jonson's treatment of Sejanus and Tiberius has some of the same ambiguity as his characterisation of the amoral tricksters in his middle comedies, who appeal to the audience through their wit and ironic superiority, but his clear-sighted presentation of political intrigue resists being read as an endorsement of Machiavellian policy. Tiberius' wit may make him deserving of victory over Sejanus, but not of ruling. The voices in the play that protest against his lust and his tyranny are muted but intense, and his temporary triumph is seen as a continuation of Rome's suffering. Jonson's viewpoint toward princes who place all 'under the law of their spoil, and licence' seems to be continuous with that in *The Discoveries* (ll. 1430–1524), where Machiavellian precepts are subjected to moral evaluation. There he remarks, 'Princes that neglect their proper office thus, their fortune is oftentimes to draw a Sejanus . . . who will at last affect to get above them. . . . For no men hate an evil prince more than they that helped to make him such. . . . The same path leads to ruin which did to rule when men profess a licence in governing.' (ll. 1513–24). His later moral objections to Machiavellian policy are thus not a reversal of his position in *Sejanus*, but a clarification.[32]

The most politically volatile material in *Sejanus* – that which offers the greatest number of parallels to the late Elizabethan and early Jacobean context – is the destruction of the Germanicans at the hands of Sejanus' informers and toadies in the Senate. The accusations made in Act III against Cremutius Cordus, whose history of Brutus and Cassius is alleged to criticise Tiberius 'by oblique glance of his licentious pen' (l. 404), are a direct analogue to the trial of John Hayward. Jonson underscores the futility of censorship and book burning by quoting Tacitus: those 'that use this cruelty / Of interdiction', says Arruntius, only 'purchase to themselves rebuke and shame, / And to the writers an eternal name' (ll. 467–80). The trial of Silius also recalls the recent treason trials of Essex and Ralegh, both given to the insolent boastfulness and scornful impatience that Silius exhibits. The accusation that Silius connived with the German Sacrovir, though found in Tacitus, would have reminded Jonson's contemporaries of the charge that Essex had plotted to deliver Ireland to Tyrone, while Silius' defiance of the prosecutor Varro for failing to supply proof of his treason and his complaint that the law has become a net to catch innocent men are reminiscent of Ralegh's exchanges with Attorney General Coke. The detail of Silius' supposed impiety, not mentioned in Tacitus' account, parallels Coke's claims that both Essex and Ralegh were atheists. Philip Ayres has plausibly suggested that it may have been the echoes of Ralegh's trial in particular that angered Northampton, for he had played a major role in poisoning the mind of King James against Ralegh.[33]

If Silius is reminiscent of Ralegh and Essex, then Sejanus, who plots his downfall, might be equated with Northampton or Sir Robert Cecil, the age's consummate 'politicians'. Jonson's depiction of informers and spies might thus be compared to Drayton's political beast fable *The Owl* (also written in 1603–4), where Cecil seems to be figured as the Vulture, whose agents the Parrot and the Bat practice such treacherous arts as urging 'a doubtful speech up to the worst, / To broach new treasons, and disclose them first'.[34] Jonson, however, prevents easy identifications by describing Sejanus' cultivation of military men in terms that recall Essex' behaviour before his rebellion, while giving Macro, the agent of his downfall, some hints of Francis Bacon, originally Essex' client but later one of his prosecutors. At the same time, the noble Germanicus, sent away from Rome under 'fair pretext, / And honourable colours of employment' so that he might 'purge and lessen' in another air (I.162–3, 166), offers another parallel to Essex' frustrating service in Ireland as his enemies gained power at home. Jonson has thus dramatised Tacitus' story so that it defies consistent allegorisation, but provides 'flashes of insight' into the current political scene, exposing the sleights by which courtiers destroyed their enemies and perverted justice with the aid of ambitious lawyers.[35]

For Tacitus, however, the key features of Tiberius' reign were his erosion of Roman liberty and his creation of a climate of fear that stifled resistance. Jonson follows Tacitus in lamenting the public servility and greed that allowed Tiberius to extend imperial power, but he is even more responsive to Tacitus' sense that individuals lose the ability to oppose tyranny once informers and spies are given free rein and any expression of discontent against a regime is defined as treason. As Richard Dutton has noted, the play's complex dialectic forces the audience to consider responses to oppression in an almost Brechtian fashion; *Sejanus*, however, offers no easy solutions but reveals the contradictions in Jonson's and the age's thought.[36] Arruntius praises Brutus for striking 'So brave a blow into the monster's heart / That sought unkindly to captive his country' (I.95–6), and Latiaris, seeking to entrap his cousin Sabinus into treason, urges that 'It must be active valour must redeem / Our loss, or none' (IV.157–8). Sabinus, like Richard Hooker, seems to conceive of kingship as grounded in a social contract between people and monarch, but he maintains the orthodox position, also reaffirmed by Jonson in *Discoveries*, that 'No ill should force the subject undertake / Against the sovereign' (ll. 163–4).[37] Despite his orthodoxy, his unguarded words lead to his arrest by spies hiding in the ceiling of his own house, and his execution serves as the climactic demonstration of state-sponsored terror.

From the perspective of modern readers accustomed to democratic freedom, the Germanicans' passivity seems reprehensible, and it has been argued that Jonson means us to condemn figures like Arruntius, whose indignation is expressed in talk without action. However, when Lepidus, who wins praise from Arruntius (and from Tacitus) for moderating the confiscation of Silius' estate, is later asked what 'arts' have preserved him from harm, he answers, 'None, but the plain and passive fortitude, / To suffer, and be silent' (IV.294–5).[38] Such passivity in the face of tyranny was widely endorsed by Renaissance commentators. So Thomas Gainsford, in his *Observations of State and Military Affairs . . . Collected out of Tacitus* (1612) urges that 'the safest way to live under tyrants is to do nothing', and Lipsius advises those under an assured dictatorship 'Not to fight against God': 'If thou be a good citizen or commonwealth-man preserve thyself to a better and happier end'.[39] This solution of Stoic withdrawal had a recurring appeal for Jonson, who alternated between humanist optimism that society might be reformed by an educated elite and an underlying pessimism that the political and social order was incurably corrupt. On the one hand, believing that 'they are ever good men, that must make good the times' (*Disc.*, ll. 303–4), he sought to encourage virtue and condemn vice through poetic praise and blame. On the other hand, while trusting that 'God did never let [good men] be wanting to the world', he casts them in the role of spectators, not actors, looking 'down on the stage of the world' and contemning 'the play of fortune' (ll. 1358–68). The ways of the world, he seems to acknowledge in translating 'A Speech Out of Lucan', are not for idealists: 'He that will honest be, may quit the court, / Virtue and sovereignty, they not consort' (*M.P.* CXXVI, ll. 17–18).[40] *Sejanus* is a protest against that separation and the tyranny that can follow from it.

That Jonson was not punished for *Sejanus* but did get into considerable trouble for his next play, his collaborative comedy *Eastward Ho*, is one of the paradoxes of early Stuart censorship, which tolerated generalised treatments of tyranny so long as they did not encourage rebellion but came down hard on representations of particular persons or groups.[41] Apparently staged sometime in early 1605 by the Children of the Queen's Revels without the approval of the Lord Chamberlain, *Eastward Ho* was the joint work of Jonson, Chapman and Marston, with whom Jonson had been reconciled in 1604.[42] Both a burlesque of prodigal son plays that preach thrift and hard work and a satire on upstarts claiming nobility, the play contained at least two passages of satire that touched sensitive nerves. The first, ironically praising Scots as the greatest friends in the world 'to Englishmen and England, when they are out an't' and wishing that 'a hundred thousand of 'em' were in Virginia (III.iii.38–40), reflects the growing hostility to James' Scottish entourage, which engrossed the offices controlling access to the King and received rewards of money and land on a previously unheard of scale.[43] The second passage, a speech by an anonymous 'gentleman' who remarks, 'I ken the man weel, he's one of my thirty pound knights' (IV.i.155–6), comments on James' lavish distribution of honours and raises the possibility that he had been impersonated satirically on the stage by one of the boy actors.

King James had been surprisingly permissive about allowing satire on his person, but in this case his anger was apparently fanned by his Scottish courtiers. Jonson later reported to William Drummond that 'He was delated [accused] by Sir James Murray to the king for writing something against the Scots in a play, *Eastward Ho*, and voluntarily imprisoned himself with Chapman and Marston, who had written it amongst them. The report was, that they should then have their ears cut and noses' (*Conv.*, ll. 270–4).[44] The printed text of the 1605 Quarto (entered 4 September) was censored, and Jonson and Chapman languished in prison until James 'high displeasure' cooled.[45] Their defence was that they had not written the offending passages, though they avoided mentioning Marston, whose whereabouts at this time are uncertain, despite Drummond's statement that he was in gaol. Chapman appealed directly to King James' 'Caesar-like bounty (who . . . was glad of offences that he might forgive)' and to the Lord Chamberlain, the Earl of Suffolk. Jonson, whose patronage network was much more extensive, wrote not only to Suffolk but also to the Earl of Salisbury, the Earls of Pembroke and Montgomery (with whom his letters show a greater familiarity), Lord D'Aubigny and an unnamed lady (probably Lucy, Countess of Bedford). His letter to Salisbury betrays some embarrassment at again being in hot water so soon after his interrogation for *Sejanus* and denies (somewhat disingenuously) that he has 'ever (in any thing I have written, private or public) given offence to a nation, to any public order or state, or any person of honour or authority'.[46] It was James' fellow Scot, Lord d'Aubigny, who seems to have interceded most successfully with the King on Chapman's and Jonson's behalf, and they were ultimately released from prison on the authority of the Lord Chamberlain, to whom James apparently delegated the matter.[47]

Jonson's release was the occasion for celebration, tempered by sober reflection on his near escape from mutilation. He told

Drummond, 'After their delivery, he banqueted all his friends; there was Camden, Selden and others. At the midst of the feast his old mother drank to him, and shew him a paper which she had (if the sentence had taken execution) to have mixed in the prison among his drink, which was full of lusty strong poison, and that she was no churl, she told, she minded first to have drunk of it herself' (*Conv.*, ll. 275–81). Fortunately, her bravery was never put to the test, but Jonson's second imprisonment for his satiric indiscretions left him obligated to the 'bounty' of those who helped secure his release. To Robert Cecil, Lord Salisbury, he soon had occasion to repay the benefit.

Some time early in October 1605 Jonson had been a guest in the Strand at a Catholic dinner party whose members included Robert Catesby, Sir Jocelyn Percy, Francis Tresham – gentlemen who had actively supported the Essex rebellion in 1601. A month later Catesby, Tresham and Thomas Winter, another guest, were all implicated in the Gunpowder Plot, which sought to restore England to Catholicism by killing the King and the peerage at the opening of the House of Lords on 5 November. It is possible Jonson knew members of the group through his friendship with Sir John Roe (apparently not a Catholic), who had dined with many of them the previous Lent, although Roe was serving bravely in the Low Countries in October and so could not have been the 'unknown' gentleman listed as attending.[48] Jonson's presence could have many possible explanations; it cannot by itself be taken as evidence of his knowledge of the plot or of his activity as a government spy. However, in his letter to the Earl of Suffolk over *Eastward Ho* he had affirmed his affection as 'a most zealous and good subject', and when the Plot was uncovered, he acted as Cecil's agent in attempting to contact a priest 'that offered to do good service to the state'.[49] He tried to reach the priest through the chaplain of the Venetian ambassador, but the priest was overcome with caution and sent word that he would 'not be found'. Jonson's efforts to contact others were equally unsuccessful, leading him to conclude that 'they [priests?] are all so enweaved in it, as it will make five hundred gentlemen less of the religion within this week, if they [the gentlemen] carry their understanding about them'.[50]

Jonson's actions place him with the many moderate Catholics who, despite Papal encouragement to rebel, saw no inconsistency between their faith and their allegiance to the English monarchy. After the Gunpowder Plot, however, loyalty was no protection against the government's efforts to impose conformity. On 10 January Jonson and his wife were cited by the London Consistory Court for recusancy: 'they refuse not to come to divine service, but have absented themselves from the communion, being oftentimes admonished, which hath continued as far as we can learn ever since the King came in'. Perhaps betraying the age-old suspicion of creative writers, the record adds, 'he is a poet and is by fame a seducer of youth to the popish religion'. Jonson utterly denied the last charge, but confessed that he had 'heretofore been of some other opinion in religion, which now upon better advisement he is determined to alter; he desireth such learned men to be assigned unto him to confer withal, he promising to conform himself according as they shall advise him and persuade him.'[51] The court assigned five prominent clergymen, including the Dean of St. Paul's and three doctors of divinity, with whom he could choose to consult and required that he meet one of them twice a week.

The conferences must have been intense, for Jonson was widely read in theology. Among the losses he lamented in 'An Execration upon Vulcan' (*Und.* XLIII) were his 'humble gleanings in divinity; / After the Fathers, and those wiser guides / Whom faction had not drawn to study sides' (ll. 102–4). His interest in patristic studies is confirmed independently by John Selden, whom Jonson later asked for background on the Levitical prohibition against men wearing women's clothes. Selden concentrated in his reply primarily on Hebrew and Syrian sources, explaining that he did not touch on European theology and the church fathers because 'your own most choice and able store cannot but furnish you incidently with whatever is fit that way to be thought of in the reading'.[52] Undoubtedly some of Jonson's book collecting had been motivated by his desire to work out the intellectual and historical basis of his faith, and he would have been a difficult man to persuade. The Consistory Court records do not indicate the final disposition of his case; according to his own account he remained a Papist for twelve years (that is, until 1610) and then made an emotional return to Anglicanism: 'After he was reconciled with the church, and left off to be a recusant, at his first communion, in token of true reconciliation, he drank out all the full cup of wine' (*Conv.*, ll. 313–15). There is no need to interpret this extravagant gesture as a tongue-in-cheek allusion to his drinking; it surely expresses his relief that his intellectual struggle and the political pressures toward conformity had finally been resolved.

6
Learned Inventions

At the same time that *Sejanus* and *Eastward Ho* provoked difficulties with the authorities, Jonson's royal entertainments and masques – those festive shows combining poetic fable, scenic display and dancing by the nobility – won him favour and reward in the new Jacobean court. Jonson's confidence in his skill as a masque writer is shown by his boast to Drummond 'that next himself only Fletcher and Chapman could make a masque' (*Conv.*, ll. 43–4). In this genre as in others he achieved success by setting a new standard of competition for his rivals – a standard based on his conviction that even such ephemeral entertainments demanded the ingenious application of the poet's learning in ways that would both honour and instruct their noble participants. His belief that the poet's role was central to masque-making and that masques were an educative ritual for the masquers inevitably brought him into conflict with his artistic collaborators and the social realities of such occasions. Yet partly through force of personality and partly through skill at invention he established himself as the leading Jacobean masque writer. In the theatre, too, he gained a striking success with his comedy *Volpone, or The Fox* (1606), which pleased both popular and learned audiences in London, Oxford and Cambridge.

The development of the court masque as a major artistic form in the early Stuart period was the result of royal patronage and the combined talents of Jonson and the scene designer Inigo Jones. Queen Anne, an excellent dancer, aspired to commission for the Jacobean court entertainments that would rival the splendour of those presented in France and at the Medici court in Florence.[1] She was indulged by King James, who viewed the masque partly as an expression of his own magnificence and partly as an opportunity to display her physical grace and that of his male favourites. Jones, who had studied in Italy and was skilled as an artist, architect, scenic and costume designer, introduced the new mode of proscenium-arch staging along with astounding effects of lighting and scenic transformation, while Jonson's scholarly, classical bent made him an ideal collaborator in mythologising the participants into emblems of grace and virtue. Together they transformed the court masque from its simpler Tudor form as a 'disguising' into a highly theatrical 'spectacle of state'.

Jones, however, did not enter Anne's service until 1604, and the first major masque commission of the new reign went not to Jonson but to his rival Samuel Daniel for *The Vision of the Twelve Goddesses*, presented on 8 January 1604. Possibly it was this masque from which Jonson and his friend Sir John Roe were ejected for creating a disturbance; he at least seems to have criticised it openly, for Daniel's highly defensive dedication to Lucy, Countess of Bedford (who recommended him to the Queen) responds to exactly the kind of objections Jonson might have raised.[2] To meet successfully the artistic challenges posed by the form, the masque poet not only had to supply speeches of introduction and song lyrics to be interspersed with the dancing but also to create a fiction that explained the visit of the masqued dancers to the hall, drawing on mythology or history for identities appropriate to the occasion. Daniel's twelve goddesses, led by Anne herself as Pallas, were aptly chosen to present 'the hieroglyphic of empire and dominion' and 'those blessings, and beauties that preserve and adorn it'.[3] However, Daniel's portrayal of Somnus (or Sleep) without his traditional ivory horn seems to have provoked Jonson's criticism, which Daniel answers both by citing his classical guides and by claiming that disagreement among the mythographers left poets free to choose the 'aptest representations that lay best and easiest for us'.[4] Moreover, Daniel had announced the identity of his twelve goddesses in four-line poems that were all read at once before the masquers appeared 'so that the eyes of the spectators might not beguile their ears'. He excuses this long undramatic description on the grounds that 'pomp and splendour' are 'most regardful in these shows'.[5] Although he concedes that masques furnish 'state and greatness' with 'the necessary complements' of 'glory and majesty', he disparages their literary value, claiming that 'whosoever strives to show most wit about these punctilios of dreams and shows are sure sick of a disease . . . and would fain have the world to think them very deeply learned in all mysteries whatsoever.'[6]

Daniel, whom Jonson characterised as 'a good honest man . . . but no poet' (*Conv.*, ll. 21–2), received no further masque commissions until 1610, when his *Tethys' Festival* was performed at the celebration of Prince Henry's investiture as Prince of Wales. He comforted himself with the thought that if the 'deep judgments' of his 'captious censurers . . . ever serve them to produce any thing, they must stand on the same stage of censure with other men, and peradventure perform no such great wonders as they would make us believe'.[7] However, Jonson, who was asked to write *The Masque of Blackness* for 1605, proved more than equal to the task. From then until 1613, when he was out of the country as the travelling companion to Sir Walter Ralegh's son, he was called upon almost annually for the Twelfth Night masque, producing *Hymenaei* in 1606, *The Masque of Beauty* and *The Haddington Masque* in 1608, *The Masque of Queens* in 1609, *The Speeches at Prince Henry's Barriers* in 1610, *Love Freed from Ignorance and Folly* and *Oberon The Fairy Prince* in 1611, and *Love Restored* in 1612.

Jonson's masques are superior precisely because he did not accept his rival's definition of the masque poet as 'a poor engineer for shadows'.[8] His prefatory matter to *Hymenaei* (published 1606) is a direct reply to those, like Daniel, who 'squeamishly cry out that all endeavour of learning and sharpness in these transitory devices . . . is superfluous':

> It is a noble and just advantage that the things subjected to understanding have of those which are objected to sense that the one sort are but momentary and merely taking, the other impressing and lasting. . . . This it is hath made the most royal princes and greatest persons . . . not only studious of riches and magnificence in the outward celebration or show, which rightly becomes them, but curious after the most high and hearty inventions to furnish the inward parts, and those grounded upon antiquity and solid learnings; which, though their voice be taught to sound to present occasions, their sense or doth or should always lay hold on more removed mysteries. (*Masques*, pp. 75–6)

By defining spectacle merely as the 'body' of the masque and poetry as its soul, Jonson claims credit for creating the masque's most enduring part and justifies his attention to detail.

Jonson's emphasis on artistic invention in this manifesto is directly related to the occasional nature of masques. Most were designed for particular state occasions honouring members of the royal family or celebrating the marriages of leading courtiers. His first artistic challenge was to devise a fable appropriate to the occasion and conformable to the wishes of the patrons or participants. In *The Masque of Blackness* the Queen required him to supply a fictional excuse for her appearance in black-face, while in its sequel *The Masque of Beauty* the 'limits' to which he 'apted' his invention (l. 7) were her requests to add four more masquers and to justify the passage of time in his fable. The form of *The Masque of Queens* (and of most subsequent masques) was determined by Anne's command 'to think on some dance or show that might precede hers and have the place of a foil or false masque' (ll. 10–12). King James never danced in the masques, but his presence as the chief spectator was a constant consideration: Jonson's choice in *The Masque of Queens* of an anti-masque of witches was calculated to appeal to the King, whose book on *Demonology* (1591) was one of the sources that he used. Though the early masques rarely honour James so directly as later ones like *The Golden Age Restored* or *Pan's Anniversary*, Jonson always finds ways to incorporate the King into his fiction, making his throne of state a focal point of the mythology, as well as the theatrical lines of sight.[9]

The polycentric nature of the Jacobean royal household, which actually comprised three establishments (those of James, Anne and Prince Henry) each with its own officers and its own religious, political and sexual orientation, sometimes required Jonson to serve conflicting interests. In *The Masque of Queens*, for example, the ostensible celebration of the Queen and her eleven attendants is qualified by reminders of James' patriarchal power and by the misogynistic images of the witches over whom they triumph. The female masquers are glorified by their impersonation of virtuous or warlike queens from history and mythology, yet their appearance in the House of Fame is signalled by the descent of Perseus, who represents the 'heroic and masculine virtue' of King James (l. 342), and the King's distrust of women, linked to his belief in witchcraft, is reinforced by the hags of the anti-masque.[10] Jonson's masque thus seems to have satisfied both his royal patron and patroness, despite their conflicting sexual politics.

Another difficult commission proved to be that for *Prince Henry's Barriers*, anticipating Henry's investiture as Prince of Wales. Here Jonson found it necessary to arbitrate between Henry's militant Protestantism, encouraged by the anti-Spanish bias of the old Essex followers who surrounded him, and the King's self-image as the *Rex pacificus* who would play an instrumental role in reconciling European Protestants and Catholics. Jonson presents Henry under his favourite title 'Meliadus' (an anagram, when spelled

'Moeliades', on the Latin phrase *miles a deo* or 'soldier of God'), and praises him as a successor to the warrior-princes Richard the Lion-hearted, Edward the Black Prince and Henry the Fifth. At the same time he stresses the arts of peace and makes the Lady of the Lake present the Prince not with a sword, but with a shield, 'to show / Defensive arms th'offensive should forego' (ll. 98–9).[11] After the tourney, in which the sixteen-year-old Prince and his six supporters fought fifty-six challengers across the barriers, Jonson reintroduces a martial note into Merlin's final speech, predicting that Prince Charles 'Shall second him [Prince Henry] in arms and shake a sword / And lance against the foes of God and you [James]' (ll. 416–7).[12] This vague phrase is as close as Jonson comes to crusading Protestant rhetoric, but it hardly confirms his image, now current in some circles, as an unwavering supporter of James' pacifism. His adroit balancing act seems to have satisfied the royal father and son; it may also have expressed his own complex feelings about military valour (which he always honoured), overseas adventurism, and religious politics.

Few masques or entertainments involved such conflicted issues as those in *Prince Henry's Barriers*, but all posed a challenge to Jonson's ingenuity – a challenge that he heightened for himself by insisting that the masque must 'lay hold on more removed mysteries' as well. His learned allegories invoke the Renaissance belief in correspon-dences between microcosm and macrocosm, elevating masquers, scenery, music and dancing into universal symbols. Thus the masque music metaphorically represents the harmony of the soul or cosmos, dancing the order of the planets or the internal graces of virtue and excellence, and stage lighting any kind of perfection, whether of beauty, virtue, valour or reason, as well as the god-like nature of royal power.[13] *The Masque of Beauty* exalts Queen Anne and her ladies as the eight essential attributes of beauty and places them in a stage machine that is 'an image of the turning world, presided over by Harmony, with Beauty set in the wheeling heaven which is its cause, and attended by Love moving like the planets'.[14] Its sighted Cupids, who represent spiritual love, and its fountain of 'Chaste Delight' may have been a subtle attempt to instruct a court already winning a doubtful reputation for licentiousness.[15]

The concepts of harmony and union are given their widest extension in *Hymenaei*, presented at the wedding of Lady Frances Howard (daughter of the Lord Chamberlain) and the young Earl of Essex. As he does in his plays, Jonson here seems to have built on the motifs of others, turning in this case to the lost wedding masque for Sir Philip Herbert and Lady Susan Vere (given a year earlier on 27 December 1604), where the scene was imagined as Juno's temple and the masquers were brought in by the four seasons and Hymeneus.[16] Jonson typically transmutes this simple concept into something grander by playing on the Iuno–Unio anagram, thereby parallelling the Essex–Howard match, which reconciled two hostile political factions, to the proposed union of England and Scotland that was then being debated in Parliament. This in turn is placed in cosmic perspective by analogies between the physical and the political order drawn from court sermons and tracts supporting James' scheme.[17] Jonson and Jones also adapt the device of a hollow globe containing figures of the various estates of England employed by Dekker and Harrison in their Fleet Street arch in *The Magnificent Entertainment*, but convert it into the 'little world of man' (l. 111) from which issue the male masquers as the four humours and the four affections. Jonson's reworking of Dekker's device no doubt confirmed the latter's opinion of him as a 'plagiarist', but as usual Jonson makes more of the motif than his rival had. The affections and humours are tamed by Reason and joined by Order with the lady masquers, who represent the eight properties of marriage. The licentious and disorderly behaviour of crowds at masques testifies that on the personal level the court badly needed his instruction.[18] The dancers' formation into a chain and circle ritually confirms their commitment to the ideal of rational self-control and symbolically links the union of the married couple and of the two kingdoms to cosmic harmony.

Hymenaei is still comprehensible today because its central idea is clear even to readers unaware of its political backgrounds. Some of Jonson's other masques employ a more arcane symbolism drawn from the ancient poets and mythographers, and their meanings have only recently been deciphered as modern scholars have recovered the language of Renaissance iconography and the particular contexts of the masque occasions. The symbolic qualities of the masquers are indicated by their allegorical names, by their costumes and properties, or by the 'hieroglyphics' or symbolic pictures carried on their fans or shields; the action of the masques, like that of Spenser's *The Faerie Queen*, forms a 'continued allegory, or dark conceit' intended to be unraveled by the spectator.[19] For example, in *The Masque of Blackness* Queen Anne held a picture of 'a golden tree laden with fruit' and was given the name of Euphoris or 'abundance' (l. 245); recognising that she was six months pregnant at the time, as many in the original audience would have known, clarifies these symbols and much of the imagery in the masque as a celebration of her fertility.[20] Of course, not every spectator was attentive to Jonson's symbolism. Dudley Carleton found the presentation of the Queen and her ladies as the Daughters of Niger 'a very loathsome sight'; he passed over the masque's elaborate mythology to comment on the dancers' 'light and courtesanlike' apparel.[21] In general, however, Renaissance courtly audiences were intrigued by the challenge of puzzling out hidden meanings; their interest in such riddles explains the sudden vogue for emblem books in the later sixteenth century and the use of *impresas* (symbolic pictures and mottoes) on the shields of tilters.

Jonson liked to test his audience's powers of interpretation, and he insisted on authenticating his poetic mythology. His strategy is to avoid direct announcements and to identify his figures in the course of his dramatic dialogue, designing their symbolic attributes so 'as upon the view, they might, without cloud, or obscurity, declare themselves to the sharp and learned'.[22] It troubled him when details were inaccurate, and he went to unusual lengths to research the rituals and mythology of his masques. In *Hymenaei* he recreated a complete Roman marriage ceremony according to the descriptions of Renaissance antiquaries; in *The Masque of Queens* he prescribed most of the magical properties of the witches 'out of the authority of ancient and late writers' (ll. 33–4), adding a few details from rumours and tales remembered from his Westminster childhood. His fussiness about authenticity is often dismissed as pedantry, but he saw himself setting a higher standard for art – if the poet could be inventive and still be historically correct, so much the better! The malignant energy of his witches, who compare well with their Shakespearean counterparts in *Macbeth*, and his sprightly lyric 'The owl is abroad, the bat and the toad' (ll. 66–86) demonstrate that scholarship did not inhibit his inspiration.

Jonson's early masques, in fact, are notable not only for the artful application of his learning, but also for their variety and for their dramatic effectiveness. Considering that he often ridiculed medieval romance and popular superstition, his treatment of Arthurian legend in *Prince Henry's Barriers* and his handling of witch and fairy lore are surprisingly deft. The masques praising love, beauty and marriage draw on such diverse sources as neo-Platonic love theory, classical epithalamia and the Greek Anthology, and range in tone from the high serious to the playful. With the encouragement of Queen Anne he gradually evolved the antic-masque or anti-masque that preceded the masque proper; its comical or grotesque dancers assure a lively beginning and symbolise the forces of disorder dispelled by the entrance of the masquers in all their splendour. As he explains in his preface to *The Masque of Queens*, he chose his twelve witches to sustain 'the persons of Ignorance, Suspicion, Credulity, etc., the opposites to good Fame . . . not as a masque but a spectacle of strangeness, producing multiplicity of gesture, and not unaptly sorting with the current and whole fall of the device' (ll. 15–19). In contrast to their hellish charms, the mischievous Cupids of *The Haddington Masque* and the satyrs of *Oberon* provide a comical touch; they are not driven offstage, but integrated into the final vision of their masques.

There was, of course, more to masque writing than merely working up a text; the form demanded a close collaboration between the poet, the scene designer, the composer and the dancing master. Paradoxically, Jonson's sense of the poet's function made him both a valuable and a difficult collaborator. By giving symbolic significance to the various media in which his fellow artists worked, he integrated their contributions as aspects of the masque's central theme. At the same time, by insisting on his role as 'inventor' of the masque's central concept, he sometimes aroused professional jealousies. Alphonso Ferrabosco, the composer for most of the early masques, became a good friend: Jonson paid him a warm tribute in Epigram CXXX, and he gave his 'judicial care' and 'absolute performance' of the musical compositions in *Hymenaei* generous recognition in the printed text (*Masques*, p. 475). With Inigo Jones, however, he seems from the first to have had a cooler relationship, if one can judge from the much briefer reference to him in the same passage. As Jones gained experience and an extensive knowledge of European entertainments from his frequent travels abroad, their collaboration was to break down into outright rivalry, for Jones' sense of 'design' was very close to Jonson's sense of 'invention' and neither wished to yield creative control to the other.[23] In the early masques Jones was content to realise Jonson's conceptions, and Jonson makes it very clear that the choice of setting was his alone; thus he notes in *The Masque of Beauty*, 'Here . . . the scene [was] discovered, which (because the former was marine, and these yet of necessity to come from the sea) *I devised* should be an island floating on a calm water' (ll. 144–6, italics mine).

Jonson sustained his claim that poetry was the 'soul' of masques in large part because no other media were available to preserve them besides printed texts. These were sought by the Jacobean public as mementoes of the occasion and as court news to send to inquiring friends in the country, but Jonson used them to promote the masque as a literary form and to publicise his own art. He had received a painful lesson in authorial privilege in 1604 when Dekker's *The Magnificent Entertainment* was recognised as the official narrative of King James' entry into London and his own version was suppressed; Dekker gave Jonson's pageants only a brief description, omitting his verses entirely but including a full text of his own.[24] In turn, Jonson's early masque texts describe the costumes and scenery and identify the masquers, but they give primacy to the poetry and its meaning. The Quartos of *Hymenaei* (1606), *The Masque of Blackness* and *The Masque of Beauty* (printed together by Thomas Thorpe in 1609) and *The Masque of Queens* (also 1609) include extensive side-notes that clarify their symbolism and identify Jonson's classical sources, thereby justifying his claim to 'most high and hearty invention . . . grounded upon antiquity and solid learnings'.[25]

Jonson must have been aware, of course, that his high seriousness about masques was not shared by the public or even the participants, for whom the dancing and the dressing-up (not to mention the satisfaction of having been chosen as one of the inner circle around Queen Anne or Prince Henry) would have been the most absorbing aspects. In the end his pursuit of masque commissions would prove a Faustian bargain, in which he traded his artistic and political independence for the benefits of court patronage. Those benefits were considerable: his reward for composing a masque was forty pounds (at least four times higher than his payment for plays), and he may have received extra gratuities for the elegant copies of the texts that he wrote out for the Queen or for other noblemen upon request. Moreover, just as his duties as masque poet placed him in the very centre of the production of *Hymenaei* to turn the globe revealing the masquers, so they also drew him into contact with the leading officers and court ladies, expanding his opportunities for patronage and new commissions.[26] It would have been through such informal encounters as masque rehearsals or planning meetings that he gradually became the familiar 'Ben', increasingly absorbed into the courtly world whose manners he had criticised in the 'Comical Satires'. In the early years of James' reign, however, it was the artistic challenge that was uppermost, and he threw himself into the task of composing masques that were 'apted' to their occasions, yet worthy of continuing admiration for their poetry and doctrine.

Jonson's stress on the enduring literary merits of his works, as opposed to their brief stage life, is nowhere seen more clearly than in the printed text of his comedy *Volpone, or The Fox*, first acted to great applause in early 1606 by the King's Men and taken on tour by them to Oxford and Cambridge in the summer of 1606 or 1607.[27] Like the *Sejanus* Quarto, the *Volpone* Quarto (published in February 1607) contains a number of English and Latin commendatory poems (which, before his example, were never published with plays from the commercial theatre), as well as a dedication to 'the two famous universities for their love and acceptance shown to his poem in the presentation' (*Plays*, III, x). Jonson describes *Volpone* as a 'poem' rather than a play because, as he explains in the dedicatory epistle, he desires to 'stand off' from 'the present trade of the stage, in all their misc'line interludes' – a trade corrupted by 'ribaldry, profanation, blasphemy' (ll. 81, 34–5).[28] The epistle is his boldest literary manifesto to date, borrowing from Erasmus and the Italian critic Minturno to define 'the offices and function of a Poet' and to defend his satire against 'the imputation of sharpness' (ll. 19–20, 44). As in the preface to *Sejanus*, he stresses his play's classical correctness, claiming 'to reduce ['bring back'] not only the ancient forms, but manners of the scene' (ll. 98–9) and promising to 'raise the despised head of Poetry again, and stripping her out of those rotten and base rags, wherewith the times have adulterated her form, restore her to her primitive habit, feature, and majesty' (ll. 119–22). In contrast to *Every Man out of His Humour*, where he had rejected the ancient 'laws' of comedy as 'too nice observations' (Ind., l. 237), the Prologue now claims that Jonson presents 'quick comedy, refined, / As best critics have designed' and observes 'the laws of time, place, persons' (ll. 29–31). The classic stature of *Volpone* is further suggested by his acrostic 'Argument', imitating the Latin acrostics in Renaissance editions of Plautus' plays.

With this edition, then, Jonson completed a triad of publications – *Sejanus* (1605), *Hymenaei* (1606) and *Volpone* (1607/8) – that demonstrated his powers of learned invention in three different genres. In each case he gave classical material a contemporary application, combining his sources into a richer and more complex whole and inviting comparison with English analogues too. The spirit of emulous rivalry in which he adapted his materials is most noticeable in *Volpone* because it distils the 'quintessence' of all previous treatments of its central motif – the folly of legacy hunting – thereby seeking not only to apply the matter of classical satire to his own time but to outdo its form as well. Yet his change in focus from the affectation ridiculed in the 'Comical Satires' to lust and avarice would also seem to be a reaction to the City Comedy of Thomas Middleton, in which roguery and sharp practice initiate an ironic cycle of cheating and being cheated.

Middleton's plots are rooted in a sense of class warfare between citizens who aspire to become landed gentry and prodigal gallants who squander their estates in pursuit of London pleasures. Jonson's *Eastward Ho*, written in collaboration with Chapman and Marston, had combined burlesque of citizen morality and the prodigal-son plays with satiric intrigue centring around the upstart courtier Sir Petronel Flash and the usurer Security, but in the plays he wrote alone he is less interested in dramatising actual social and economic tensions than in commenting generally on the corrupting power of gold in late Elizabethan and early Jacobean society. He had perceived the quickening scramble for wealth as early as 1599, when in his 'Epistle to Rutland' (*For.* XII) he satirised people's willingness to give 'life, conscience, yea, souls' for gold and remarked on the short-lived benefits of New Year's gift-giving by clients to patrons (l. 3). His vision of 'this, our gilt, [or] golden age' proved to be prophetic of the reign of James, whose reckless liberality depleted the treasury and increasingly transformed court patronage and office-seeking into a money-exchange.[29] In such a climate classical satire on the practice of courting rich old men had a particular relevance, especially since Jacobean gift-giving sometimes did take the form of legacy-hunting. John Aubrey, for example, claimed that the businessman Thomas Sutton (died 1611) was the model for Volpone: 'he was much upon mortgages, and fed several with hopes of being his heir. The Earl of Dorset (I think Richard) mightily courted him and presented him, hoping to have been his heir, and so did several other great persons'.[30] Sutton's character has been shown to be quite different from that of Jonson's trickster, but Aubrey's story is valuable nevertheless as a contemporary example of the drawing power of gold.

In the spirit of City Comedy in general and of Jonson's play in particular, his friend John Hoskyns is also reported by Aubrey to have said 'that all those that came to London were either carrion or crows'.[31] Hoskyns is quoting from the description in Petronius'

Satyricon of the fictional town of Croton, where the rogue Eumolpus stages 'a little farce' for the legacy-hunting inhabitants by pretending that he is a bachelor millionaire near death.[32] Whether inspired by *Volpone* or the inspiration for it, Hoskyns' remark points up the imaginative transformation Jonson worked on his sources. He elaborates Petronius' metaphor of legacy hunters as carrion-eaters into an extended beast fable in which the greedy Voltore, Corbaccio, and Corvino (vulture, raven, and crow) are outwitted by his Fox, whose wiliness is inspired in part by Caxton's *The History of Reynard the Fox* and by Aesop's fables. Additional details of the cheats played by and on his unscrupulous suitors are derived from Horace and from Lucian's *Dialogues of the Dead*, which also supplies hints for Volpone's parasite Mosca. With his characteristic attention to authenticating detail, Jonson updates the Mediterranean locale of his models to contemporary Venice, noted both for its commercial wealth and its rigorous justice.[33] The Venetian setting is linked to the world of his audience by his sub-plot of the English travellers, Sir Politic and Lady Would-Be – the latter a version of the domineering, talkative women ridiculed by Juvenal and the Greek rhetorician Libanius, the former a satire on pretenders to intelligence about political intrigues. The pair are integrated into the beast fable by their parrot-like chatter and by Sir Pol's absurd device of disguising himself as a tortoise, while the whole play is further unified around the Erasmian theme of folly.[34]

It should be obvious from even this brief and incomplete accounting that *Volpone* is indeed, as George Parfitt puts it, 'a triumph of creative assimilation'.[35] Parfitt's close analysis demonstrates how artfully Jonson's borrowings are fitted to their dramatic contexts, but in focusing on the details of the imitative process one must be careful not to suggest that Jonson's mode of composition was coldly calculated and laborious. The early 1600s were for him a period of intensive classical reading – reading that he was able to hold in his memory better than most men – and in *Volpone* at least, the various hints from his studies came together in a lightning flash of illumination that fused them into a new and brilliant whole. Having been taunted by Dekker in *Satiromastix* about the slowness of his composition, he must have taken a special pleasure in being able to announce in the Prologue that only two months previously *Volpone* was 'no feature' and that 'five weeks fully penned it' (ll. 14–16).

Jonson's creative approach to satiric imitation is best seen in his development of complex ironic structures from the simple effects of his sources. By ridiculing men and women who wasted their own wealth in the hopes of getting others', classical satire on legacy-hunting exposed the delusions of greed. Yet the satires of Lucian and Horace turn on fairly obvious ironies, such as the gold-diggers' hypocrisy in pretending concern for those whose death they wish or their blindness in believing that they are healthier and will be longer-lived than those they court. Jonson's plot incorporates all of these ironies while also stressing the self-delusion of his three carrion-eaters, who each believe, despite competition, that they will be Volpone's exclusive heir. Moreover, as in Petronius, where the legacy-hunters are asked to eat what passes for Eumolpus' dead body if they wish to inherit his non-existent wealth, they are all pushed to extremes by Volpone and Mosca before being left empty-handed in the end. Corbaccio's disinheritance of his son Bonario and his denunciation of him in open court, Corvino's testimony that his wife Celia has cuckolded him (the very thing he feared most) and Voltore's perjury show that gold does indeed transcend 'All style of joy, in children, parents, friends' and that it takes precedence over 'virtue, fame, / Honour and all things else' (I.i.17, 25–6). Yet the mockery of the will-reading scene, in which the suitors discover that they have been disinherited for a parasite, is here not the end of the action as it is in Jonson's sources, but the start of fresh complications that eventually bring down Volpone and Mosca too.

Jonson, in fact, adds an entirely new level of irony to his satire by extending the cheater-cheated formula to Volpone and Mosca. In contrast to Eumolpus, who stages his death to escape from his role, Volpone's announcement that he is dead and his nomination of Mosca as his heir proves to be 'the fox-trap' in which he is caught. Here Jonson seems to be following Middleton, whose comedies frequently demonstrate the maxim of the roguish Follywit in *A Mad World My Masters*: 'craft recoils in the end . . . and maims the very hand that puts fire to't'.[36] The closest analogue to Volpone in Middleton's comedies is Ephestian Quomodo from *Michaelmas Term*, most probably produced sometime in 1604 or 1605.[37] Having gulled a young heir out of his lands, Quomodo falsifies his death to test the response of his wife and son, only to find that his wife marries his former victim and that his son is promptly cheated of Quomodo's ill-gotten estate. Like Volpone, Quomodo reveals himself, but finds his losses upheld in the play's final judgement scene.

Jonson viewed Middleton as a 'base fellow' (*Conv.*, l. 157–8), and he undoubtedly took pleasure in enriching and refining Middleton's comic plot. Quomodo's elaborate deception of the naive Easy, aided by the virtuoso disguising of his accomplices Shortyard and Falselight, depicts commercial fraud with the zest of the cony-catching pamphlets, yet Quomodo's impulsive decision to fake his death is inadequately motivated.[38] By contrast, Volpone's over-reaching is not just an arbitary device to end the play, but is consistent with his masquerade as a dying man and with his characterisation throughout. From the first, Volpone plays a double role, serving both as a satiric agent who exposes the folly of others and as a foolish worldling blinded by his own self-love. His function at any given moment is signalled, among other means, by classical echoes meant to delight the 'sharp and learned'. Thus he ridicules Corbaccio's prayers for long life in a direct quotation from Pliny, while his promise that Celia will drink dissolved pearl and feast on nightingales is an ironic application of Horace's *Satires* II.iii, where such extravagance is dismissed as a form of madness. Jonson's technique of mixing straightforward borrowings and ironic ones is established in Volpone's opening hymn to gold, composed of passages from Lucian's *The Dream, or The Cock*, Seneca's moral epistles and Horace.[39] Still, the play's irony can be appreciated even by auditors who cannot follow Jonson's classical allusions because Volpone's folly is also indicated dramatically by his susceptibility to Mosca's artful flattery and by the way his various disguisings hasten his exposure and ruin.[40]

It is, of course, Volpone's lust for Celia that starts his downhill slide, and here Jonson's workmanship illustrates his extraordinary skill at seizing on parallels between seemingly disparate materials. The Celia plot is built on hints from no less than four different sources and blends them into an action that serves his moral purpose while creating suspense about which of their possible outcomes he will follow. Lust and legacy hunting are linked in two of his sources: in Horace's *Satires* II.v Teiresias suggests to Ulysses that, in courting a rich libertine, he should hand over Penelope (the classical pattern of a virtuous wife), and in *The Satyricon* Eumolpus ingeniously gains sexual satisfaction from the daughter of a suitor even while supposedly impotent and immobile. Jonson betters his models by making Corvino insanely jealous at first so that his offer of Celia is a comically shocking reversal and by using her resistance to expose the perversity of Corvino's and Volpone's values. Wives are also victimised in *The History of Reynard the Fox*, where Reynard catches the Raven's wife by pretending to be dead and rapes the Wolf's wife after luring her into a trap; Volpone's offered violence is thus consistent with his 'wolvish nature', but the parallel with the Reynard story would build tension about whether Volpone might escape punishment like his model or be caught.

Suspense about Volpone's fate is heightened further by Jonson's use of another Elizabethan dramatic analogue – his friend George Chapman's *The Blind Beggar of Alexandria* (written 1596, revived 1601). Produced by the Lord Admiral's Men, Chapman's comedy depicts the exploits of Duke Cleanthes, who assumes three masks – those of Irus the blind beggar, the humourous Count Hermes and Leon the usurer. In the latter role he engages in amours very much like Volpone's, courting the maiden Samathis and then slyly cuckolding himself by seducing Elimine, the wife of his alter ego Count Hermes. As does Volpone, Chapman's protagonist conducts his wooing while disguised as an old man, demonstrates his virility in song and dance, argues that stolen love is no sin and offers jewels as a temptation.[41] The parallels between the two works highlight the superiority of Volpone's dramatic rhetoric and illustrate once again Jonson's complex relationship to popular drama. Chapman's Cleanthes uses his disguising to gain power, wealth, and sexual pleasure, and no moral considerations are allowed to diminish the audience's delight in his tricks. In the end he successfully kills off his various false identities, though he is momentarily alarmed by his brother Pego, who teasingly threatens to reveal his role as Leon. Jonson's treatment of disguise, on the other hand, manifests what Jonas A. Barish has called his 'deeply rooted antitheatricalism', which condemns spectacle and shape-shifting as transitory and inauthentic.[42] Although Volpone's appearance as Scoto of Mantua is theatrically persuasive and his skill at impersonating a dying man convinces the Venetian court and amuses the audience, his disguisings prove unfortunate. Thus his impersonation of Scoto gains him a beating, his attempted seduction of Celia brings on the first trial scene, and his jeering at his victims while disguised as a commandatore leads Voltore to betray the conspiracy to the Venetian court. Unable to persuade Mosca, as Cleanthes persuades Pego, to co-operate with his story, he must choose between being outwitted by his parasite or confessing his roguery and receiving justice.

Jonson's defence of his ending in the dedication indicates that Volpone's harsh sentence troubled contemporary audiences as it has continued to trouble modern readers. As we shall see in the next chapter, its rigour can be explained partly by Jonson's own psychological investment in the attempted seduction of Celia, but Jonson justifies it as a response to critics 'that cry out, we never punish vice in our interludes' (ll. 107–8). Although he shares Middleton's ironic faith that roguery will overreach itself, his refusal to dismiss Volpone, as Middleton does Quomodo, merely with the confiscation of his goods threatens the delicate balance between our awareness of Volpone's vices and our delight in his deception of the fools. That Jonson recognised the problem is evident in the Epilogue, where the actor playing Volpone asks the audience to distinguish between his punishment 'by the laws' and the pleasure provided by his fiction itself, but this ingenious solution is inadequate to override the play's defiance of comic convention.[43] Despite its troubling ending, however, *Volpone* stands as a magnificent achievement, one that shows Jonson responding directly to Elizabethan dramatic models while weaving his varied literary materials into a texture rich in irony and literary allusion.

7

Jonson and London Life

Jonson's letter dedicating *Volpone* to 'The Two Famous Universities' is signed 'From my house in the Blackfriars this 11 of February 1607'.[1] His style no doubt reflects his pride in acquiring a residence in this fashionable London enclave. Blackfriars was located along the western wall of the old city, close to Baynard Castle (the London address of the Earl of Pembroke) and convenient to the Inns of Court and the great noble mansions and genteel residences spreading westward along the Strand. His move to Blackfriars may be seen as one step in his campaign to reclaim the social status that he felt was his by right of his natural father. Though his critics might still taunt him with his old trade of bricklaying, he had begun to call himself a gentleman and to associate himself publicly with gentleman-scholars and wits.[2] His participation in the lively intellectual and social life of this genteel urban milieu, whose growth in the early seventeenth century is a noticeable feature of London's development, is reflected in his *Epigrams* and in his comedy *Epicoene* (1609/10), while Blackfriars itself is the setting for *The Alchemist* (1610).

Jonson's Blackfriars' address raises some puzzling questions about his domestic arrangements, which seem to have been troubled. In their citation for recusancy on 10 January 1606 Jonson and his wife Anne are both identified as members of the parish of St. Anne's, Blackfriars, but Jonson's statement in his examination of 26 April 1606 that 'for any thing he knoweth' she 'hath gone to church and used always to receive the communion' implies some estrangement between them.[3] Drummond reports Jonson as saying, 'He married a wife who was a shrew yet honest, five years he had not bedded with her, but remained with my lord Aubigny' (*Conv.*, ll. 249-51). Jonson also told him that his translation of Horace's *The Art of Poetry* had been done in D'Aubigny's house in 1604.[4] D'Aubigny's house was located in Blackfriars, which might explain why Jonson and Anne could both have been identified as members of St. Anne's even if they were not living together. On the other hand, the separation Drummond mentions must either have been shorter than he indicated, or begun earlier than Jonson's stay with D'Aubigny, or have occurred after Jonson's return from France in 1613, for D'Aubigny could not have taken up residence in Blackfriars until after James' accession in 1603, and Jonson must have bedded with his wife at least one night in May 1607, when the 'Benjamin Johnson son to Benjamin' christened at St. Anne's on 20 February 1608 was conceived.[5] Equally perplexing are the records of baptisms for 'Elisab. daughter of Ben Johnson' on 25 March 1610 at St. Mary Matfellon, Whitechapel, and for 'Benjamin Johnson fil. [son of] Ben.' on 6 April at St Martin-in-the-Fields. These may or may not be children of Ben Jonson the poet, but it is unlikely, though not impossible, that they were born to the same mother.

What is clear is that the wife who attracted the young bricklayer did not hold the undivided love of the mature poet. Although he valued Anne's 'honesty' and praised marital fidelity in his poetry, he lived by the age's double standard of chastity for women and sexual licence for men. In his conversations with Drummond he recounted his adulterous affairs without apology:

> He thought the use of a maid nothing in comparison to the wantonness of a wife [that is, 'a married woman'], and would never have another mistress. He said two accidents strange befell him: one, that a man made his own wife to court him, whom he enjoyed two years ere he knew of it, and one day finding them by chance, was passingly delighted with it; one other, lay diverse times with a woman, who shew him all that he wished, except the last act, which she would never agree unto. (*Conv.*, ll. 287–93)

Jonson's preference for other men's wives as mistresses may be explained not only by their sexual experience, but also by their relative freedom, in an age before birth control, from anxiety about the consequences of a liaison. The phrase 'the use of a maid', if Jonson's, is also revealing and sheds light on Volpone's wooing of Celia, where his description of their imagined lovemaking is largely a description of the various erotic roles in which Volpone will 'have' her (see III.vii.220–31). Indeed, the presence in his later collection *The Forest* of three songs to 'Celia', including the verses that Volpone sings during the seduction scene, suggests that he identified with Volpone's lust and with the Catullan mode of its expression.

David Riggs has interpreted Jonson's dramatisation of seduction as evidence that the poet who had previously rejected Ovidian eroticism was now psychologically mature enough 'to confront and utilise impulses that he had hitherto kept at bay'.[6] Certainly he was to feel increasingly free about imitating classical and neo-Latin amatory verse and incorporating its prototypes of the seductive lover into his own poetic persona.[7] Yet in 1606 in *Volpone*, he still, as in *Poetaster*, projected his libidinous impulses on to a figure whose vices require punishment. The harsh ending of *Volpone* hints not so much at a resolution of his personal conflicts as at an ongoing effort to repress desires that at some level disturbed him. Though his extra-marital affairs may have been encouraged by the literature of seduction and condoned by the genteel mores of his day, his addiction to 'venery' was in conflict with his public endorsement of rational self-control in 'The Epode' (*For.* XI) and of marital harmony in *Hymenaei*. Jonson's stance as a spokesperson for his culture's official values was of course encouraged by the occasional nature of his poetry and masques, but it may also have been a method of wrestling with moral weakness – an attempt to shore up his resolve by reminding himself of the ideal standards at which he aimed. Father Thomas Wright had recommended that 'it were good to dispraise in words before others that passion thou art most addicted unto . . . not . . . because I would have a man to do one thing and speak another, but [because] . . . it may be a good way to recall him again and not to fall so often'.[8] Read carefully, the 'Epode' (originally contributed to *The Turtle and the Phoenix* in 1601) strikes a confessional note when Jonson admits that the 'true course' of love is scarce 'embraced . . . by any' because 'our affections do rebel' (ll. 19–21). He concludes by cautioning the Phoenix that 'a noble, and right generous mind . . . / That knows the weight of guilt' will control his sexual impulses with this maxim: '*Man may securely sin, but safely never*' (ll. 111–13, 116); his sententious ending may have been an exhortation to himself as well. Still, his defiant answer to the 'vicious fool' who denies the existence of 'this chaste love we sing' (ll. 66–8) has the same repressive force as the condemnation of Volpone. Both in art and in life, Jonson's attempts to master his sensual appetites remained problematic.

Although Jonson was an indifferent husband, he worked harder at friendship, yet here again his personal insecurities often complicated his relationships. Like many Renaissance men he turned to male friendship for intellectual companionship, for conviviality, for assistance in obtaining patronage and – in his case – for public confirmation of the dignity and artistry of his poetry. His declaration in an inscription to Sir John Roe that a parent was not better to him than a friend is revealing – he seems to have looked to other men for the support and affirmation that he might have received from his natural father.[9] Friendship is an important topic in his poetry, and his publishing strategies invoke his friendships in various ways. The Quarto editions of *Sejanus* (1605), *Volpone* (1607), and *Catiline* (1611) were printed with commendatory poems that serve as a body of 'witnesses' to their merit, thereby neutralising their public-theatre failure or confirming their success, while his *Epigrams*, by interspersing poems to friends and patrons with satiric poems of ridicule, imply a community of readers who share his values.[10] These commendatory poems and epigrams may exaggerate or idealise the nature of his relationships, but they do help to identify his many associates.

Jonson's close friends in the period 1605–1615 came from three interconnected circles of scholars, wits, and professional poets. With his old Westminster teacher William Camden and his circle Jonson remained on good terms, as we know from his description of the banquet given after his release from prison in the *Eastward Ho* incident.[11] His relations with his Blackfriars neighbour Sir Robert Cotton may have been complicated when Cotton became a client of Henry Howard, the Earl of Northampton, described by Jonson as 'his mortal enemy for brawling, on a St. George's Day, one of his attenders' (*Conv.*, ll. 324-5), but Cotton's influence may still be seen in *Prince Henry's Barriers* (1610).[12] Also present at the 1605 banquet was the young jurist and antiquarian John Selden. Like other members of Cotton's circle he was distinguished by wide-ranging legal and historical interests and at the age of twenty-one was already at work on the treatise *On the Gods of the Syrians* that would establish his credentials as an orientalist and Biblical scholar.[13] In the preface to his *Titles of Honour* (1614), Selden describes researching a doubtful passage in Euripides 'in the well-furnished library of my beloved friend, that singular poet Master Ben Jonson, whose special worth in literature, accurate judgment and performance, known only to that few which are truly able to know him, hath had from me, ever since I began to learn, an increasing admiration'.[14] Jonson returned that admiration in a poem originally prefixed to the same work, praising Selden for redeeming truth from error and for rectifying 'Times, manners, customs' (*Und.* XIV, l. 44). Another young acquaintance of Selden's and Cotton's was the Catholic poet and historian Edmund Bolton, author of a treatise on

The Elements of Armories (1610), an unpublished life of Henry II and a translation of the Roman histories of Julius Florus. His praise (in his commendatory poem on *Volpone*) of Jonson for 'studying Greek antiquities and the monuments of Latin theatre *as an explorer*' is typical of how Jonson's friends helped to interpret his goals to a wider public and evidence that he was accepted in the circle of antiquaries as a scholarly peer.[15]

With his fellow playwrights and professional poets Jonson's relationships were complicated by his strong sense of rivalry, which issued in ridicule of those whose works he thought inferior or in jealousy of those whose accomplishments he admired.[16] Still, he formed a close friendship with George Chapman, whose Stoical tragedies and translations from Homer and Hesiod made him a kindred spirit, and with John Fletcher, whose pioneering tragi-comedy *The Faithful Shepherdess* (1608) he defended publicly when its neo-classical conventions displeased the theatre audience.[17] He told William Drummond in 1619 'that Chapman and Fletcher were loved of him' (*Conv.*, l. 159). He also served as something of a mentor for Fletcher's young collaborator Francis Beaumont, who wrote commendatory verses for *Volpone*, *Epicoene* (printed in the 1616 Folio) and *Catiline*. Beaumont's verse epistle to him from the country, later printed in the Beaumont and Fletcher Folio of 1647, prayed that fate would bring him again to Jonson 'who wilt make smooth, and plain / The way of knowledge for me' (ll. 76–7).[18] Jonson later criticised Beaumont to Drummond because 'he loved too much himself and his own verses' (*Conv.*, ll. 143–4), but whatever his private reservations, he paid tribute to him in Epigram LV ('How I do love thee Beaumont, and thy muse'), confessing to fears that he is 'not worth / The least indulgent thought thy pen drops forth' and acknowledging – as evidence of Beaumont's merit – that 'even there, where most thou praisest me, / For writing better, I must envy thee' (ll. 3–4, 9–10).[19] The mutual praise shared between Chapman, Beaumont, Fletcher and Jonson points to their status as a literary avant-garde, challenging even the elite private theatre audiences with new modes of Stoical tragedy, Italianate pastoral and ironic comedy.

Another of Jonson's literary friendships sealed with an exchange of commendatory poems was that with Donne, who composed a Latin poem on *Volpone*. Jonson, who thought Donne 'the first poet in the world, in some things' (*Conv.*, ll. 101–2), praised his talents in two epigrams (XXIII and XCVI) and wrote another to accompany a copy of Donne's satires sent to the Countess of Bedford (XCIV). He told William Drummond that Donne's 'verses of the lost chain he hath by heart; and that passage of 'The Calm', that dust and feathers do not stir, all was so quiet. [He] affirmeth Donne to have written all his best pieces ere he was twenty-five years old' (*Conv.*, ll. 102–5). The 'verses of the lost chain' are Elegy XI ('The Bracelet: Upon the Loss of his Mistress's Chain for which He Made Satisfaction'), a satire on avarice and the corrupting effects of gold like his own 'Epistle to Rutland'. His preference for Donne's early poetry, rather than the 'conceited' love poems of Donne's middle period, is explained by his attraction to satire and epigram. Perhaps because he and Donne mined the same poetic veins, he also esteemed Donne's critical judgement. In the lost 'Apology' for his comedy *Bartholomew Fair* written to accompany his translation of Horace's *Art of Poetry*, he cast Donne in the role of 'Criticus' (*Conv.*, ll. 71–3, 421–3). His Epigram XCVI celebrates Donne ('That so alone canst judge, so alone dost make') as the ideal audience for his epigrams: his willingness to submit his poems to Donne for evaluation, he says, will erase any doubts that he is a poet, and Donne's approval of even one will 'seal' his claim to the title. Yet while both men were acknowledged by contemporaries as pioneers of the 'masculine' or 'strong' verse line, Jonson's preference for the plain style put him at variance with Donne's rougher metrics and metaphysical wit. With his characteristic vehemence, he told Drummond 'that Donne, for not keeping of accent, deserved hanging' and 'that Donne himself, for not being understood, would perish' (ll. 42, 187–8). Such differences, however, apparently did not threaten their friendship as they threatened Jonson's ties with Daniel or Marston; the fact that Donne was a gentleman-poet who wrote only for manuscript circulation may have eliminated the factor of direct competition that proved so destructive to many of Jonson's professional relationships.

With Donne, Jonson was linked to an extensive network of London wits – courtiers, soldiers and lawyers who comprised the 'small poets' of the time. Several of Donne's correspondents from 1605 to 1615 – Sir Henry Goodyer, Sir Thomas Roe and Sir Edward Herbert – either penned verses to Jonson or received them from him.[20] Among those identified as possible contributors to the *Conceited News* of Jonson's friend Sir Thomas Overbury, Donne, Roe, John Cooke and William Strachey also wrote commendatory poems for *Volpone* or *Sejanus*, while Benjamin Rudyerd was praised by

Jonson for his manners and wit.[21] Sir Thomas Roe, the future explorer and diplomat, was the subject of two of Jonson's epigrams (XCVIII and XCIX) and the cousin of Jonson's 'well-approved friend' Sir John Roe. Jonson told Drummond that Sir John 'died in his arms of the pest [that is, the plague], and he furnished his [funeral] charges, £20; which was given him back' (*Conv.*, ll. 176–8). Possessed of a combative personality and satiric inclinations like Jonson's, Sir John had survived 'two brave perils of the private sword' and had been commended for valour in Flanders; he had also written a verse satire reminiscent of Donne's and two verse epistles, addressed to Jonson and composed in a plain style like his, that condemn 'the time's unthrifty rout' and defy wrongs done him by 'great men'.[22] Jonson showed his loyalty to this kindred spirit by trying to prevent his brother William (the subject of Epigrams LXX and CXXVIII) from being cheated of his estate, and he worked through his grief at Roe's death by writing three epigrams in his praise (XXVII, XXXII, and XXXIII).[23] Jonson's relationships with the Roe family contradict Dekker's accusation that he exploited his young admirers; his admonitions and encouragement (in verse and in person) to Sir Thomas and William, his warm inscription in his gift copy of Persius to Sir John and his presence at his death-bed despite the risk of infection show that he could live up to the age's ideal of male friendship.

Jonson was also loosely connected to a continuing fraternity of old Inns-of-Court acquaintances that included Donne and Sir Robert Cotton. In a letter from India written in 1615 and addressed to 'the Sireniacal Gentlemen, that meet the first Friday of every month, at the Mermaid in Bread Street', the traveller Thomas Coryat mentions Jonson along with Donne, Sir Robert Cotton, Christopher Brooke, Richard Martin, John Hoskyns, Hugh Holland, Inigo Jones, the parliamentarian William Hakewill, John Bond, secretary to Lord Chancellor Egerton, and a number of others.[24] Unfortunately, Coryat does not specify who were members of the 'Sireniacal Gentlemen', but the probability that Jonson was included in the group is increased by his active role in the publication of Coryat's *Crudities* (1611), the account of Coryat's travels in Germany and Italy. On the other hand, his name is conspicuously absent from a poem of 1611 that describes a 'philosophical banquet' held at the Mitre Tavern and attended by Coryat, Jones, Holland, Martin, Hoskyns, Brooke, Donne and others, including the London financiers Arthur Ingram and Lionel Cranfield, who had encouraged publication of the *Crudities*.[25]

This network of wits, then, contained many different cliques, and one cannot assume that Jonson was equally intimate with everyone. With Ingram and Cranfield, who were the type of projectors he satirised in *The Devil Is an Ass* (1616), he seems to have had no other connections, and his contacts with them through the 'Sireniacal Gentlemen' may only have provided material for his comedies.[26] A letter from Donne to an unnamed correspondent in July of 1613 indicates that Jonson's tendency to ridicule acquaintances had caused some friction with his old friend Hugh Holland.[27] The subject of the complaint may possibly have been Inigo Jones, whose behaviour in the Mermaid and Mitre groups seems to have irritated Jonson, and it is possible that his ongoing hostility toward Jones originated partly in his jealousy at being excluded from gatherings of friends to which Jones was admitted. His Epigram CXV, 'On the Town's Honest Man', glances at Jones' occupations when attacking its subject for being 'its own fame's architect' and 'An engineer, in slanders, of all fashions, / That seeming praises, are, yet accusations' (ll. 30–3); Jones is presented as an anti-type of true sociability, ingratiating himself with present company by backbiting absent friends, talking 'loud, and bawdy' and engaging in a 'fit' of miming to get 'the opinion of a wit' (ll. 9, 27–8).[28]

As is so often true of Jonson's method, his satire here is set against ideal norms expressed more fully in his poems of praise, in this case ideals of intellectual community and urbane conviviality. Informal clubs and tavern gatherings like those of the 'Sirenaical Gentlemen' are thought of as more typical of the Restoration and eighteenth century, but they had already begun to appear in early seventeenth-century London, and Jonson is the chief poet associated with this new urban sociability. His most elevated expression of the ideals that informed such gatherings is Epigram CI, 'Inviting a Friend to Supper', which is inspired by classical and humanist models of dining and good conversation. Addressed to an unnamed 'grave sir' like Camden or Cotton whose 'worth will dignify our feast / With those that come' (ll. 4–5) it reworks passages from Martial and Horace into an appealing image of civilised fellowship, where friendly trust and innocent freedom are the foremost values. As Sara van den Berg points out, his allusions to London cooks' stalls and pastry shops presume an urban setting, while his description of the conviviality around 'our mirthful board' communicates the Erasmian ideals of humanity, simplicity and liberty.[29] Jonson's teasing catalogue of the 'cates' that might be served humorously acknowledges his limited resources and reinforces the classical theme of enjoyment in moderation, but he stresses that it is 'the fair acceptance' of the guests that 'creates the entertainment perfect' (ll. 7–8). With self-deprecating irony Jonson promises that he will repeat none of his own verses but will instead have his man 'read a piece of Virgil, Tacitus, / Livy, or of some better book to us, / Of which we'll speak our minds, amidst our meat' (ll. 21–3).[30]

This promise of learned entertainment, derived from Erasmus' colloquy *The Poet's Feast*, may seem merely to be humanist window-dressing, but at least some Jacobean and Caroline gentlemen held to the classical tradition of 'table-talk' as a mixture of playful joking and serious discussion. Edward Hyde, later Earl of Clarendon, who joined Selden's and Jonson's circle in the 1620s reports in his autobiography that 'he always gave himself to dinner to those who used to meet together at that hour, and in such places as was mutually agreed between them; where they enjoyed themselves with wonderful delight and public reputation, for the innocence, and sharpness, and learning of their conversation'.[31] Of Jonson himself Hyde reports, 'His conversation was very good, and with the men of most note'.[32] Unfortunately Hyde was no Boswell and did not record any of Jonson's sayings, but some of Selden's remarks were preserved by his secretary Richard Milward and published in 1689. Though collected years later, his pithy observations on constitutional and ecclesiastical matters, expressed in vivid but homely analogies and informed by his broad knowledge of scriptural backgrounds and of medieval history, give us some idea of what the conversation at Jonson's suppers may have been like.[33]

In 'Inviting a Friend to Supper' Jonson promises his guest 'a pure cup of rich canary wine' from the Mermaid Tavern in Bread Street; its reputation is confirmed by Francis Beaumont's verse letter from the country, where Beaumont – able to obtain only watered-down claret sold by Puritans – lies dreaming 'of your full Mermaid wine' (l. 6). Beaumont's epistle describes a more high-spirited mode of conviviality than 'Inviting a Friend to Supper', one in which wit is compared to 'a rest / Held up at tennis, which men do the best / With the best gamesters':

> What things have we seen
> Done at the Mermaid? Heard words that have been
> So nimble, and so full of subtle flame,

As if that every one from whom they came
Had meant to put his whole wit in a jest
And had resolv'd to live a fool the rest
Of his dull life.

(ll. 43–51)

The essential features of the fellowship described by Beaumont were later formalised in the Apollo Club that Jonson established at the Devil Tavern in 1624. The poem he wrote to be placed over the door at the Apollo Room of the tavern (*M.P.* CXIII) praises wine as 'the true Phoebian liquor' that 'Cheers the brains, makes wit the quicker' (ll. 15–16). His Latin rules for the club, engraved in gold letters over the mantelpiece, command ignorant fools and gloomy or base persons to stay away and welcome those who are learned, urbane, cheerful and virtuous; guests are urged to contend with each other more in conversation than in drinking. Noisy quarrels and bitter jokes are forbidden, while the 'liberty' of the participants is to be preserved by the expulsion of anyone who blabs abroad what is done or said.[34]

The veil of secrecy over the Apollo Club meetings has not been breached, but from their surviving works it is evident that the earlier circle of Mermaid wits inclined to clever sophistry, ironic satire and mock encomia. The sophistical arguments of Donne's *Paradoxes and Problems* were described by him as 'swaggerers', designed to make the reader 'find better reasons against them'.[35] *The Courtiers' Library*, generally attributed to Donne, uses mock learning to gibe at occultism, pseudo-science, Puritans and self-serving politicians like Bacon. Mock encomia of a more occasional type are represented by the prefatory matter in Coryat's *Crudities* and by Jonson's long epigram 'On the Famous Voyage' (*Epig.* CXXXIII). The latter, cast as a burlesque of epic voyages to Hell, seems to have been written not too long after 1607 to celebrate the malodorous journey by rowboat up the Fleet Ditch made by two gallants named Shelton and Heyden, who dined 'at Bread Street's Mermaid' before departing.[36] Its vivid evocation of London's sanitary arrangements has been touted as evidence of Jonson's compulsions by Freudian critics, but its learned parody and its satiric allusions of the kind also found in *The Courtiers' Library* would seem to establish it as a coterie piece of high-spirited joking for his fellow Mermaid wits.

Members of this same group were involved in the publication of Coryat's *Crudities*, which was printed at Prince Henry's command with ironic commendatory poems in English, Latin, Greek, French, Spanish, Italian and Welsh by some fifty-six gentlemen and knights. A chatterbox and pretentious fool who paraded his knowledge of Greek and Latin, Coryat was the target of much ridicule for revealing every embarrassing mishap that occurred to him during his journey to Italy and back. Hugh Holland, John Hoskyns and Lawrence Whitaker (later the 'High Seneschal' of the 'Sireniacal Gentlemen') contributed some of the more extensive and ingenious entries, but Jonson's contributions were given pride of place. Together with Whitaker he composed verses explaining the illustrations of Coryat's adventures on the title-page, and his 'Character of the Famous Odcombian, or rather Polyptopian, Thomas the Coryat' and his acrostic verses, 'To the Right Noble Tom, Tell-Troth of His Travels', follow Coryat's dedication to Prince Henry and the epistle to the reader. His prose 'character', supposedly 'done by a charitable friend', is a mock encomium that commends Coryat as 'a spectacle grateful above that of Niniveh, or the City of Norwich' (common puppet shows) and as a frequenter 'at all sorts of free tables, where though he might sit as a guest, he will rather be served in as a dish' (that is, to be laughed at) 'and is loth to have any thing of himself kept cold against the next day'.[37]

The ironic ridicule of foolish pretension and the sense of rivalry among 'the best gamesters' at wit that is exhibited in the contributions to Coryat's *Crudities* provide a useful context for understanding Jonson's *Epicoene, or The Silent Woman*, produced in late 1609 or early 1610 at the Whitefriars Theatre by the Children of the Queens Revels, which included his young protégé Nathan Field.[38] Abandoning the sharp antagonism between Crites' Stoic virtue and the foolish courtiers of *Cynthia's Revels*, Jonson now criticises fashionable society from within, employing as satiric agents three gentlemen – Clerimont, Dauphine and Truewit – who comprise a little fellowship of urbane wits. Like the speakers in Baldassare Castiglione's *The Book of the Courtier*, whose views they echo, none is given complete authority, but they function collectively to defeat the antisocial tyranny of Dauphine's uncle Morose and to expose the shallowness of the Ladies Collegiates and the fatuous knights Sir Amorous La Foole and Sir John Daw.[39] Clerimont, whose indolent lifestyle is condemned by Truewit at the beginning of the play, nevertheless enunciates the ideal of natural beauty against which the cosmetic artifice of the Collegiates is measured. Dauphine, whose attitude toward their victims seems excessively cruel at times, not only frustrates Morose's efforts to disinherit him but also deflates Daw's and La Foole's sexual boasting when he reveals that Morose's bride Epicoene is a boy dressed as a woman. Truewit, though 'lurch'd . . . of the better half of the garland' as chief wit by Dauphine's revelation (V.iv.191–2), demonstrates his inventiveness through his many plots, which turn the torment of the noise-hating Morose into 'an excellent comedy of affliction', unmask the cowardliness of Daw and La Foole, and expose the Collegiates' judgement as 'crude opinion, without reason or cause'(IV.vi.58). That each of the three seems slightly flawed perhaps indicates Jonson's continuing social uneasiness; his refusal to write City Comedy that merely offers idealised models of court gallantry may well be a reaction to his own marginality even among friends like Donne or Sir Edward Herbert, who were reluctant to be seen, in Jack Daw's words, as 'poor fellows that live' by their verses.[40]

On the other hand, as a private theatre play directed at auditors like the Mermaid and Mitre wits, *Epicoene* is calculated to appeal to such sophisticated sensibilities as those required for Donne's poetry, which invites 'both an imaginative involvement in and a critical attitude toward' its subject matter.[41] Jonson's use of indirection and surprise in his plotting parallels the witty turns Donne gives his poems: like Donne's shocking disclosure of the speaker's nakedness at the end of 'To His Mistress Going to Bed' or the sudden shift from Platonic spiritualising to a plea for physical gratification in 'The Ecstasy', the stripping off of Epicoene's wig to reveal his boyish identity elicits admiration for Dauphine's cleverness and forces a re-examination of what has gone before. In this dramatic world, where surfaces prove notoriously untrustworthy, characters must be judged by what they do, not by their teasing banter. Dauphine's claim to be in love with all of the Collegiates is belied by his scornful reaction when they solicit him, and his request that Truewit make him 'a proficient' in the knowledge of women's behaviour (IV.i.48) is revealed as mere dissembling by his own skill in constructing Epicoene's female identity. The play's dialogue also requires auditors who are alert to irony, paradox and literary allusion. Dauphine and Clerimont encourage the 'humours' of Daw and La Foole while mocking them in ironic asides, much as the 'Sirenaical Gentlemen' derided Tom Coryat's pretensions. Reproved by Clerimont at the outset for his Stoic sermonising, Truewit reverts to paradoxical praise, turning Ovidian advice on cosmetics and

seduction into subtle satire on fashionable deceit. His recommendation that women be allowed privacy to put on 'their perukes . . . ,
their false teeth, their complexion, their eyebrows, their nails'
(I.i.104–5) catalogues female deceptions even as he seems to defend
them. His ironic satire on women is balanced at IV.i.86–96 by his
analysis of male vanity, which masks as instruction in courtship but
commends practices that Jonson consistently satirised, such as
plagiarising love poetry, performing feats of activity, or devoting
excessive attention to grooming and foreign fashion.[42]

Unfortunately, like Francis Beaumont's equally ironic *The Knight
of the Burning Pestle*, *Epicoene* seems to have puzzled more of its
original audience than it pleased; Jonson told William Drummond
that when it was first acted, 'there was found verses on the stage
against him, concluding that that play was well named *The Silent
Woman*, there was never one man to say 'plaudite' to it'(*Conv.*, ll.
697–700).[43] Its general pattern, however, should not have seemed
strange to Elizabethan playgoers. Although *Epicoene* is generally
held to owe little to the contemporary theatre other than a few
borrowings from Shakespeare's *Twelfth Night*, Jonson's device of
using a group of wits to castigate the follies of foppish men and
shrewish women is another instance of his creative rivalry – in this
case a clever reworking of the formula employed in the anonymous
Every Woman in Her Humour (published 1609), itself an imitation of
his own early humour comedy. Supposedly set in Rome but
stripped of all classical detail, *Every Woman in Her Humour* contains a
few romantic scenes depicting a love triangle between Lentulus,
Cicero and Terentia. Most of the play, however, is a satire on the
blurring of sexual roles, and the grouping of the remaining
characters exactly parallels *Epicoene's* division of the cast into
foolish gallants, 'masculine women', tyrannous and hen-pecked
husbands and intriguing wits. There are three effeminate fops: the
swearer of affected oaths, Servulus; the cowardly Scilicet; and 'this
gentlewoman gallant' Philautus. The female 'humours' include a
Gentlewoman, whose face is painted on-stage by her servant; a
Citizen's Wife, who is full of advice about how to control men; and
the Hostess, strictly confined by her husband but eager for
independence and an affair with Philautus. The husbands of the
latter two women, Cornutus and the Host, exemplify the submissive
and the dominant male respectively. All of these figures are
manipulated by the gallants Acutus and Gracchus, who humiliate
Philautus with several plots and arrange for the Host, Cornutus and

Scilicet to appear in the concluding wedding masque as the horned Actaeon and his hounds.

Like so many of Jonson's Elizabethan dramatic models, *Every Woman in Her Humour* served not as a direct source of the incidents in *Epicoene* but as a dramatic pattern for creative development. Though they perform the same function, his three witty gallants are far subtler than Gracchus and Acutus, who indignantly assault the fops and rail against women's pride, lustfulness and extravagance in the spirit of contemporary anti-feminist tracts. No doubt the topic of gender roles appealed to Jonson because of his own difficulties with the wife he described as 'a shrew but honest'. His treatment of female domination and male submissiveness in Mrs. Otter and her 'subject' Tom has the crude energy of John Heywood's Tudor farces, and there is much in *Epicoene* that reflects his own misogynistic tendencies and those of his fellow wits.[44] Yet he also goes further than the author of *Every Woman in Her Humour* in balancing his anti-feminist satire with ridicule of male folly and patriarchal tyranny. Morose's marriage to Epicoene, inspired by Libanius' declamation on 'The Unsociable Man who Marries a Talkative Woman', is handled in a quite different spirit from its classical source, where the emphasis is on the woman's endless chatter. Jonson had already drawn on this aspect of Libanius' work for Lady Politic Would-Be's torment of Volpone; in *Epicoene* it is Morose's anti-social nature that is stressed, and Truewit rebukes him: 'Nay, look you, sir: you would be friends with your wife upon unconscionable terms, her silence' (IV.iv.38–9).[45] If Morose describes Mrs. Otter as 'that Gorgon, that Medusa', he himself is conceived as a 'prodigy' and a 'portent': his monstrosity is underscored by Truewit's remark to Dauphine that he is 'Strook into stone, almost . . . with tales o' thine uncle' (I.ii.2–3). The Collegiates' lack of judgement in assessing 'the Wits and Braveries o' the time' is exposed by demonstrating the cowardice of Daw and La Foole, and in the end, Truewit's harshest words are directed not at the ladies, but at the two fops for defaming women's honour. Admittedly, there is no virtuous woman or female wit in the play to balance the three male satirists, but at least Jonson articulates through Clerimont the Cavalier ideal of natural beauty, which potentially liberates the Renaissance lady from the erotic fetishism of farthingales, head-tires and face-painting.

Jonson's ridicule of feminine artifice is linked directly to the London setting through Captain Otter's account of his wife, whose beauty, like Lady Haughty's, is 'piec'd': 'All her teeth were made i' the Blackfriars: both her eyebrows i' the Strand, and her hair in Silver Street. Every part o' the town owns a piece of her' (IV.ii.80–3). Jonson is translating Martial IX.xxxvii here, but the local colour is his own. His references to the Blackfriars and the Strand ground the play in the stylish milieu of the emerging West End, where the chief characters reside.[46] Sir Amorous La Foole has a lodging in the Strand for the purpose of inviting his guests to plays or suppers 'as they ride by in coaches. . . . Or to watch when ladies are gone to the China houses or the Exchange, that he may meet 'em by chance, and give 'em presents' (I.iii.31–4). His cousin Mistress Otter, who lives nearby, is 'the rich Chinawoman, that the courtiers visited so often' (I.iv.23–4). The Exchange to which Jonson refers is undoubtedly the New Exchange or 'Britain's Bourse', an arcade containing shops for such purveyors of luxuries as the 'embroiderers, jewellers, tire-women, sempsters, feather-men [and] perfumers' whom Truewit catalogues for Morose at II.ii.94–5. Constructed by the Earl of Salisbury on the grounds of Durham House in the Strand, it officially opened on 11 April 1609 with an entertainment for King James written by Jonson himself. The use of coaches to visit it and other London attractions was another recent innovation, one that would lead to protests by Jonson's neighbours about congestion around the Blackfriars Theatre in 1619.

Such details point up the extravagance and shallow display of a fashionable urban existence, but Jonson's London references extend far beyond the West End. His allusions to the bells of Westminster, the ordnance at Tower Wharf, the bustle of London Bridge and Billingsgate market, the drums and trumpets of the public theatres, the sounds of bear-baiting and cock-fighting, and the cries of street-vendors conjure up the vast pageant of the Jacobean city in all its shrill cacophany. After locating *Volpone* in exotic Venice, his return to the London setting employed in his collaboration with Chapman and Marston on *Eastward Ho* marks a shift toward greater use of local colour. His next comedies – *The Alchemist* (1610), *Bartholomew Fair* (1614), *The Devil Is an Ass* (1616) and the revised version of *Every Man in His Humour* published in the 1616 Folio – vividly portray London's teeming life, providing the audiences at the Blackfriars, the Globe and the Hope with a mirror-image of themselves. Like Dickens, to whom he is often compared, Jonson also offers evocative glimpses of the city's seamier side. The dialogue of *The Alchemist* invites us to picture poor rogues picking rags out of muck-heaps, taking their 'meal of steam in from cooks' stalls' at Pie Corner, or lurking in alehouses as dark as Deaf John's (I.i.25–6, 85). In *Bartholomew Fair* the tawdry pleasures of the fair at Smithfield assault the fairgoers' senses, while the stage is peopled not only with a crowd of pleasure-seekers, but also with the bawds, punks and cut-purses who prey on them.

Jonson's local allusions, however, are not merely 'atmospheric', but are instrumental to his satire, and although his humour characters are increasingly particularised, they are conceived as contemporary manifestations of enduring follies and vices, given new artistic life by the realistic detail with which they are invested.[47] As he explains in the Prologue to *The Alchemist*:

> Our scene is London, 'cause we would make known
> No country's mirth is better than our own.
> No clime breeds better matter, for your whore,
> Bawd, squire, impostor, many persons more,
> Whose manners, now called humours, feed the stage:
> (ll. 5–9).

His whore (Dol Common), bawd (Face, the servant turned 'Captain') and impostor (Subtle, the pretended alchemist) are imagined as working their cheats in Jonson's own Blackfriars district, where the play was performed by the King's Men in 1610. Their victims form a cross-section of London life, from the fish-wives, oyster-women and 'the bawd of Lambeth' who are only mentioned in the dialogue through Drugger the tobacconist, Dapper the law-clerk (who dines nearby in Holborn at the Dagger Inn), the two puritans Ananias and Tribulation Wholesome, the country squire Kastril and his widowed sister Dame Pliant (come up to the city to learn manners and fashions), the gamester Surly and Sir Epicure Mammon. In the tradition of the 'estates morality', Jonson uses this representative sample to demonstrate how greed and credulity pervade society at all levels.[48]

The deceptions worked upon these victims satirise a broad range of popular superstitions and pseudo-sciences. Jonson's chief target, alchemy, claimed to achieve through the repeated distillation and purification of matter a refined elixir or 'quintessence' (the philosopher's stone) that could transform base metal into gold and work miraculous medical cures. Queen Elizabeth and several nobles invested in alchemical projects, and its possibilities continued to fascinate learned men into the late seventeenth

thematician John Dee, whose preface to Euclid
actised alchemy and attempted to communicate
Aubrey considered him to be the model for
wever, Subtle is not only a pretended alchemist, but also
counterfeit 'cunning man' – a practitioner of folk medicine,
magical arts and astrology, which appealed to all classes of Jacobean
society.[50] A well-known example of this type is Simon Forman, to
whom Jonson refers at *Epicoene* IV.i.130 as a purveyor of love-
potions. Largely self-educated and unable to gain entrance into the
Royal College of Physicians, Forman was an astrologer, necroman-
cer, magician, distiller of strong waters and healer. His casebooks, in
which he kept systematic records of his astrological calculations,
document a lucrative London practice in medicine and in casting
horoscopes to answer clients' queries about everything from their
love life to the whereabouts of lost dogs. They also record his
disappointment when on 27 April 1596 'in subliming, my pot and
glass broke, and all my labor was lost *pro lapide* [for the
philosopher's stone]'.[51]

Jonson's satirical temperament inclined him to view alchemy and
astrology as delusions and to judge those who were taken in by
them as worthy of being cheated. In regard to astrology, he reported
to William Drummond: 'He can set horoscopes, but trusts not in
them. He, with the consent of a friend, cozened a lady, with whom
he had made an appointment to meet an old astrologer, in the
suburbs, which she kept; and it was himself disguised in a long
gown and a white beard at the light of dim burning candles, up in a
little cabinet reached unto by a ladder' (*Conv.*, ll. 305–10). We do not
know whether this incident came before or after he wrote *The
Alchemist*, but it implies a personal identification with his tricksters'
deception of the credulous fools.

Jonson's attitude toward alchemy is indicated in Epigram VI, 'To
Alchemists': 'If all you boast of your great art be true; / Sure, willing
poverty lives most in you'. Like Chaucer, whose Canon Yeoman
learns from his alchemical experience only how 'To multiplie, and
brynge his good to naught', he ridicules both the false hopes
aroused by alchemy and the metaphorical jargon in which
alchemists clothed their principles. Widely read in alchemical
literature, Jonson seems to have been particularly amused by the
inflated claims of Paracelsus, who rhapsodised about 'the Spagyric
art' (alchemy) and promised to teach 'all . . . philosophers,
astronomers, and spagyrists . . . the tincture, the arcanum, the

quintessence, wherein lie hid the foundations of all mysteries and of all works'.[52] The confrontation in II.v between Ananias and Subtle, who opposes Ananias' zeal with a defence of '*Chrysopoeia*, or *Spagyrica*, / Or the pamphysic or panarchic knowledge' (ll. 14–15), is an amusing reduction to the absurd of two competing systems of private inspiration – the Puritan and the Paracelsan.

Subtle, of course, is only a fraudulent alchemist who has no real aspirations to achieve the philosopher's stone. His deceptions link *The Alchemist* to other examples of Jacobean City Comedy based on cony-catching pamphlets. Once again Jonson set out to rival his predecessors. Here his immediate model seems to have been the anonymous play *The Puritan, or the Widow of Watling Street* (published 1607), which stages several incidents from *The Merry Conceited Jests of George Peele*.[53] As usual, Jonson treated it more as a dramatic paradigm than as a narrative source, freely adopting three of its basic elements – two swindlers posing as a captain and a conjurer, an intrigue plot involving the marriage of a rich widow, and incidental satire on Puritan hypocrisy and casuistry. By combining these motifs with the satire on alchemy in *The Canon's Yeoman's Tale* and in Erasmus' *Colloquies* and with additional frauds gleaned from rogue literature and from actual court cases, he sublimed his relatively simple model into the quintessential trickster play.

For the short time that their 'venture tripartite' holds together, Subtle, Face and Doll operate as virtuoso swindlers, presenting new faces to each of their victims as they (and Jonson) work creative variations on conventional urban cheats. Dapper is lured by a variant of 'barnard's law', in which a group of rogues co-operate to entice a victim deeper into dice-play.[54] His hopes of favour from the Queen of Fairy are based on the actual case of Thomas Rogers, bilked of ten or twenty pounds in gold by tricksters who promised him marriage to the Fairy Queen, but his confinement in the privy while awaiting Dol's appearance as Her Grace was probably suggested by the amusing pamphlet, *The Bridling, Saddling and Riding of a Rich Churl in Hampshire, by the Subtle Practice of One Judith Philips, a Professed Cunning Woman, or Fortune-Teller* (1595), where Judith (or Dol, as she was known in contemporary ballads) makes her victims grovel in the mud for three hours while she escapes with their goods.[55] Sir Epicure Mammon is caught through a version of 'cross-biting', in which a woman lures a man into a sexually compromising position so he can be blackmailed by another trickster posing as the woman's husband (or, like Subtle, as a pious alchemist horrified by vice). His misadventures are based on Erasmus' colloquy 'Alchemy', where the rich Balbinus, a believer in alchemical theory, is gulled by a priest who continually asks for fresh materials and equipment, using his own sexual sins as excuse for the work's delay; by making Mammon both the gull and the sinner, Jonson turns the fraudulent explosion in the laboratory into a comical judgement on vice and folly.

Jonson's satire on Ananias and Tribulation Wholesome is developed from *The Puritan, or The Widow of Watling Street*, but it was also undoubtedly inspired by his own difficulties with the puritanical congregation of St. Anne's, Blackfriars, whose non-conforming pastor, Stephen Egerton, was silenced sometime after 1607.[56] Jonson took his revenge for their persecution of his recusancy in Doll's description of Blackfriars' residents as 'A sort of sober, scruffy, precise neighbours / (That scarce have smiled twice, sin' the king came in)' (I.i.163–4). He was probably reconciled to the Church of England around the time he composed *The Alchemist*, but even then he would have had little sympathy for Puritan extremism and rabid anti-Catholicism. By equating his two representatives of 'the silenc'd saints' with the most anarchic of Anabaptists, the leaders of the Munster uprising, he makes Puritans in general appear to be a lunatic fringe. The decision of Tribulation Wholesome and his Elders that 'casting of dollars is . . . lawful' (IV.vii.43), even though 'coining' by private citizens is illegal, repeats the attack on Puritan casuistry in *The Puritan*, where Nicholas Saint-Tantlings and Simon Saint-Mary-Overies refuse to steal a gold chain, but do agree to 'nym' it. Jonson's critique of Puritanism, however, is far more penetrating than his model's superficial ridicule of hypocrisy. To a humanist poet, for whom 'ignorance . . . of the arts and sciences' was 'the darkener of man's life: the disturber of his reason, and common confounder of truth' (*Disc.*, 1. 992–6), there is heavy irony in representing a mere 'botcher' (a tailor who does repairs) like Ananias as 'a man, by revelation, / That hath a competent knowledge of the truth' (III.ii.113–14). Ananias' insistence that 'All's heathen, but the Hebrew' (II.v.17) comically subverts the authority of the Greek New Testament, while his warning that Subtle 'bears / The visible mark of the Beast in his forehead' (III.i.7–8) parodies Puritan apocalypticism.[57] His zealous reaction to anything that smacks, however distantly, of Catholicism (bells, traditions, the term 'Christmas') is ridiculed as a blind energy that can be directed at will by those shrewd enough to manipulate him, as Face does when he incites him against Surly, whose Spanish disguise makes him look 'like Antichrist' (IV.vii.55) to Ananias. Though not intended as political allegory, their comical confrontation foreshadows the growing opposition to James' Hispanophile policies from dissenters whose uncompromising Protestantism was fortified by apocalyptic myth.

The satire in *The Alchemist* thus cuts in many directions at once, mocking fantasies of self-gratification and power, as well as particular forms of credulity and ignorance. Jonson here seems more at ease with his own erotic drives and impulses toward witty superiority than he did in *Volpone*, and consequently he achieves a more satisfying balance of comedy and satire. Despite the 'small strain' it imposes on 'his own candour' (V.v.151–2), Lovewit's willingness to forgive Face in exchange for winning Dame Pliant marks a noticeable softening of judicial rigour. For many of Jonson's younger contemporaries *The Alchemist* was to stand as the apex of his comic achievement. Along with *Othello* it was chosen for performance by the King's Men at Oxford in September of 1610, where it was acted 'with greatest applause, in a full theatre', and it was often revived.[58] Nevertheless, its skilful blend of comic and satiric traditions appears to have been too rich a dish for some theatre-goers to digest. In the epistle 'To the Reader' in the 1612 Quarto, Jonson speaks scornfully of those who 'think rude things greater than polished: or scattered more numerous than composed' (ll. 29–30).[59] Robert Herrick refers to the ignorance of those 'who once hissed / At thy unequall'd play, *The Alchemist*', and Jasper Mayne implies that it took a second viewing for audiences to fully appreciate Jonson's art: 'We, like the Actors did repeat, the Pit / The first time *saw*, the next *conceiv'd* thy Wit'.[60] It is not clear whether Mayne is referring to performances at the Blackfriars or at the Globe; the King's Men were playing at both after 1608, and the dense ironies of *The Alchemist* may have taxed the capacities of play-goers accustomed to simpler fare.[61] If Jonson's complaint in 'To the Reader' about 'the concupiscence of dances and antics' in contemporary drama is, as it seems, an allusion to Shakespeare's late romances, it indicates that they were more accessible to the mixed audience now served by the King's Men, however much his own pieces pleased the literate. Even when writing for the enclosed hall theatres, he had to campaign hard for readers and auditors who were also 'understanders'.

8

The Poet and His Patrons

Following a practice established with his dedication of *Volpone* (published 1607) to Oxford and Cambridge, *The Masque of Queens* (1609) to Prince Henry and his tragedy *Catiline His Fall* (1611) to William Herbert, the Earl of Pembroke, Jonson printed *The Alchemist* in 1612 with a dedicatory epistle to Lady Mary Wroth, the niece of Sir Philip Sidney. His dedication of plays to individual patrons was unusual in the period and served as another sign that he considered his plays 'classic' pieces worthy of the recognition accorded serious literature. It also points to his complex role in the transition from an older system of literary patronage to a new market-orientated print culture.[1] No contemporary playwright did more than he to raise the literary status of drama or maintained a greater independence from the usual conditions of theatrical employment, but the absence of a royalty system made it impossible for him to earn a living from the print audience he courted so assiduously.[2] For this reason he seems to have asked for partial payment in presentation copies like those surviving examples of *Cynthia's Revels* that contain inserted tributes to William Camden and the Countess of Bedford, and (as noted in Chapter 3) he cultivated a network of patrons to whom he addressed odes, epistles and epigrams of praise.[3] The commissions or gratuities he received from his noble patrons and the forty pounds he was paid for composing each of his court masques liberated him from the economic pressures of commercial play-writing at ten pounds per play, allowing him to lavish more care on the inventive synthesis of his great middle comedies and on the historical authenticity of his two Roman tragedies.

Yet although the patronage system provided income and gave him entry into the aristocratic world on the basis of his artistic skill, it also threatened both his autonomy and his integrity. It was only through his force of character, and perhaps also his satire, that he was able to maintain some degree of independence. Willing to glorify the Stuart court and to dignify with his entertainments or poems of praise major events in the lives of its leading members, he

114

nevertheless fought against the very conditions of his employment by insisting on his role as moral commentator. If modern readers are often troubled by the suspicion that his poems retail unmerited flattery, their uneasiness springs in large part from Jonson's own self-consciousness about the issue. Signing himself the court's 'servant, but not slave' in the Folio dedication to *Cynthia's Revels*, he struggled 'to write / Things manly, and not smelling parasite'.[4] Although he was often conscious of failing to meet his own high standards of moral probity, his conflicted attitudes toward the court were to prove, in J. C. A. Rathmell's words, 'the source of a highly fruitful tension in his poetry'.[5] His tragedy *Catiline*, his collected *Epigrams*, and many of the poems of praise in *The Forest* and *The Underwoods* gain interest from his complex strategies of asserting his independence while working within a patronage context.

The traditional system of literary patronage relied on the nobility's sense of obligation to support the arts and placed poets in the demeaning position of petitioning for aid. Writing from the perspective of the courtly amateur whose fortunes had not yet reduced him to solicitation in verse, the young John Donne had criticised this practice in 'Satire II', where he asked, 'And they who write to lords, rewards to get, / Are they not like singers at doors for meat?' (ll. 21–2).[6] Jonson avoided the stigma of begging by conceiving of patronage as an exchange. Just as contemporary political patronage was seen as the exercise of the patron's influence in return for the client's deference and service, so he defined the poet–patron relationship as one in which his patrons' generosity was rewarded with counsel and praise that guaranteed abiding fame. 'Learning needs rest', he said in *Discoveries*, 'sovereignty gives it. Sovereignty needs council: learning affords it. There is such a consociation of offices, between the prince, and whom his favour breeds, that they may help to sustain his power, as he their knowledge' (ll. 81–6). Though he at times shows deference by understating his role, as when he asks Robert Cecil, 'What need hast thou of me, or of my muse, / Whose actions so themselves do celebrate?' (*Epig.* XLIII, ll. 1–2), he just as often draws attention to the rarity of poetic skill and the poet's ability to confer lasting honour. And even such seemingly self-effacing queries as that to Cecil could also serve as a subtle reminder that an entertainment or epigram by him was just as enduring an expression of his patrons' magnificence as a prodigy house by Robert Smythson or a portrait by Van Dyke. In fact, recent studies have suggested that the rhetoric of Jonson's patronage poems, like the rhetoric of Elizabethan suitors' letters in general, is distinguished by manipulative strategies that not only promote his worthiness, but play on his patrons' anxieties and their sense of self-interest.[7]

In transactions between poet and patron, in other words, power was not wholly on the patron's side. Jonson's ability to mythologise his subjects as emblems of heroic virtue, domestic harmony, or classic grace and beauty made his services desirable. In the masque, in particular, his aristocratic patrons were to some extent also *his* clients, in the modern sense of 'someone who engages the service of a professional'. His inventiveness at devising matter appropriate for particular occasions, his authoritative, dignified poetic voice and his ability to gauge what would please King James and Queen Anne led those who entertained the royal couple to seek his talents. The records of the Merchant Taylors Company for July 1607, for example, document his employment 'about a speech . . . to welcome his Majesty and for music and other inventions which may give liking and delight'.[8] The Company's records show that he was paid twenty pounds (twice the going rate for a play) and that he not only composed a short verse welcome, but also hired the singers, arranged the rehearsal dinner and had his man write out copies of the speech and songs to be given to the King and his attendent lords. Throughout his career he often performed these functions for nobles who desired to win royal favour or entertain visiting dignitaries, serving (among others) Robert Cecil, Earl of Salisbury; James Hay, Lord Doncaster; George Villiers, Duke of Buckingham; and William Cavendish, Earl of Newcastle.

Yet even though Jonson's talent gave his masques and poems considerable market value, he refused to reduce the exchange between poet and patron to a purely commercial transaction. Like his contemporaries he ideally conceived of patronage in terms of the Senecan language of benefits.[9] This is seen most clearly in 'An Epistle to Sir Edward Sackville, now Earl of Dorset' (*Und.* XIII), where he contrasts Sackville's readiness to aid him with the pride or reluctance of other nobles and repays Sackville's generosity 'By thanking thus the courtesy to life' (l. 159). Stanley Fish has argued that Jonson's poems 'declare unreal the network of dependencies and obligations' that direct his actions, but since Jonson ends by acknowledging that he owes Sackville 'all', he does not seem to be evading his indebtedness.[10] Rather, by stressing the generous or grateful spirit in which giving or receiving should be conducted, he insists on the mutuality of the patronage relationship.

Some of those who employed his talents did not pass this Senecan test. Of the Earl of Salisbury, for whom he wrote four royal entertainments between 1606 and 1609, he complained to William Drummond: 'Salisbury never cared for any man longer nor he could make use of him' (*Conv.*, ll. 357–8). He also resented his impersonal entertainment: 'Being at the end of my lord Salisbury's table with Inigo Jones, and demanded by my lord why he was not glad, 'My Lord', said he 'You promised I should dine with you, but I do not', for he had none of his meat; he esteemed only that his meat which was of his own dish' (*Conv.*, ll. 316–19).

By contrast, his favourite patrons were those who, like the Sidneys and the Herberts, loved 'not alone the arts, but the men' and admitted him to their company on a familiar basis.[11] His poem 'To Penshurst' contrasts Cecil's distant hospitality with the warm personal associations he enjoyed in Sir Robert Sidney's household. There 'the same beer, and bread, and self-same wine, / That is his lordship's' was given to Jonson and he was 'not fain to sit (as some, this day, / At great men's tables) and yet dine away' (*For.* II, ll. 63–6). Sidney's daughter, Lady Mary Wroth, his niece Elizabeth Sidney Manners, the Countess of Rutland (Sir Philip Sidney's daughter), and his nephew William Herbert, the third Earl of Pembroke (his sister Mary's son) were all amateur poets who composed in one or more of the genres practised by Sir Philip: versified psalm-translations, Petrarchan love-poetry, pastoral drama and prose romance.[12] Jonson's relationship with them all was marked by cordiality and mutual respect. He told Drummond that 'The Countess of Rutland was nothing inferior to her father, S[ir] P. Sidney, in poesy' (*Conv.*, ll. 205–6), and he complimented Lady Wroth by claiming that since he had 'exscribed' (copied out) her sonnets, he had become 'A better lover, and much better poet' (*Und.* XXVIII, l. 4). A glimpse of his intimacy with Pembroke and his wife is provided by Jonson's report that his 'Song. That Women Are but Men's Shadows' (*For.* VII) resulted from a disagreement between the Earl and the Countess: 'Pembroke and his lady discoursing, the Earl said the women were men's shadows, and she maintained them. Both appealing to Jonson, he affirmed it true; for which my lady gave a penance to prove it in verse, hence his epigram' (*Conv.*, ll. 368–71). In such congenial company Jonson could imagine himself as an equal member of the aristocracy of virtue and knowledge envisioned by Renaissance humanists.

Though Jonson clearly preferred some patrons over others, he understood the realities of court life too well to become a partisan of any one clique. Recent historical studies have made us keenly aware of the importance of faction at the late Elizabethan and early Stuart court, interpreting many contemporary events in terms of conflict between the militant Protestant lords (Essex, Ralegh, Southampton, Pembroke) and the pro-Spanish Howards – conflict that was complicated in turn by the interests of King James' Scottish courtiers and the influence of his male favourites.[13] In turn, our awareness of shifting alliances has brought a new sophistication to discussions of the literature of patronage, allowing us to locate poems, plays and masques much more precisely in relation to current factional tensions and to recover aspects of their significance that have hitherto been lost.[14] The process, however, is not without its pitfalls. The resulting temptations for students of Jonson are either to explain individual works wholly as an expression of some patron's concerns or to view his career in general as an opportunistic progress, in which he threw in his lot with one group or another as their prospects altered. Yet while he was no doubt keenly aware of factional interests and served them on occasion, he also maintained a degree of impartiality, and he rarely allowed a work's political import to become its whole meaning.

One way Jonson preserved his autonomy was to avoid commitments that made exclusive claims on his services, choosing instead to cultivate patrons from many different centres of power. Lord D'Aubigny, with whom he lived for a period, was one of the four Gentlemen of the Bedchamber, who controlled access to the King. The Earl of Salisbury (both Secretary of State and, after 1607, the Lord Treasurer) and Thomas Howard, Earl of Suffolk (the King's Lord Chamberlain) were members of the inner circle of the early Jacobean Privy Council. Lucy Russell, Countess of Bedford (to whose influence he may have been indebted for his early masque commissions) and Sir Robert Sidney (later Viscount L'Isle and Earl of Leicester) were the Queen's chief lady-in-waiting and Lord Chamberlain, respectively. Sidney's friend Sir Walter Ralegh, whose son Wat he took on a continental tour in 1612–13, was admired by Prince Henry even though imprisoned in the Tower by King James. The Earl of Pembroke was favoured by the Queen, his brother Philip by the King. Jonson's familiarity with both may have begun in 1597 when he was a member of Pembroke's Men (then in the service of their father Henry, the second earl). Their early assistance is attested by his letters during the *Eastward Ho* affair in 1605.[15] Their aid of Jonson, then a Catholic, along with support from such members of the old anti-Spanish Essex alliance as the Bedfords and the Rutlands, indicates that literary patronage in the Jacobean court was not strictly a matter of ideology or religious orientation.

It is true that as a court masque-poet, Jonson was called upon to celebrate occasions that promoted particular factions and that at times political realities dictated his fictions. For example, in writing *Hymenaei* for the marriage of the Earl of Essex and Frances Howard (daughter of Lord Chamberlain Suffolk) he recognised the greater power of the Howards by casting their party as the champions of Truth in the accompanying *Barriers*. But Jonson's composition of *Hymenaei* can no more be taken as evidence of commitment to the goals of the Howard faction than his later composition of *Mercury Vindicated from the Alchemists at Court* in 1614, discussed in Chapter 9, can be taken as evidence of his conversion to the principles of the militant Protestant faction led by Pembroke and Archbishop Abbot. Jonson could have his private opinions about the character of various courtiers; he could even allegorise them as he did when he characterised Suffolk's wife as an enchantress in his lost pastoral *The May Lord*.[16] As a masque poet, however, he used his inventive powers to serve members of different factions as occasion or the King demanded, just as Pembroke and Suffolk put aside their differences and served together as the King's proxies at the christening of Sir Robert Wroth's son.[17] If Jonson was truthful when he told Drummond in 1619 that 'He was Master of Arts in both the universities, by their favour, not his study' (*Conv.*, ll. 247–8) Suffolk and Pembroke may both have had a hand in his degrees. The Oxford degree was apparently granted at the request of Pembroke, the university's chancellor; the chancellor of Cambridge from 1614 to 1626 was Suffolk.[18]

Suffolk's possible role in his honorary Cambridge degree (which is not recorded in any case) is, of course, sheer speculation. The important point here is that Jonson wrote in a court milieu full of competing noblemen and noblewomen with whom he needed to remain on good terms regardless of their (and his) personal or political differences. In a world not unlike that of *King Lear*, where 'packs and sects of great ones, / . . . ebb and flow by th'moon' (V.iii.18–19), no poet could work for more than twenty-five years as

Jonson did without maintaining an inclusive patronage network. If Jonson was closer to Pembroke than to Suffolk, the Lord Chamberlain, he still had to appease the latter, who had the ultimate authority over court entertainments. If Pembroke helped to raise George Villiers to his position as Duke of Buckingham but then became one of his chief political enemies, Jonson had to remain on good terms with both. Given his satire on homosexuality in *Sejanus*, James' male favourites – Philip Herbert, James Hay, Robert Carr and Villiers – must have posed a special problem, even though they took a leading role in his masques and sometimes commissioned entertainments from him. A surviving poem written to Carr on his wedding day (*M.P.* XXVI) indicates that courtly realities required him to cultivate the good will of James' young men, whatever his moral reservations. He expressed his distaste for sycophancy by refusing to dedicate anything to them publicly and by leaving poems to them out of his collected editions or, in the case of Philip Herbert, by praising his wife instead (see *Epig.* CIV). In his publishing practice, at least, he could be his own man.

Perhaps the best example of the tension between accomodation to courtly realities and resistance to subservient clientage is Jonson's relationship with Robert Cecil. Though in *Sejanus* the young satirist seems to have glanced bitingly at the role of Salisbury and Northampton in furthering the downfall of Ralegh and Essex (see Chapter 5 above), his perspective on court politics gradually shifted from that of a detached critic to one implicated in court life and forced to compromise with authority by his own vulnerability. Salisbury could have broken him for his Catholicism, for his satire on the Scots in *Eastward Ho* or for his allusion to Lady Arabella Stuart in *Epicoene*. His appeal to Salisbury from prison in the *Eastward Ho* incident asks Salisbury's aid in securing his release and Chapman's, promising that 'Freeing us from one prison, you shall remove us to another, which is eternally to bind us and our Muses, to the thankful honouring of you and yours to posterity'.[19] He repaid that debt in three epigrams of praise and the four royal entertainments that helped cement Salisbury's relationship with King James. Yet when read carefully these pieces reveal critical undertones. *The Entertainment of the King and Queen at Theobalds*, written to mark Salisbury's transfer of his ancestral home to James in May 1607, raises uneasy questions about Cecil's motives even as it praises his sacrifices for James and the common good. His epigrams to Salisbury (*Epig.* XLIII, LXIII and LXIV) are equally complex in tone, applauding Salisbury's virtue or merit and praising 'the constant suffering' of his 'equal mind' (*Epig*. LXIII, l. 8) while acknowledging that his eminence aroused envy and that his actions were not acclaimed by popular opinion.[20]

Still, the greater willingness of the mature Jonson to see things from Salisbury's perspective is evidenced by his tragedy *Catiline His Fall*, written in 1611 after the assassination of Henri IV of France had led to repressive measures against English Catholics – measures that apparently precipitated his own reconversion to Anglicanism.[21] Having earlier been accused at the time of the Gunpowder Plot 'both of popery and treason' by the Earl of Northampton when examined before the Privy Council over *Sejanus* (*Conv.*, ll. 324–7), he apparently decided in 1610 that writing a play about the preservation of the Roman state from conspiracy would demonstrate his loyalty once and for all. Like *Sejanus*, *Catiline* is a Senecan tragedy about a monstrous villain driven by depraved ambition. Echoing Seneca's *Thyestes*, the play begins with the ghost of Sulla presenting Catiline as his heir in cruelty and ends with the narration of his 'brave bad death' (V.688). However, *Catiline* marks a significant shift in Jonson's political vision by focusing for the last three acts on the leader whose surveillance preserves the commonwealth. Though its framing action follows the pattern of rise-and-fall tragedy, its real hero is Cicero, who exposes Catiline's plots to fire the city and murder the senators, as Salisbury had exposed the role of Catesby and the other Gunpowder Plotters.

Once again Jonson makes 'truth of argument' (that is, historical authenticity) the hallmark of his tragedy. *Catiline* is an intricate synthesis of his historical sources – mainly Sallust's *The War with Catiline*, Plutarch's *Lives* and the orations of Cicero, one of which he reproduced at length in Act IV to the great discontent of his public-theatre spectators.[22] Yet while he seems to exercise the poet's licence by simplifying Catiline into a vicious monster and by painting Caesar and Crassus as shadowy supporters of his revolt, he does so under the influence of the Renaissance account – included in his edition of Sallust – of *The Conspiracy of Catiline* by Constantius Felicius Durantinus. Sulla's ghost catalogues Catiline's vices of murder, rape and incest at the beginning of the play much as Felicius condenses several discrete passages from Sallust into his opening chapter. Moreover, in contrast to Plutarch, who characterises Cicero as vain and cowardly, Jonson follows Felicius in emphasising Cicero's skill in mixing promises and threats to win over Curius, in stressing the unfair criticism he received and in repeatedly affirming the involvement of Caesar and Crassus in Catiline's conspiracy.[23]

Felicius' narrative thus offers an alternative perspective on Jonson's Cicero, whose character has been read negatively either as a Machiavellian statesman whose noble ends are undercut by his unscrupulous means or, with Plutarch, as a timid leader whose decision not to pursue the evidence against Caesar makes Caesar's later tyranny possible.[24] The former judgement reflects an ideal of political purity not held by any of Jonson's Roman sources; the latter assumes that the audience's responses will be determined by their knowledge of Rome's subsequent history. Jonson *may* have expected his audience to recognise Cicero's refusal to take action against Caesar as a failure of political nerve; he certainly shared the view of Caesar as an enemy to 'Rome, and her liberty' (*Epig.* CX, 1. 4). Yet nowhere in *Catiline* does he include any prophecy foreshadowing Caesar's destruction of republican institutions. When Cicero first questions whether it is wise to prove the falsehood of Caesar and Crassus, Cato asks indignantly, 'What honest act is that, / The Roman Senate should not dare and do?' (IV.526–7), but he assents without further protest when Cicero replies that it is 'an unprofitable, dangerous act, / To stir too many serpents up at once' (ll. 528–9). Like Felicius, Jonson allows no reference to later events to qualify his presentation of Cicero as a diligent and courageous statesman willing to die, if necessary, to preserve the commonwealth.[25] At the end of Act IV the Chorus confesses, in words inspired by Felicius' commentary on the instability of Roman public opinion, that they have made 'the careful magistrate / The mark of slander'.[26] Even though Jonson's view of Cicero differs from some of his Roman sources, therefore, his imaginative reconstruction of Roman history has good authority.

Yet in 1611 a play on Catiline's conspiracy that defended Cicero would inevitably have reminded auditors of the Gunpowder Plot and the allegations that it had been fomented by Robert Cecil, the 'careful magistrate' who foiled it. Contemporaries often compared the two events, and for this reason Barbara N. De Luna has argued that *Catiline* is an elaborate 'parallelograph' in which Robert Catesby, Guy Fawkes and their fellow Gunpowder Plotters are portrayed allegorically by Roman counterparts, with Jonson himself in the role of Quintus Curius, the turncoat who betrays Catiline's plans to Cicero.[27] De Luna's overingenious reading is based on the misguided assumption that Jonson can be proven to have worked as a double agent for Cecil and on forced parallels between some of Catesby's confederates and the Catilinarian conspirators.[28] Nevertheless, she does demonstrate convincingly that Jonson's handling of his subject is calculated to evoke memories of the Plot. By giving the proposed date of Catiline's destruction (28 October) in accurate, but ambiguous terms as 'the fifth (the kalends of November)' (IV.246), by describing it repeatedly as a sudden 'blow', by playing up the role of sulphur (mentioned only once in Plutarch) in the conspirators' preparations to fire the city, by calling the ritual of drinking blood to seal their pact a 'sacrament' and by having Cicero reassure Curius that 'no religion binds men to be traitors' (III.369), he reinforces the analogy between Catiline's conspiracy and Catesby's.[29]

Furthermore, by portraying Caesar and Crassus as supporters of Catiline and by having them make the same accusations against Cicero that had been levelled against Cecil, Jonson implicitly answers the allegation that the Gunpowder Plot was a 'state intrigue' designed to strengthen Cecil's position and to make Catholics the object of popular hatred. Crassus' charge that 'Treasons and guilty men are made in states / Too oft, to dignify the magistrates' (III.102–3) has no validity at all in a dramatic context in which Crassus is later proven to be complicit with the traitors. Moreover, the Chorus' wonder at the slanderous accusations against Cicero parallels Cecil's own query in his *An Answer to Certain Scandalous Papers, Scattered abroad under colour of a Catholic Admonition* (1606): 'To what end do princes admit of counsellors' care or secretaries' vigilance (whose offices are to stand sentinel over the life of kings and safety of states), if their endeavours to countermine the secret mines of treason be thus exposed to misconstruction?'.[30] By depicting Cicero's use of 'policy' as a purely defensive effort 'to countermine the secret mines of treason', Jonson has come full circle from his position in *Sejanus*, where accusations of treason *were* fabricated for political purposes. Further links between Cecil and the ideal of statesmanship represented by Cicero can be found in 'An Epigram on William, Lord Bur[ghley], Lo[rd] High Treasurer of England (Presented upon a Plate of Gold to His Son Rob[ert], E[arl] of Salisbury, When He Was also Treasurer)' (*Und.* XXX). Here Jonson echoes Cato's praise of Cicero as steersman of the state (III.61–74) by praising Burghley as 'The only faithful watchman for the realm, / That in all tempests, never quit the helm' (ll. 9–10). Cicero's lament that he must bribe Antonius to oppose Catiline because 'So few are virtuous, when the reward's away' (III.480) is also a variant of Jonson's assertion that Burghley 'still was good for goodness' sake, nor thought / Upon reward, till the reward him sought' (ll. 13–14). Jonson undoubtedly knew that Burghley had reaped massive profits from his offices; as was so often the case, his praise is probably a subtle way of instructing his son, who was much more rapacious.[31] Whatever their actual shortcomings, however, the Cecils are depicted in terms of the same statesmanlike virtues dramatised through Cicero.

Yet while *Catiline* affirmed Jonson's loyalty to the government by celebrating the vigilant exposure of treason, he asserted his independence in two ways. First, by adopting Sallust's theme that Catiline's conspiracy was symptomatic of an underlying moral degeneration, he presented his audience with a looking-glass for London and the court. The Chorus at the end of Act I blends passages from Sallust with sections of Petronius' satire on Roman lust, effeminacy and greed:

> And now ambition doth invade
> Her state, with eating avarice,
> Riot, and every other vice.
> Decrees are bought, and laws are sold,
> Honours and offices for gold;
> The people's voices, and the free
> Tongues in the Senate, bribed be.
>
> (I.576–82)

Jonson's favourite theme of the Golden Age corrupted by greed and ambition is here given memorable expression. Despite the historical authenticity of his Roman Chorus's sentiments, their application to the Jacobean context is unmistakable. In effect, Jonson levels a powerful indictment at the contemporary social and political scene, where royal extravagance and the venality of office-holders would lead eventually to the repudiation of Stuart rule.

Secondly, given the ease with which his dedication might have played up the analogy between Salisbury and his Roman counterpart, Jonson's choice of the Earl of Pembroke as the dedicatee of *Catiline* is a notable refusal to pursue the obvious possibilities for public flattery. Barbara De Luna has suggested that his depiction of Cicero angered Salisbury, but aside from Caesar's brief allusion to

Cicero's excessive love of glory at III.28 there is little in Jonson's portrayal at which he could take offence and no evidence at all that he did so.[32] It is conceivable that by 1611 Salisbury's failing health and his inability to negotiate the Great Contract with Parliament made him seem a less promising patron than the rising Pembroke, but the widespread assumption among historians that Salisbury was in disgrace with King James after 1610 has recently been questioned.[33] A better explanation is that Jonson's disillusionment with Salisbury's personal traits made him balk at the public endorsement implied by a dedication and turn to Pembroke instead. Where Salisbury was viewed as the arch-politician of his age, Pembroke acquired a reputation for learning, wit and integrity. Jonson's praise of his 'noblesse', which 'keeps one stature still, / And one true posture, though besieged with ill / Of what ambition, faction, pride can raise;' (*Epig.* CII, ll. 13–15), is confirmed by the Earl of Clarendon's description: 'He was exceedingly beloved in court, because he never desired to get that for himself, which others laboured for, but was still ready to promote the pretences of worthy men. And he was equally celebrated in the country, for having received no obligations from the court which might corrupt or sway his affections and judgement'.[34] In a move we might call 'the king's secretary declined', therefore, Jonson's dedication of *Catiline* to Pembroke marks his refusal to proceed beyond a tacit accomodation with Salisbury to open flattery and distinguishes between a patron he preferred by choice and one he served by necessity.

To Pembroke Jonson also gave 'the honour of leading forth so many good, and great names . . . to their remembrance with posterity' by dedicating to him 'the ripest of my studies, my *Epigrams*' in the 1616 Folio.[35] A separate edition may already have appeared, for the Stationers' Register contains an entry for 15 May 1612 of 'a book called, Ben Johnson his Epigrams'; in a manuscript note of 'books read by me, anno 1612' William Drummond includes 'Ben Jonson's Epigrams' and Arthur Throckmorton mentions ordering a copy for sixpence.[36] Jonson's collection of individual pieces into *Epigrams, I Book* transformed private praise into public celebration and emulated Martial, the order of whose *Epigrams, Book I* he initially copies.[37] Moreover, by heightening the idealised praise of his subjects through contrast with the vices and follies ridiculed in the many satiric epigrams and by selecting subjects that ranged from great officers of state and noble ladies to members of the gentry and the professions, he redeemed the epigram from its function in amateur circles as a vehicle for bawdy wit and set forth a comprehensive vision of the good society lacking in his Roman model. Once again he tacitly asserted his independence through the arrangement of the collection. Although the first thirty-six poems contain three in praise of King James (including one [XXXVII] that paradoxically flatters by declaring that he 'cannot flattered be'), they also contain six (VIII, X, XI, XV, XXVIII and XXIX) that satirise courtly injustice, parasitism and false greatness, sometimes through mock titles such as 'My Lord Ignorant' and 'Courtworm'. In addition, Jonson makes good his claim to William Drummond that 'he never esteemed of a man for the name of a lord' (*Conv.*, l. 338) by placing poems to personal friends like Camden, Sir John Roe and Donne before the patronage poems that begin with XL 'On Margaret Ratcliffe' and XLIII 'To Robert, Earl of Salisbury'.

Whether writing to friends or to patrons, however, Jonson's purpose is the same. His subjects are presented not as individuals, but as types of virtue – as exemplars of the good poet, historian, soldier, statesman, judge or friend and as models of feminine grace or chastity. The 'great names' that Pembroke leads forth are discovered to stand, through an almost magical equation of name and nature, for admirable moral qualities.[38] So the military commander Sir Horace Vere (*Epig.* XCI), whose name has 'a Roman sound', is said to embody 'Roman virtue', and Lucy, Countess of Bedford, is nominated the 'brightness of our sphere' (*Epig.* XCIV) through a word-play on the etymology of 'Lucy' from 'light'. When their names or deeds yield less promising matter for praise, Jonson finds something in their activities or associations from which to generalise: so Donne's friend Sir Henry Goodyer is applauded for 'making thy friends books, and thy books friends' (*Epig.* LXXXVI, l. 4), and his invitation to Jonson to share a few days' hawking becomes a lesson that men 'to knowledge so should tower upright, / And never stoop, but to strike ignorance' (*Epig.* LXXXV, ll. 6–7). Such strategies invite admiration at Jonson's wit in finding matter for praise, but they do not result in actual likenesses. As a portrait painter, he frequently poses his subjects in heroic postures but leaves their faces in deep shade; we finally know little about them beyond the idealised roles they are said to perform.[39] Keenly aware that his praise was sometimes exaggerated or unmerited, he apologised for the misrepresentation in his dedication to the *Epigrams*: 'if I have praised, unfortunately, anyone, that doth not deserve; or, if all answer not, in all numbers, the pictures I have made of them: I hope it will be forgiven me, that they are no ill pieces, though they be not like the persons' (ll. 19–22).

Jonson's apology seems to be the product of some painful self-examination in the period from 1612 to 1616 about his mode of addressing patrons. His Epigram LXV castigates his Muse for having 'betrayed' him 'to a worthless lord' and made him 'commit most fierce idolatry / To a great image through thy luxury' (ll. 2–4), and in his 'An Epistle to Master John Selden' (*Und.* XIV), originally prefixed to Selden's *Titles of Honour* in 1614, he confesses 'I have too oft preferred / Men past their terms, and praised some names too much, / But 'twas with purpose to have made them such' (ll. 20–2). Having once been deceived, he declares, he is determined to 'turn a sharper eye' upon himself and 'vex it many days / Before men get a verse: much less a praise' (ll. 23, 25–6). His vow provides assurance that 'I now / Mean what I speak' (ll. 27–8) in commending his friend Selden, but it was a vow that was almost impossible to keep for long in a cultural context where 'patronage required the performance of the role of a devoted follower and exaggerated language of alliance even if the client did not feel it'.[40]

The thoughts with which Jonson consoles himself in these two self-critical pieces, however, are not merely idle excuses. By declaring in the epistle to Selden that his purpose in praising 'twas . . . to have made them such' and by reminding himself at the end of Epigram LXV that 'Whoe'er is raised, / For worth he has not, he is taxed, not praised' (ll. 15–16), he underscores the coercive function of compliment as a standard to which the recipient is expected to conform. Here he may be echoing Erasmus' letter to Jean Desmarez (Paludanus), printed with his *Panegyric* to the Archduke Philip in 1504, which sets out the Renaissance theory of praise as a diplomatic mode of instruction and reproof:

This kind of composition . . . consists in presenting princes with a pattern of goodness, in such a way as to reform bad rulers, improve the good . . . and cause even the hopelessly vicious to feel some inward stirrings of shame. . . . How could one reproach a wicked ruler for his cruelty more safely, yet more severely, than by proclaiming his mildness; or for his greed and violence and lust, than by celebrating his generosity, self-control, and chastity?[41]

According to Erasmus, panegyrics – even when untrue – are valuable as patterns of virtue for future generations of readers and because they move the persons addressed to emulate their praise.

Jonson's adherence to the Erasmian theory of panegyric means that his masques and his encomiastic verse are often at variance with the 'facts' of his patrons' lives, and this may be so even when he was writing to those whom he generally respected. Investigations into the background of two of his most notable patronage poems – *The Forest* II, 'To Penshurst' and III 'To Sir Robert Wroth' – have revealed that their commendations are not as straightforward as they initially seem. Both translate Roman poetic models into memorable images of English country life and celebrate their subjects as exemplary 'housekeepers' whose generous hospitality recalls the innocent cheer of the classical golden age. The theme was one that would appeal to King James, who regularly urged the gentry to return to their rural homes, but 'To Sir Robert Wroth' in particular betrays Jonson's customary ambivalence about the court and seems unlikely to have been an attempt to curry royal favour.[42] The poem commends Wroth for being 'no ambitious guest' at city banquets or state dinners and for refusing to join the throng

> (when masquing is) to have a sight
> Of the short bravery of the night;
> To view the jewels, stuffs, the pains, the wit
> There wasted, some not paid for yet!
> (ll. 5-6, 9–12)

These lines are a remarkably candid confession of the vanity of the entertainments on which Jonson expended so much artistic energy. No doubt his aside about 'the wit . . . not paid for yet' was inspired by bitter personal experience with the slow workings of the nearly bankrupt Jacobean Exchequer. Yet he also seems to be warning the Wroths against a vain pursuit of courtly extravagance. Though not one of the Queen's inner circle of ladies-in-waiting, Lady Wroth was enough enamoured 'of the short bravery of the night' to have danced in *The Masque of Blackness* (1605) and to have her portrait painted in masquing attire; Sir Robert spent a great deal on his estate and died twenty-three thousand pounds in debt. Jonson's urging that he live 'at home, in thy securer rest, / . . . with unbought provision blest' (ll. 13–14) was apparently much needed.[43]

'To Penshurst' contrasts the home of the Sidneys with the prodigy houses – 'proud, ambitious heaps' Jonson calls them – built by leading Elizabethan and Jacobean courtiers. The opening catalogue of the architectural features that Penshurst lacks ('polished pillars, or a roof of gold', a glass upper-storey 'lantern', imposing stairwells or courts) recalls the splendours of the Sackvilles' Knole, Lord Burghley's Theobalds, and Suffolk's Audley End – estates built as much to entertain the sovereign as for the use of the owners.[44] In praising Penshurst for standing 'an ancient pile' Jonson may be thinking in particular of Robert Cecil's Hatfield House, where an older medieval manor was destroyed to provide bricks for Cecil's new construction. Like Cecil, Sidney represented the third generation of Tudor 'new men' (his father was Lord Lieutenant of Ireland), yet his aspirations of improving his estate to match his growing influence at court were constrained by his limited income. His decision to expand rather than rebuild Penshurst and to link the new wings to the older structure by continuing the crenelations of the ancient fortress was probably dictated by considerations of economy and architectural unity. Even so, however, Sidney's steward advised him to curb his remodelling, and Jonson's strictures against 'envious show' reinforce those cautions.[45] By lauding Sidney and his wife as exemplars of 'manners, arms, and arts' and by stressing their hospitality and the goodwill they enjoy from their tenants, he attempts to persuade them that they are truer embodiments of aristocratic greatness than lords who build imposing, but empty edifices.

Like the acid used to make an etching, then, the hidden counsel in the poetry of praise may be washed away in time, leaving its patrons to stand as images of the social or moral ideals against which they were originally judged. Jonson's subjects served as the vehicles by which he could convey his beliefs that titles and family names were empty things without virtue, piety, or learning, that life is loaned and not possessed, that one must 'live to conscience, not to show', that the real heroes are those whose inner integrity helps them to 'stand' against the folly or vice of the crowd, and yet that there is wisdom in retiring from 'the press' into a 'centred self', where Fortune can do one little harm.[46] These humanistic and Stoic sentiments were hardly original; they spoke to Stuart culture – and to Jonson himself – because they offered consolation and stiffened moral resolve in a courtly society where ambitious seeking and extravagant display were the norm, not the exception. Jonson's art was manifested in the skill with which he consistently assimilated such classical maxims into his own poetic voice; his integrity, in the appropriateness of his concealed instruction to the figures he addressed. Although the moral compromises necessarily involved in any system of patronage continued to trouble him, he could take some satisfaction in knowing that his seeming adulation was often really surreptitious criticism or private advice.

Given his satiric temperament, of course, Jonson was more inclined to ridicule than to praise. Having 'eaten with the beauties, and the wits, / And braveries of court' and come 'so nigh to know / Whether their faces were their own, or no' (*Und.* XLII, ll. 33–6), he often could not resist mockery. The virtues extolled in his patronage poetry are opposed to the vices of the courtlings who are derided in the satiric epigrams. Don Surly of Epigram XXVIII is a study in aristocratic arrogance; Fine Lady Would-Be of Epigram LXII prefers to induce abortions rather than let pregnancy interfere with her pleasures at court. Fine Grand of Epigram LXXIII has employed Jonson to create various trifling forms of wit, but has failed to reward him for his assistance. Despite their generic names, these figures of courtly vice or folly were no doubt often composite caricatures of persons Jonson had encountered at Whitehall. Though he claimed in the dedicatory epistle of his *Epigrams* to have 'avoided all particulars' (ll. 24–5), his constant warnings against 'applying' the satire in his plays and poems to individuals point to his engagement with the actual manners of the time. The satire on the Ladies Collegiates in *Epicoene*, for example, inverts the praise of female rulers in *The Masque of Queens* and indirectly criticises the behaviour of Queen Anne's associates. Described as 'an order between courtiers and country-madams, that live from their husbands; and give entertainment to all the Wits and Braveries o' the time' (I.i.67–9), the Collegiates' independence mirrors that of Lady Bedford, whom Jonson praises in Epigram LXXVI for possessing a 'learned, and a manly soul' that controls her own destiny and spins 'her own free hours' (ll. 13–16). Like Lady Haughty, Lady Bedford referred to her women friends by their husbands' last names, and Jonson's allusions to the Collegiates' face-painting gains new resonance in relation to John Chamberlain's report of 1 August 1613 that after counsel from her Puritan physician Lady Bedford 'is somewhat reformed in her attire, and forbears painting, which they say makes her look somewhat strangely among so many visards, which together with their frisled, powdered hair makes them [Queen Anne's attendants] look all alike, so that you can scant know one from another at the first view'.[47] The Collegiates, of course, can not be identified specifically with members of Queen Anne's court; here, as elsewhere, Jonson altered or generalised details to evade charges of lampooning particular individuals.

One instance where he failed to generalise his satire, with damaging consequences for his patronage relationships, is *Underwoods* XLIX, 'An Epigram on the Court Pucell' – an attack on Cecelia Bulstrode, an intimate of the Countess of Bedford and one of the ladies of Queen Anne's bedchamber. A former love of Sir John Roe and of his cousin Sir Thomas, Mistress Bulstrode was also one of Sir Thomas Overbury's circle of 'conceited news' writers: Jonson describes her chamber as 'the very pit / Where fight the prime cocks of the game, for wit' (ll. 3–4) and condemns her as 'epicoene' for participating equally.[48] Writing to show the 'world' that he dare answer Bulstrode's previous 'censure' of him, he deprecates the laboured wit of her discourse on 'state, religion, bawdry' and accuses her of feigning 'fits o'th'mother' (hysteria) in order to lure clergymen into sexual liaisons. Since, among his other charges, he accuses her of accepting 'velvet gowns' and 'spangled petticoats' 'as new rewards of her old secrecy' (ll. 18–20), his satire implicates the Queen and Lady Bedford by hinting that they had something to hide. His intemperate epigram 'brought him great displeasure' when it 'was stolen out of his pocket by a gentleman who drank him drowsy, and given Mistress Bulstrode' (*Conv.*, ll. 673–5). It may have been this offence to which Jonson refers in a letter to Donne, where he speaks of the threatened loss of Donne's friendship and complains that 'My Lady may believe whisperings, receive tales, suspect and condemn my honesty; and I may not answer, on the pain of losing her; as if she, who had this prejudice of me, were not already lost'.[49] Lady Bedford's anger at Jonson would have been compounded by grief when Bulstrode died at Twickenham on 4 August 1609. Her death was celebrated with elegies by Donne, Lord Herbert of Cherbury and Lady Bedford herself.[50] Jonson's contrition is indicated by the epitaph he wrote at George Garrard's request, praising her as the embodiment of wisdom and modesty rarely found at court. In the accompanying letter to Garrard, he exclaims 'Would God, I had seen her before, that some that live might have corrected some prejudices they have had injuriously of me'.[51] His letter suggests that his praise of Bulstrode's chastity, which he had impugned in 'On the Court Pucell', was an act of penance directed at Lady Bedford, Donne and his friends.

This whole episode reveals the social anxieties that a patronage poet could experience when he offended a major patron, but it seems not to have taught Jonson prudence. If *Epicoene* was performed, as most scholars agree, in the winter season of 1609/ 10, he must have written it during or after his troubles with Lady Bedford. Its anti-feminist satire and his foolhardy allusion to Lady Arabella Stuart may well have irritated the Queen and her ladies and lost him the masque commision for Prince Henry's creation as Prince of Wales in June 1610.[52] Given the tact and grace of Epigram LXXVI, which praises Lady Bedford as the 'kind of creature I could most desire, / To honour, serve, and love' (ll. 4–5), and XCIV, which commends her virtue and judgement for being among the few that read satires like Donne's with approval, the risks Jonson took of offending her is all the more surprising. It is almost as if the pressures built up by the necessity of idealising his patroness became so great that he vented them in a reckless manner.

Jonson's inability to check his satiric impulse toward Lady Bedford and Cecelia Bulstrode may have been compounded by his conflicted attitudes toward women. Like Donne, who betrayed his own prejudices in praising her virtue because 'It ransoms one sex, and one Court preserves', Jonson's hostility to court fashions was reinforced by a streak of misogyny.[53] Though he might celebrate his patronesses for their learning and chastity, he shared the traditional condemnation of intellectual, assertive women as unnatural, and his own experience as a seducer seems to have left him with the suspicion that all women were unfaithful (see Epigram LXXXIII). At the same time, the conventions of patron–client discourse demanded deferential worship of his patronesses' beauty and feminine grace, to which his temperament was all too responsive anyway. Jonson manages Petrarchan compliment skilfully, avoiding the hyperbole that distinguishes Donne's poems to Lady Bedford, but his strong sexual drive seems to have created tensions even as it gave credence to the sublimated eroticism that was part of the conventional stance. His admiration for Lady Mary Wroth is evident from his praise of her as a composite of all the goddesses in Epigram CV and from the 1612 dedication to *The Alchemist*, where he calls her 'The grace, and Glory of women'.[54] As Margaret Hannay points out, such compliments could be an indirect way of bidding for (or rewarding) the patronage of the husband.[55]

Jonson's epistle to Katherine, Lady D'Aubigny (*For.* XIII) and his epigram on Susan, Countess of Montgomery (*Epig.* CIV) clearly fall into this category. Wroth, however, seems not to have been flattered by the attention to his wife; Drummond records Jonson's opinion that she was 'unworthily married to a jealous husband' (*Conv.*, ll. 359–60).[56] In light of 'An Elegy' (*Und.* XIX), where Jonson justifies adultery because 'You have a husband is the just excuse / Of all that can be done him' (ll. 22–3), his term 'unworthily' resonates suspiciously.

With Lady Rutland there is clearer evidence that Jonson had engaged in a brief flirtation, despite the correctness of his two poems to her. Her husband, Roger Manners, proved impotent, and in the 1616 Folio Jonson tactfully cancelled the ending of his first epistle (*For.* XII, written a few months after her marriage), where he wishes that she might bear a son. His *Underwoods* L, 'An Epigram. To the Honoured –, Countess of –', written some time before her husband's death in 1612, praises her as a new Penelope, living chastely as 'a widowed wife' and thereby shunning even the suspicion of ill-doing while her husband is abroad. Nevertheless, the *Conversations with Drummond* contains two interesting entries concerning his relationship with the Countess. The first reports that 'Sir Th. Overbury was in love with her, and caused Ben to read his "Wife" to her, which he, with an excellent grace, did, and praised the author. That the morn thereafter he discorded with Overbury, who would have him to intend a suit that was unlawful. The lines my lady kept in remembrance, "He comes too near, who comes to be denied"' (ll. 205–12). This incident may be the reason why 'Overbury was first his friend, then turned his mortal enemy' (*Conv.*, ll. 160–1). Overbury's 'The Wife' places chastity high on the list of feminine virtues: the line the Countess remembered concludes two stanzas stressing the need to act so that advances from men are never even invited.[57] Overbury's belief that such didactic instruction would be a suitable prelude to wooing might seem to place him with Sir John Daw in *Epicoene*, who would lie with his mistress and yet praises her modesty (see I.iii.14), but Jonson's indignation at his request to solicit the Countess for him may have been fuelled by his own jealous desire. In this connection, it is perhaps worth noting that *Underwoods* XXII, 'An Elegy' ('Though Beauty be the Mark of Praise'), celebrates its unnamed addressee for fidelity 'to the love of one' (l. 8) and ends by contrasting her adoringly to another less worthy love of his own. Is it possible that he originally addressed this poem to Lady Rutland? Drummond's second entry gives definite evidence that his relationship with her angered the Earl: 'Ben one day being at table with my lady Rutland, her husband coming in, accused her that she kept table to poets, of which she wrote a letter to him, which he answered. My lord intercepted the letter, but never challenged him' (*Conv.*, ll. 361–4).

All of this may have been innocent enough, but the possibility that Jonson did become romantically involved with one or more of the aristocratic women who patronised him forms an intriguing backdrop to 'A Celebration of Charis in Ten Lyric Pieces' (*Und.* II), where the poet conducts an amour with a courtly lady. The sixth poem, 'Claiming a Second Kiss by Desert', identifies her through her hairstyle as a married woman or a widow and places her at a wedding in Whitehall, where she is said to have aroused envy at her dancing and to be 'more the eye, and talk / Of the court' than anyone else (ll. 14–15). A reference in the fourth poem, 'Her Triumph', to 'the chariot at hand here of Love / Wherein my lady rideth' (ll. 1–2) might seem to connect her with *The Haddington Masque* of 9 February 1608 or *A Challenge at Tilt* of 27 December 1613, where Venus entered in a pageant wagon pulled by swans and doves, but those roles would have been played by a boy actor.[58] Since her name equates Charis both with the Graces and with Venus, Jonson has apparently imagined her in a similar fictional setting as a way of celebrating her beauty, which Cupid also praises in playful Anacreontic fashion in the fifth poem. Echoing the praise of Lady Mary Wroth in Epigram CV, Cupid ascribes to Charis the beguiling smile of Venus, the stately walk of Juno and the wise speech of Minerva, yet his claim that she corresponds exactly to Venus except for her chastity (see l. 42) relieves any doubts about her character. The sixth poem reveals that she has granted Ben 'a morning kiss', but in Sidneian fashion, Jonson's plea for another shifts the spotlight on to him as a witty, but incorrigibly sensual lover like Astrophil. The move to social comedy in the last three poems imposes a tactful vagueness about the degree of Ben's intimacy with Charis, who demonstrates her wit and playfulness by describing her ideal man as a courtly youth entirely unlike the ageing poet. Her resolve to 'rest me where I am' until she finds her ideal gallant leaves her acceptance or rejection of Ben, like her identity, an impenetrable mystery and proves Jonson to be skilful at courtly riddles.[59]

'A Celebration of Charis' was apparently not completed until the early 1620s, when Jonson could claim 'I now write fifty years', but two stanzas of 'Her Triumph' and sections of 'His Discourse with Cupid' were included in Act II, Scene vi of *The Devil Is an Ass* (1616), where the gallant Wittipol attempts to seduce the wife of the foolish Fitzdotterel.[60] Possibly any real-life incidents on which it was based occurred much earlier and were transmuted into various fictional forms as Jonson gained distance from them. In neither *The Devil Is an Ass* nor 'A Celebration of Charis' is the seduction pressed to its conclusion, and we may therefore assume that the actual basis for both works may have been one or more brief attractions that were sublimated into poetry and enhanced by fantasy. What is noteworthy about the sequence, however, is the freer treatment of Jonson's erotic impulses and his closer relation to the court. In contrast to *Cynthia's Revels*, where Crites–Jonson stood in sharp opposition to the shallow courtiers, Jonson is now the familiar 'Ben' of poem nine. Though he mocks the disabilities of his age and size in poem two, 'How He Saw Her', by describing himself as 'Cupid's statue with a beard, / Or else one that played his ape, / In a Hercules his shape' (ll. 30–2), he moves easily in the courtly world he describes. In poem six, 'Claiming a Second Kiss by Desert', Ben teases Charis by making her guess which of his praises is true, as he does again through his urbane raillery at her vanity in poem eight, 'Urging Her of a Promise', where she is accused of scrutinising her curls in her 'idol glass' and of peeping out the window with her 'emissary eye, / To fetch in the [male] forms go by' (ll. 17–18, 22). In contrast also to his youthful rejection of the Ovidian elegy as 'too loose, and cap'ring' for the 'stricter vein' of his muse, Jonson now imitates the erotic geography of Anacreon's lyrics and identifies with the ageing lover of Horace's *Odes*.[61] These changes illustrate how his dependence on patronage would eventually lead the formerly stern critic of court vices into an increasing identification with the world of courtly play.

9

The King's Poet

Jonson's identification with the Jacobean court developed gradually, accelerating after he was awarded a court pension in 1616. Always anxious to outdo his rivals and envious of others' accomplishments, he achieved enough recognition in the years from 1612 to 1621 to satisfy his considerable ego, but he found, as did other members of the Jacobean opposition who accepted court preferment, that reward had its price. In his masques he had necessarily endorsed royal policies, yet as the focus of court entertainments shifted from Queen Anne and Prince Henry to the King's favourites and as the court became more isolated and embattled, his freedom to act as an arbiter of morals diminished. The poor reception of one masque where he did so – *Pleasure Reconciled to Virtue* (1618) – illustrates how a court audience that valued novelty and spectacle resisted his sententious humanism. Plays and poetry allowed him freer scope, but even his comedies were more and more designed for the King's ear.

All this is not to say that the second decade of the century were years of complacent accommodation on Jonson's part. Despite his adulation of the King in his masques, Jonson teasingly criticised James in *Bartholomew Fair*, while in *The Devil Is an Ass* he risked attacking the current rage for monopolistic projects. After 1616 the hazards of satire led him to abandon comedy for a while, but the internal pressures of serving a court whose conduct he often disapproved of can be seen in his remark to Drummond that 'He hath a mind to be a churchman, and so he might have favour to make one sermon to the king, he careth not what thereafter should befall him: for he would not flatter though he saw death' (*Conv.*, ll. 330–3). Artistically, too, he was not entirely in sympathy with court tastes, and his masques contain some subversive criticism of his audience's aesthetic judgement.

Jonson received a brief respite from his usual activities when he travelled to France and the Low Countries in 1612–13 as the companion of Sir Walter Ralegh's high-spirited son Wat. Despite his imprisonment Ralegh seems to have become one of Jonson's major

patrons in the period from 1611 to 1614, for at some time during
those years Jonson also contributed to Ralegh's *History of the World*.[1]
He told Drummond that 'The best wits of England were employed
for making of his *History*. Ben himself had written a piece to him of
the Punic War, which he altered and set in his book' (*Conv.*, ll. 191–3).
His contribution, which may have comprised a large part of Book
Five, has been de-emphasised by students of Ralegh, but his
absorption in the subject of the Punic War is attested by his report
that 'he hath consumed a whole night in lying looking to his great
toe, about which he hath seen Tartars and Turks, Romans and
Carthaginians, fight in his imagination' (*Conv.*, ll. 321–3). Possibly he
also had some part in designing the iconography of Ralegh's title-
page, whose symbolism is interpreted in his poem 'The Mind of the
Front[ispiece]' (*Und.* XXIV).

Unfortunately, his duties as the 'governor' of the ungovernable
young Ralegh were to prove a less congenial use of his talents. Sir
Walter himself, in a witty sonnet, had warned his 'wag' of a son
against death by hanging, and Jonson's report of their travels in
France confirms the elder Ralegh's concerns about Wat's mischievous behaviour. In addition to such knavish pastimes 'as the
setting of the favours of damsels on a cod-piece', Jonson's youthful
charge exploited his weakness for sack, taunting the French for their
Catholicism by displaying his drunken chaperone stretched out like
a crucifix on a cart drawn through the streets (*Conv.*, ll. 295–304). In
a soberer moment, Jonson attended on 4 September 1612 a
disputation over the Catholic doctrine of the Real Presence of
Christ in the Mass, in which the debaters were D. Smith and Daniel
Featley, a Calvinist divine who had been Wat's tutor at Oxford.[2]

Jonson's travels with Wat gave him a chance to meet some
continental men of letters, but his characteristic bluntness may have
startled some of his hosts. Drummond reports 'that he told Cardinal
de Perron, at his being in France anno 1613, who shew him his
translations of Virgil, that they were nought' (*Conv.*, ll. 59–61). His
habit of exalting his own talents by putting down those of others is
perhaps glanced at in a letter of commendation supplied to him
from Jean Beaulieu, secretary to the English ambassador at Paris.
Dated 3 March 1613 and directed to William Trumbull, Beaulieu's
fellow in Brussels, it praises Jonson's 'extraordinary and rare parts
of knowledge and understanding which make his conversation to be
honoured and beloved in all companies, specially for the
commendation he hath not to abuse the power of his gifts, as

commonly other overflowing wits use to do, to the prejudice of
other men's honour'. Beaulieu himself may have been engaging in a
bit of instruction through praise here: a private note about Jonson he
sent to Trumbull a few days later reported that 'what is good in him
I was content to relate, and indeed he hath many worthy parts, for
the rest you shall soon make a discovery thereof'.[3] From Brussels,
the travellers proceeded to Antwerp and Leiden, where Jonson met
Daniel Heinsius, the Dutch humanist whose views on tragedy and
comedy he was to adapt at the end of his *Discoveries*.[4]

Jonson and young Ralegh were back in London by 29 June 1613,
when Jonson witnessed the burning of the Globe Theatre. The
English court to which they returned was much changed. Prince
Henry had died of typhoid fever on 6 November 1612; during the
following February his sister Elizabeth had married Frederick, the
Elector Palatine. The Earl of Salisbury's long administration as
Secretary of State was over; at his death in 1612 he had been
replaced by Jonson's old enemy the Earl of Northampton. The
ascendancy of the Howards was sealed by the marriage of
Northampton's niece Frances Howard to the King's current
favourite, Robert Carr, the Earl of Somerset. The scandalous
proceedings of her divorce from the Earl of Essex (on the grounds
of his supposed impotence) were in full swing in the summer of
1613. For opposing the match and exerting undue influence over
Somerset, Sir Thomas Overbury had been imprisoned in the Tower
of London, where he was secretly poisoned at Frances Howard's
initiative.

Though morally questionable and politically divisive, the
Somerset–Howard marriage went forward under the King's
sponsorship during the Christmas season of 1613/14 with masques
by Campion, Middleton and others. Jonson sent a short congratulatory poem to Somerset and wrote *A Challenge at Tilt* for the
ceremonial combat at barriers between friends of the bride and
groom on New Year's Day, as well as *The Irish Masque at Court*, a
glorification of King James' policy of Irish settlement, performed on
29 December and 3 January. The commission for *A Challenge at Tilt*
was especially problematic since he had previously composed
Hymenaei for Frances Howard's marriage to Essex.[5] His strategy, like
that of Donne's ambiguous epithalamion for the same occasion, was
to highlight the couple's strong erotic attraction through a
contention between two Cupids, who are finally discovered to be
Eros and Anteros, emblematic of mutual desire.[6] The entertainment

ends with a wish for harmony in the affections between bride and groom and in the 'humours' of the court in general. The latter reference to factional tensions may allude not only to hard feelings between the Howards and the Essex faction, but also to the division between Somerset and his ally the Earl of Pembroke on the one hand and the pro-Spanish Howards on the other over the appointment of a Secretary of State.[7] Jonson's tact here contrasts with his accidental blunder in his congratulatory poem to Somerset (*M.P.* XXVI), which wishes the couple lasting happiness and expresses the hope that Lady Frances may 'Outbe that *Wife*, in worth, thy friend did make' (l. 12). This reference to Sir Thomas Overbury's praise of wifely chastity may inadvertently have touched the conscience of the bridegroom, who is suspected of having played some role in Overbury's imprisonment.

Although Somerset's alliance with the Howards and his subsequent appointment as Lord Chamberlain brought him to the height of his advancement, his power was to prove short-lived, and Jonson's next two masques would mark his eclipse and fall. In the summer of 1614 James' eye had been caught by the beauty of young George Villiers – 'the handsomest bodied man in England' – whose fortunes at court were thereafter promoted by the Earl of Pembroke, George Abbot, the Archbishop of Canterbury, and Lady Bedford as a means of reducing the influence of the pro-Spanish Howards.[8] On 1 December the letter-writer John Chamberlain reported plans for 'a masque this Christmas towards which the King gives 1500 pounds, the principal motive whereof is thought to be the gracing of young Villiers and to bring him on the stage.'[9] The masque, unfortunately misdated by Jonson's Oxford editors and most subsequent commentators, was *Mercury Vindicated from the Alchemists at Court*, performed on 6 January 1615 and repeated, at the King's insistence, on 8 January. Chamberlain only found the 'excellent dancing' (at which Villiers excelled) worth praising, but Jonson's invention, which takes its cue from alchemical claims to remedy the deficiencies of nature, provided an excellent backdrop against which to highlight the talents of a new favourite.[10] Though the masque's title derives from the antimasque, where Vulcan and his troop of threadbare alchemists try to capture Mercury, it could just as well have been called 'Nature Vindicated by the Gentlemen at Court', for the masquers are introduced as proof that Nature is still 'young and fresh' (l. 176). The Chorus urges them to 'prove all the numbers then / that make perfection up, and may absolve you men', while the second antimasque 'of imperfect creatures, with helms of limbecks on their heads', serves as a foil to set off their physical graces (ll. 184–5, 161–2). The focus of the text is on the dancers' attractions expressed in heterosexual terms – the 'winding ways and arts . . . Of stealing fire from ladies eyes and hearts' (ll. 186–8) – but the main object of their Promethean theft was the favour of the royal spectator.

James' affections, however, were not permanently alienated from Somerset until the autumn of 1615, when evidence of Overbury's murder was discovered. James appointed a commission of councillors to investigate the case, and prosecutions followed promptly. On 18 October the Earl was placed under custody, and on 25 October the first of his wife's accomplices was executed. On 17 December, after three more confederates had been hanged, his goods were seized. James' judicial rigour is celebrated in *The Golden Age Restored*, performed (as we now know for certain from references in the correspondence of the Savoy ambassador) on 1 and 6 January 1616.[11] The masque's central fiction is the return of Astraea (Justice) to earth, ending an Iron Age in which such vices as Ambition, Pride, Scorn, Force, and Treachery were 'masters of the skies' (ll. 40–7). Pallas' opening speech declares that

> Jove can endure no longer
> Your great ones should your less invade,
> Or that your weak, though bad, be made
> A prey unto the stronger;
>
> (ll. 7–10)

Lacking definite evidence of date, the Oxford editors assumed that *The Golden Age Restored* could not have been written after the discovery of the Overbury murder because an allusion to it would have humiliated the King. In fact, James' letters to Somerset reveal his determination to prove himself an impartial judge: 'I never had the occasion to show the uprightness and sincerity that is required in a supreme judge as I have in this. If the delation prove false . . . no man among you shall so much rejoice at it as I. . . . But that I should suffer a murder (if it be so) to be suppressed and plastered over to the destruction both of my soul and reputation, I am no Christian'.[12] By celebrating James' proceedings against the Somersets and their accomplices, *The Golden Age Restored* publicly vindicated James' integrity and warned his courtiers that 'The great should still be good for their own sake' (l. 103).

James expressed his appreciation on 1 February 1616 by the grant to 'our well-beloved servant Benjamin Jonson' of a yearly pension of 100 marks (66 pounds), beginning the previous Christmas and payable in four quarterly instalments.[13] In a court where few rewards were given without the intercession of powerful advocates, Jonson's pension may have been encouraged by the Earl of Pembroke, who had assumed the duties of the Lord Chamberlain in December 1615. The patent's mention of 'good and acceptable service done and to be done unto us' implies that Jonson was expected to continue producing an annual masque. Even though the title of 'poet laureate' was not used, the grant effectively recognised him as the official court poet. When in 1620 the Dutch visitor Joachim Morsius, an expert on Greek antiquities, asked him to sign his autograph album, Jonson proudly signed himself 'Poeta Regius' – the King's Poet.[14]

The Golden Age Restored completed the selection of Jonson's drama, poetry and masques that was printed by William Stansby as *The Works of Benjamin Jonson* late in 1616. First associated with Jonson as the printer of *Catiline*, Stansby had published a series of elegantly-printed folios on philosophical, theological and historical subjects, including Ralegh's *History of the World* and Camden's *Annals*.[15] By offering his collection of plays and masques in a similar folio format (the first such collection by an English playwright) and by calling them 'works', Jonson was once again asserting that his dramatic pieces were enduring intellectual achievements. He had a precedent for his title in Samuel Daniel's collected poems of 1602, also called 'Works', but the inclusion of stage-plays under such a heading was so daring that it did not pass without comment. One contemporary wit inquired, 'Pray tell me, Ben, where doth the mystery lurk, / What others call a play you call a work?'; he was answered by another, who declared, 'Ben's plays are works, when others' works are plays'.[16] This response catches perfectly his air of confident superiority and his strategy of opposing his own 'laboured' art to the less substantial productions of his rivals. The 1616 Folio was his most audacious piece of literary self-presentation, one that claimed classic status for his plays, masques and poems and presented them as parts of a unified corpus inspired by his high conception of the poet's calling.

Jonson's *Works* included revisions of the two *Every Man* plays, *Cynthia's Revels*, and *Poetaster*, the previously unpublished *Epicoene*, and reprints of *Volpone*, *The Alchemist* and the two Roman tragedies. By omitting all of his collaborative plays and early comedies like *The Case is Altered*, he created the illusion that he had suddenly appeared on the late Elizabethan theatrical scene as a crusading playwright dedicated to the classical unities and to 'realistic' commentary on contemporary manners. This illusion was strengthened by the London setting of the revised *Every Man in His Humour* and by its new prologue, which offered his work as a model of what 'other plays should be' (l. 14). Its opposition between comedy based on 'deeds, and language, such as men do use' (l. 21) and the freewheeling treatment of time and space in the Elizabethan history play continued his ongoing campaign – begun in the dedication to *Volpone* – against the escapist spectacle of the public theatres. He reinforces his point in his closing allusion to Shakespeare's Caliban when he hopes that viewers 'that have so graced monsters, may like men' (l. 30). In addition to Aristotle's *Poetics*, Jonson's models here are Horace, who criticises the inflated rhetoric and spectacular excesses of Roman drama, and Martial, whose fourth epigram in Book X contrasts the monstrous subjects of mythology with satire that promotes self-knowledge.[17]

Jonson's assault on contemporary theatrical practice expresses his deeply-held beliefs about the proper ends of comedy, but it is also calculated to overcome his readers' prejudice against stage plays, still considered by many to be a sub-literary genre. By inscribing on the Folio title-page the Horatian motto, 'Content with a few readers, I do not labour that the crowd may admire me', he once again advertises his difference from mere play-makers for the commercial troupes. His appeal beyond the playhouse to a discriminating print audience has recently been interpreted as a reflection of his fundamental 'anti-theatricality', but one must be careful not to overstate his alienation from the stage.[18] After all, each play's individual title-page names the dramatic company that performed it, and a list of the principal actors is given at the end of each text. Moreover, the iconography of the Folio title-page invites us to consider Jonson primarily as a *dramatist* by giving pride of place to the flanking figures of Tragedy and Comedy, surmounted by emblems of the lesser dramatic genres in the persons of a satyr, a shepherd and (at top centre in reduced perspective) Tragicomedy. These figures symbolise 'the ideal structure of art', as Sara van den

Berg puts it, rather than representing all the genres included in the volume.[19]

It is true, of course, that Jonson's iconography relates his works to the classical rather than the contemporary theatre. The depictions of a Roman amphitheatre above the central pediment and of a Greek chorus and the Thespian cart at the base are the visual equivalent of the Horatian and Aristotelian principles endorsed in the prologue to *Every Man in His Humour*. Presenting his plays as extensions of the classical tradition thus affirms that he has kept the promise, made in the dedication of *Volpone*, to restore poetry 'to her primitive habit, feature, and majesty' (ll. 121–2). Yet while he eliminates fight scenes and on-stage deaths from his tragedies, his comedies are splendidly theatrical in their dramatic pacing, opportunities for comic business, and careful orchestration of on-stage noise.[20] Moreover, as we shall be reminded again below, his deep grounding in the Elizabethan popular theatre is proven by his habit of elaborating on or playing against its customary patterns.

Although Jonson defines himself first of all as a dramatist, his lyric poetry occupies a central position in the *Works*, whose arrangement also defines his various audiences and his relationship to his patrons. The selection of his comedies and tragedies is followed by *Epigrams. I. Book*, the verse epistles and lyrics entitled *The Forest* (after the Latin *Silvae* used for poetic miscellanies by Statius and others) and the Jacobean masques and entertainments.[21] By listing the dedicatees next to the works, 'The Catalogue' following the title-page signals his intended audience – those members of the Inns of Court, the royal court, the two universities, and the gentry who understood and valued poetry. As he had done in the *Epigrams*, he honours his old master William Camden and private friends like Richard Martin before his noble patrons, rather than addressing a galaxy of 'great names' in order of precedence as was customary.[22] Equally surprising, considering his recent pension, is the omission of King James. The King's presence is felt throughout the *Epigrams* and masques and *The Golden Age Restored* concludes the volume by glorifying his reign, but Jonson avoids extreme servility by declining to make him the volume's general dedicatee.

Nevertheless, Jonson's artistic gestures toward independence became more problematic as he grew more reliant on royal favour, and his comedies, as well as his masques, were increasingly directed to James. The major acting troupes had, since 1603, all been connected to the royal household, and they may well have commissioned works with court presentation ultimately in mind; even such a thoroughly professional man of the theatre as Shakespeare seems to have kept his eye on what might win applause at Whitehall.[23] Jonson's ability to write to the King's taste may have been one reason why companies like the King's Men continued to commission his plays despite their mixed reception with the public. Though his satire on female extravagance and gender confusion in *Epicoene* (written for the Children of the Queen's Revels) would not have pleased Lady Bedford, it may have appealed to the King's misogynistic prejudices, and James would have welcomed – if he did not actually invite – the ridicule of Anabaptists in *The Alchemist*.[24] In *Bartholomew Fair* (1614) and *The Devil Is an Ass* (1616) Jonson compliments the King more openly, but subverts his flattery with satire. *Bartholomew Fair*, given successive performances by the Lady Elizabeth's Men at the Hope Theatre on 31 October 1614 and in the Banqueting House at Whitehall on the following day, is the more complex of the two. While it stages 'the zealous noise / Of your land's faction' (the Puritans) for the King's 'sport', its portrayal of the self-important magistrate Adam Overdo holds up to James a glass both flattering and critical. Poet and king are equally levelled by Jonson's criticism, however, for he includes aspects of himself in the play's characters.

Human irrationality or folly had been the broad theme of Jonsonian comedy since *Every Man in His Humour*, but *Bartholomew Fair* stands as his most comprehensive treatment of human nature because he brilliantly exploits the Fair as setting and symbol. Using medieval mansion staging to recreate the annual cloth and horse fair held annually at Smithfield on St. Bartholomew's day (24 August), he follows two groups of fair-goers – the family of John and Win Littlewit and the party of the idiotic Bartholomew Cokes – seeking to enjoy the Fair's carnivalesque pleasures.[25] Yet festive comedy gives way to satire as Jonson substitutes a grainier realism for the 'green world' of Elizabethan romance.[26] His close focus exposes the cony-catching schemes of a criminal underclass out to fleece the fairgoers with gingerbread made from stale ingredients, adulterated tobacco, and ballads that lure victims to Edgeworth the cut-purse. On another level, the Fair is emblematic of the three enemies of mankind (the World, the Flesh and the Devil) familiar from medieval symbolism. As in Jonson's poem, 'To the World (A Farewell for a Gentlewoman, Virtuous and Noble)' (*For.* IV), it is portrayed as a shop 'Of toys, and trifles, traps, and snares, / To take the weak, or make them stop' (ll. 18–19). While Leatherhead's tinselled toys and Ursula's pigs and punks (both 'piping hot') arouse their concupiscible passions, her frothy ale and the smoke of tobacco result in the thoughtless contradiction and sheer irascibility of the game of 'vapours'.[27]

Bartholomew Fair, however, is no simple morality play. The three authority-figures who denounce the Fair's attractions – the Puritan elder Zeal-of-the-Land Busy, Justice Adam Overdo, the magistrate of the Fair's court of Pie-Powders, and Humphrey Wasp, Cokes' irritable governor – are themselves exposed as self-righteous hypocrites. Partly modelled on a Puritan preacher known as 'The Roaring Boy of Banbury' and partly on John Field, the clergyman father of Jonson's protégé Nathan Field (who acted in the play), Busy is a former baker who 'does dream now, and see visions' (I.iii.105).[28] Paradoxically, his railing at Joan Trash's gingerbread and Lantern Leatherhead's hobby-horses both strengthens the moral symbolism of the play and ridicules his own excessive zeal. The mockery of his apocalyptic rhetoric and his claims to inspiration must have delighted James, who had himself condemned reformed sectarians for 'leaning to their own dreams and revelations' and for 'accounting all men profane that swear not to all their fantasies'.[29] Busy amusingly illustrates the latter tendency by engaging the puppet Dionysius in a long squabble over whether his calling as a player is or is not profane. His controversy with a puppet is an effective reduction to the absurd of Puritan arguments against the players' cross-dressing, arguments that are exploded when Dionysius, echoing St. Paul, reveals that like the fellowship of the early church they have 'neither male nor female amongst us' (V.v.89–90).[30]

Jonson's portrayal of Overdo, on the other hand, confronted James with himself, 'but in a way that challenged the monarch to become his own best self'.[31] Like Busy he is a composite figure drawn from many sources. At times reminiscent of Chief Justice Coke, Overdo also burlesques London magistrates who investigated false weights and measures – petty frauds that Overdo, echoing the Lord Mayor for 1614, hyperbolically condemns as 'enormities'.[32] His lack of discernment, demonstrated most clearly in his belief that Edgeworth is an innocent young man debauched by bad company, is aptly symbolised by his disguise as a Fool. His efforts to play the role of a disguised ruler like Vincentio in *Measure for Measure* or

Thomas Middleton's Duke Phoenix end embarrassingly when he finds his own wife has been lured into prostitution. Jonson also inverts the morality play device of 'Justice in the Stocks', used conventionally to dramatise the temporary triumph of vice over virtue, but here to bring the three would-be authorities together for a moment of humiliation. Forced to listen to complaints about his judicial rigour, Overdo's reflection that 'compassion may become a Justice, though it be a weakness' (IV.i.72–3) is preparation for Quarlous' later warning to 'remember you are but Adam, flesh and blood!' (V.vi.89). Converted to good fellowship, he ends with an echo of James' speech to Parliament in 1609: 'my intents are *Ad correctionem, non ad destructionem; Ad aedificandum, non ad diruendum'* ('For correction, not for destruction; for building up, not for tearing down').[33]

Overdo's flattering conversion to principles endorsed by James is the culmination of a teasing strategy by which Jonson alternately identifies James with and distances him from the foolish justice. Though Overdo, unlike James, holds poetry to be a 'terrible taint' in 'a commonwealth's man' (III.v.5–7), his oration on the evils of smoking sounds suspiciously like the King's tract *A Counterblast to Tobacco* (1604), just as his inflated self-image as an authority planning to 'break out in rain and hail, lightning and thunder, upon the head of enormity' (V.ii.4–5) reminds one of James' insistence that kings were earthly gods. Moreover, while Overdo's sternness may link him to Sir Edward Coke, his grudging lesson in compassion may also have been intended for the King, who had burned 'blue' with anger in the summer of 1614 at the leaders of the Parliamentary opposition. For an intemperate speech against the Scots, Jonson's friend and mentor John Hoskyns was still 'a close prisoner' in the Tower when *Bartholomew Fair* was performed at Whitehall on 1 November.

If Jonson's satire was aimed at the King, however, he eased the sting by putting something of himself into the characters of Overdo and Humphrey Wasp. Like Jonson, Overdo identifies closely with classical authorities, speaking familiarly of 'my Quint. Horace' (II.i.5) and consoling himself with Stoic sentiments from 'thy friend Persius' (IV.vi.85). In the figure of Wasp, comically unable to govern the impulses of the flighty Bartholomew Cokes as he is diverted by each new attraction of the Fair, Jonson worked out the frustrations of his journey to France. Wasp's observation, after news of his being in the stocks has reached Cokes, that 'he that will correct another, must want fault in himself' (V.iv.87) is equally applicable to the poet whose inebriated figure was displayed by his charge in the streets of Paris. The theme would have been appreciated by James, who began his advice to Prince Henry in *Basilikon Doron* with the warning that 'he cannot be thought worthy to rule and command others, that cannot rule . . . his own proper affections and unreasonable appetites'.[34] Jonson's self-satire in *Bartholomew Fair* contrasts sharply with the self-righteous poet-figures of his early comical satires and marks a welcome growth in self-knowledge.

Jonson's confession of his own frailty is also accompanied by a new tolerance toward the debased art he normally scorns. John Littlewit's adaptation of Marlowe's *Hero and Leander* for Lantern Leatherhead's puppet show reduces Leander to 'a dyer's son, about Puddle Wharf' and Hero to 'a wench o' the Bankside', inspired with love by sherry from a Cupid turned tapster (V.iii.100–7). Its crude action serves a double function – presenting the lust and aggression of the fairgoers on a yet lower level and contrasting Jonson's own satiric art with the type of 'misc'lene interludes' attacked in the dedication to *Volpone*, plays 'where nothing but the filth of the time is uttered, and that with such impropriety of phrase, such plenty of solecisms, such dearth of sense' (ll. 82–4). Yet coarse and vulgar as it is, the puppet show is defended against the anti-theatrical arguments of Zeal-of-the-land Busy. Jonson no longer makes common cause with Puritan opponents of the stage in order to distinguish his own plays from those of the popular theatre.

His vindication of the puppets, however, does not alter his impulse toward dramatic rivalry. Once again he sets out to 'quintessence' the works of his competitors, subsuming major plot elements from their comedies into a richer and more comprehensive vision of folly and roguery. The inversion of the disguised-ruler motif, mentioned above, is typical of his ingenious toying with established conventions. Though *Measure for Measure* and *Bartholomew Fair* are both meditations on the text 'Judge not, that ye be not judged', he reworks the theme while parodying the outcome of Shakespeare's plot. He thus exploits the appeal the disguised-ruler motif held for King James while reinforcing his Horatian self-image as a poet who refuses to walk in others' footsteps. He finds similar matter for revision in the multi-disguise play *The Blind Beggar of Bednal Green* (1600), a little-known analogue to the stripping of Bartholomew Cokes by the tricksters of the Fair. Written by John Day, whom Jonson considered 'a base fellow' (*Conv.*, l. 158), *The*

Blind Beggar features a sub-plot in which the foolish Tom Strowd, a Norfolk clown, is repeatedly cheated by a trio of cony-catchers including one Snip the cutpurse (no doubt the main inspiration for Jonson's Edgeworth). As in *Bartholomew Fair* the rogues trick Strowd out of his clothes, taking refuge by disguising themselves as operators of a puppet show. Strowd, however, uncovers their knavery and proves the mettle of Norfolk yeomen by helping defeat their scheme to dispossess the play's protagonist, Lord Momford. Jonson finds more varied dramatic possibilities than Day in the devices of the puppet show and the cutpurse, whose part he fleshes out with suggestions from the play book of *Sir Thomas More* and from rogue fiction.[35] Characteristically he also rejects Strowd's metamorphosis from clown to hero, leaving his own Bartholomew Cokes in the grip of childish folly.

Bartholomew Fair, in fact, offers us an Erasmian vision of life in which idiots like Cokes live happily because they are too foolish to feel their losses, while self-interested wits like the gallant Quarlous, willing to abandon his principles for Dame Purecraft's gold, come out on top. As in *The Praise of Folly* Jonson's panoramic scene reveals 'the numberless agitations among mortal men . . . quarreling among themselves, . . . setting snares for each other, robbing, sporting, wantoning', yet like Erasmus he does not abandon his fundamental belief in the ideal of human rationality, but moderates his satire by laughing at himself and by exposing the limitations of the Stoicism he elsewhere praises.[36] If his conclusion falls short of true festivity and reveals only 'the baseness and enormity of our humanity', it is because he rejects the wondrously improbable transformations of Shakespearean comedy and romance.[37] In the Induction written for the Hope Theatre the Bookholder speaks for his maker in asking, 'If there be never a servant-monster [like Caliban] i'the Fair; who can help it? . . . He is loth to make Nature afraid in his plays, like those that beget Tales, Tempests, and such like drolleries' (ll. 112–15). His dismissive allusions to *The Tempest* and *The Winter's Tale* spring partly from his reluctance to gratify 'the concupiscence of jigs and dances', but they are based primarily on his conviction that comedy should offer a critical perspective on every-day life. In *Bartholomew Fair* that perspective is broader and more inclusive than in any other of his plays.

Given the critical consensus that *Bartholomew Fair* is the culmination of Jonson's comic development, it is puzzling to find that it was not included in the 1616 *Works* and not performed again until the Restoration. We can only speculate about why it was omitted from the Folio, but one possibility is that it seemed to need a lengthy defence. Drummond reports that Jonson read him 'the preface [now lost] of his *Art of Poesy*, upon Horace *Art of Poesy*, where he hath an apology of a play of his, *St. Bartholomee's Fair*, by Criticus [his spokesman in the dialogue] is understood Donne' (*Conv.*, ll. 71–3). A letter from John Selden about the origins of the Biblical injunction against cross-dressing, dated 28 February 1615, indicates that Jonson was researching the objections made to actors by Puritans and the Church Fathers.[38] Quite possibly his 'Apology' dealt with this issue as well as with aesthetic matters and justified his ridicule of Busy. That the play was not revived subsequently may be due to its requirement for an unusually large cast, made possible in its initial performance by the recent amalgamation of the Children of the Queen's Revels and Lady Elizabeth's Men.[39] Since Jonson describes it on the 1631 title-page as having been 'dedicated to King James, of most blessed memory', it would be wrong to conclude that it displeased the King.

His next play, *The Devil Is an Ass*, was performed late in 1616 by the King's Men and marks something of a new direction despite its continuity in satiric method. It too was designed to appeal to James while satirising matters of topical interest and giving a new twist to well-worn conventions – in this case from the old devil plays. Rising ominously through trap-doors or cavorting about with fireworks, stage devils delighted the groundlings in popular theatres like the Red Bull; Thomas Dekker's anti-court morality *If This Be Not a Good Play, the Devil Is in It* (1611), referred to in Jonson's prologue, was a recent example of their continuing appeal.[40] Jonson's contempt for such sensationalism is evident in his dedicatory letter to *Volpone*, where he lumps fools and devils with 'antique relics of barbarism' (ll. 73–4). Yet just as in *Cynthia's Revels* he had ridiculed the trite conventions of children's troupe plays by introducing an impotent Cupid to show the power of self-love, so he now parodies the Tudor moralities of the 1560s in order to make a moral point. As he explained to Drummond, 'according to *comedia vetus* [old comedy], in England the devil was brought in either with one vice or another: the play done the devil carried away the vice[;] he brings in the devil so overcome with the wickedness of this age that [he] thought himself an ass' (*Conv.*, ll. 416–20). His unsophisticated devil Pug, delighted by the antics of the morality vice Iniquity, desires to be sent to earth for a day to make mischief, but is warned by Satan that

London manners are too subtle for him: 'They have their vices, there, most like to virtues; / You cannot know'em, apart, by any difference:' (I.i.121–2). Baffled at every turn, Pug hinders the adultery of the gallant Wittipol and Mrs. Fitzdotterel and is fooled by the disguises of the trickster Meercraft and his assistant Trains. In the end he makes an ignominious exit from prison on the back of Iniquity, proving that in Jacobean England 'the evil out-carries the Devil' (V.vi.77).

Jonson's clever inversion of the old morality ending is typical of his parodic strategies, but as usual he also builds on earlier dramatic paradigms. In this case an important model is William Haughton's *Grim the Collier of Croyden: or, the Devil and His Dame* (1600), which depicts the trials of the devil Belphagor, sent to earth to investigate reports of women's shrewishness, extravagance and infidelity. He is tricked into marrying the faithless Mariana, who first cuckolds him and then plots his murder. Mariana's virtuous cousin Honoria, on the other hand, rejects her lover Musgrave after being forced to marry the old Earl of Kent. Though he softens Haughton's anti-feminism, Jonson maintains his double perspective, vindicating the virtue of Mrs. Fitzdotterel while ridiculing women's face-painting, eagerness for luxuries and licentious flirtation through his characterisation of Lady Tailbush and Lady Eitherside; their interrogation of Pug about the qualities requisite for a gentleman usher leads him to exclaim, 'There is no hell / To a lady of fashion' (V.ii.14–15). Here Jonson's satire echoes King James' speech to Star Chamber earlier in 1616, which blamed 'the pride of the women' for the migration of country gentry to London, where wives 'lose their reputations, and rob their husbands' purses'.[41] Yet unlike the King, Jonson blames men as well. His heroine proves to be a virtuous figure like Honoria, but she has been made to dress 'bravely' and encouraged to dream of coaches and servants by her husband in order to gratify his own fetishism and foolish ambitions.

Jonson breaks new ground by treating the relationship between Mrs. Fitzdotterel and Wittipol as sentimental comedy, diverting the latter's attempted seduction through Mrs. Fitzdotterel's plea for friendly assistance and the timely intervention of his friend Manly.[42] Wittipol is initially presented as a clever intriguer, gaining his first interview with Lady Fitzdotterel by means of a trick from Boccaccio's *Decameron* III.vi and successfully impersonating a Spanish lady for continued access after Fitzdotterel interrupts their secret meeting. As in Jonson's *Underwoods* XIX, Wittipol argues that Fitzdotterel's character justifies adultery (see II.vi.63–6), and he woos Mrs. Fitzdotterel with excerpts from 'A Celebration of Charis', numbers 4 and 5. Jonson's identification with Wittipol is also confirmed by his revelation that he once 'struck at Sir Hierome Bowes' breast, and asked him if he was within' (*Conv.*, ll. 577–8), as Wittipol does to Manly at I.v.2–3. In contrast to *Volpone*, where his protagonist's punishment seems to be a repressive response to his own lustful actions (see Chapter 7 above), his self-projection here is a self-congratulatory idealisation of temptation resisted. Wittipol proves a true hero, saving Fitzdotterel's estate from Meercraft's plots. Manly's closing comment on human error – 'we do all ill things, / They do 'em worst that love 'em, and dwell there' (V.viii.170–1) – points as much to Wittipol's switch from seducer to rescuer as to Fitzdotterel's confession of folly. We are not so far away from 'Tales and Tempests' here as Jonson would have us think.

The satire in *The Devil Is an Ass*, however, keeps it 'familiarly allied to the time'. Its ending, where Fitzdotterel pretends to be possessed by devils in order to discredit Wittipol and his wife, flatters King James by mirroring his exposure of a thirteen year old boy responsible for the deaths of nine accused witches. Sir Pol Eitherside's unwillingness to hear the testimony of Manly and Wittipol parallels the credulity of Justices Winch and Crew in that case and perhaps glances at Sir Edward Coke as well.[43] Moreover, the play's sociology duplicates more fully than usual for Jonson the class tensions in Middleton's City Comedy, where grasping merchants prey on the gentry whose arrogance and prodigality they scorn. In such moments as the goldsmith Guilthead's instructions to his son Plutarchus, Jonson's satire cuts both ways, combining the damning admission that 'We citizens never trust, but we do cozen' (III.i.22) with bitter comments on court life: 'There / Nothing is done at once, but injuries, boy' (III.iii.12–13). The trickster Meercraft is no ordinary cony-catcher but a fraudulent 'projector' – an entrepreneur who promised the government and private investors vast profits from new technologies if granted a monopoly. Faced with a growing deficit, the Jacobean court had been receptive to all kinds of projects, some of which proved no more trustworthy than Meercraft's. Though Meercraft's delusive promise to make Fitzdotterel 'Duke of the Drowned-lands' seems like comic hyperbole, the Earl of Argyle and Sir Robert Carr (a relative of the Earl of Somerset) had in fact been granted patents to drain the fens of Norfolk and Lincolnshire and share the profits with the Crown, and such projects as Sir Arthur Ingram's alum monopoly or Alderman Cockayne's scheme to export dyed cloth had recently resulted in notorious scandals. Earlier in 1616 Jonson had been hired to write a show for Cockayne's entertainment of the King; his satire reveals what he really felt about a system in which corrupt courtiers and cunning profiteers schemed to enrich themselves at the public's expense.[44]

The topicality of *The Devil Is an Ass* proved to be both politically and artistically problematic. While satire on Carr and Argyle would have pleased the Earl of Pembroke, it risked offending the Howards and James' Scottish courtiers. Jonson told Drummond that he had been 'accused' because of it and that 'the king desired him to conceal' his discourse of the Duke of Drowned-land (*Conv.*, ll. 415, 420–1). It is not clear from this whether he was asked to suppress the text (which was not printed until 1631) or to alter its details, but his court pension made him susceptible to pressure, and his satire after 1616 seems more and more to be aimed at targets of which the King would approve. Artistically, the play's topicality is problematic because it narrows his satire's focus from the broad spectrum of folly depicted in his previous works. Although Meercraft cleverly flatters Fitzdotterel's hopes of greatness, his victim is not so magnificently self-deluded as Sir Epicure Mammon in *The Alchemist*, nor does the dramatic irony of Wittipol's disguise quite compensate for the fact that, aside from their faddish admiration for things Spanish, the parliament of women in Act IV repeats the satire on the Ladies Collegiates in *Epicoene* without adding much new. A recent revival has proven that *The Devil Is an Ass* can be highly effective in the theatre, but it does not raise Jonson's comedy to new heights.

Whether Jonson himself felt that his comic vein was becoming exhausted or whether stage satire seemed too risky, he did not produce another comedy until 1626, concentrating instead on his annual masques and on pastoral drama, lyric and narrative poetry, and translation. His decision to turn away from his greatest strength is regrettable, but he may also have wanted to strike out in new directions. His royal pension now gave him the financial security to be a man of letters in the broadest sense, a role that was soon confirmed by his honorary degrees from both Oxford and Cambridge (see Chapter 8 above) and by his nomination to Edmund Bolton's proposed Academy Royal.[45] The stage, on the other hand, had always been the scene of contention for him – with audiences, his fellow playwrights, official censors, and 'politic picklocks' who found personal satire in every character – and possibly it was a relief to direct his energies elsewhere.

Jonson's annual masques, of course, provided a continual challenge, but even here he experienced tensions between his ideal of humanistic instruction and the expectations of his courtly audience. As we saw in Chapter 6, Jonson ideally conceived of the masque as an educative ritual, but his courtly audience demanded lively entertainment. Under the influence of French and Italian models, Jacobean masque writers increased the number of anti-masques featuring monstrous or low comic characters, often unrelated to the subject of the main masques they preceded.[46] Jonson accomodated this trend by using two anti-masques, often danced by grotesques such as the phantasms of *The Vision of Delight* (1617) and the bird-men or 'Volatees' of *News from the New World Discovered in the Moon* (1620), or by adding prose comedy like Robin Goodfellow's satiric monologue in *Love Restored* (1612). The contentious Irishmen of *The Irish Masque at Court* and the low-life citizens (a Corn-Cutter, Tinderbox-man, etc.) of *Pan's Anniversary* (1620) are typical of his comic anti-masquers. Like the artisans in *A Midsummer Night's Dream*, they supposedly come to court to show their good will, but their folly and ineptitude serve primarily to confirm the superiority of the court world they invade, and there is no one like Theseus to urge toleration for them. In *The Masque of Augurs* (1622), however, Jonson comments bitingly on courtly taste while gratifying it with dancing bears and an anti-masque of 'straying and deformed pilgrims' supposedly created by the debased artist Vangoose. Whereas Jonson's anti-masques normally symbolise the negative forces opposed to the transcendent principles of the main masque, Vangoose defends his as 'all de better vor an antic-masque, de more absurd it be and vrom de purpose' (ll. 243–4).

An interesting example of how an audience that equated invention with novelty failed to appreciate Jonson's integration of the masque's elements is the response to *Pleasure Reconciled to Virtue*, performed on 6 January 1618. It was the first masque in which Prince Charles was a main dancer, and its elevated theme may well express his sober distaste for the excesses of his father's court.[47] Its central motif is Hercules' choice between Virtue and Pleasure, here represented in its cruder forms by Comus, 'the Belly-God', who introduces the first anti-masque of men dressed as bottles. Having driven off the pigmies who dance the second anti-masque, Hercules is crowned by Mercury, and the twelve masquers descend from Mt.

Atlas to participate in three dances representing the 'mazes' of human activity, beauty, and love. In this case, Jonson and Inigo Jones seem to have taken their cue from Robert White's masque of *Cupid's Banishment*, performed by young women from Ladies' Hall, Deptford before the Queen at Greenwich on 4 May 1617 and dedicated to Lady Bedford. Like Jonson's, White's setting was a mountain from which the nymphs of Diana descended 'to show their defiance to Cupid' (ll. 154–5).[48] An anti-masque of sorts was provided by Bacchus, who appeared 'in a chariot hung all with vine leaves and grapes . . . [and] riding on a barrel with a truncheon in one hand and a bowl of wine in the other' and two boy Bacchanalians wreathed in ivy (ll. 273–9).

Jonson imitated White's mountainous setting and his comical Bacchanalians but gave them far greater coherence, while Jones gave a new twist to the landscape by humanising it. Orazio Busino, chaplain to the Venetian embassy and a spectator at the performance, reports, 'there appeared first of all Mount Atlas, whose enormous head was alone visible up aloft under the very roof of the theatre; it rolled up its eyes and moved itself very cleverly'.[49] The anthropomorphic character of Jones' mountain sorts well with Jonson's mythology, for Atlas was the brother of Hesperus, by whom Jonson figures King James, and the father of the Hesperides, whom Hercules had rescued. Mt. Atlas was also the scene of Hercules' defeat of Antaeus, performed (as we know from Busino's description) in pantomime within the masque. Finally, it has thematic significance as 'the hill of knowledge', and the invitation to the masquers to make its laborious ascent at the end calls the audience to moral responsibility.[50]

Jonson's rivalry with White is also evident in his portrayal of Comus as a big-bellied Bacchus riding in a chariot and accompanied by a Bowl-bearer and other followers decked with ivy (ll. 5–7), rather than as the youthful god of Renaissance mythographers. White's Bacchus and the four modern drunkards who follow him have no relation to White's theme of chastity, but Jonson's plays a key thematic role as the patron of the sensual pleasures the virtuous Hercules must reject. His hard drinking is contrasted with Hercules' proper use of wine, and the anti-masque of men transformed into bottles makes grotesque comedy out of the subversion of human reason by the lower appetites. Their antics contrast with the elevated rites of the masque proper, whose participants are instructed as they are led through their dances by Daedalus.

Though much admired by modern critics for its skilful integration of dancing, spectacle, and poetic fable, *Pleasure Reconciled to Virtue* was not well received by its Jacobean audience. The King, irritated by the lagging steps of the dancers, complained loudly until appeased by Buckingham's capers. Other spectators, failing to appreciate Jonson's artful elaboration of White's model, objected that his invention was stale. Chamberlain found 'nothing in it extraordinary', and Nathaniel Brent wrote, 'The mask on Twelfth Night is not commended of any. The poet is grown so dull that his devise is not worthy the relating . . . divers think fit he should return to his old trade of bricklaying again'. For the repeat performance before the Queen on Shrove Tuesday, Jonson won over some critics, though not all, by adding quarrelsome Welshmen in place of the anti-masque of Comus; their only link to the occasion is the fact that Charles was Prince of Wales, but their ethnic humour was more to the court's taste.[51] With considerable irony Jonson has one of them ask, 'Is not better this now than pigmies? This is men, this is no monsters' (ll. 295–6).

Jonson's activities in the spring of 1618 are obscure, but the unenthusiastic reception given *Pleasure Reconciled to Virtue* apparently led him to try his fortunes in the north. When King James visited Scotland in May of 1617, Jonson resolved to walk to Edinburgh and back 'for his profit'.[52] In the summer of 1618 he finally set out, inspiring Sir Francis Bacon to jest that 'he loved not to see Poesy go on other feet than poetical dactylus and spondaius' (*Conv.*, ll. 334–6). His mode of travel did penance for his own habitual choice of pleasure over virtue. Swollen by sack and the ample fare of a pensioner's table he had grown to Gargantuan proportions, weighing 'twenty stone within two pound' – about two-hundred eighty pounds (*Und.* LVI, l. 11). In 'My Picture Left in Scotland' (*Und.* IX) he plays wittily on the possibility that the sight of his 'mountain belly' and his 'rocky face' had stopped his mistress' ears against his courtship, and in his 'Epistle. To My Lady Covell', quoted above, he jokes with Falstaffian self-exaggeration about breaking chairs and cracking coaches. Yet despite his girth he was still vigorous enough for an extended walking tour. He remained in Scotland four months, visiting Loch Lomond, stopping twice at Leith, and being feasted by the Edinburgh town fathers, who made him a burgess and guild-brother.[53] At the beginning of January he spent several weeks with William Drummond of Hawthornden, consuming his host's wine, gossipping and talking poetry.

Jonson's visit with Drummond was the encounter of two men divided by a common interest. Author of a panegyric celebrating James' visit to Scotland, a funeral elegy on the death of Prince Henry and a volume of sonnets, madrigals and epigrams, Drummond was, along with his friends Sir William Alexander and Sir Robert Ayton, one of the leading Scottish poets of his day and widely read in French, Italian and English literature.[54] Through Alexander, resident in London, he was also in touch with the English literary scene and had corresponded with Michael Drayton. Expecting, no doubt, to find a kindred spirit in Jonson, he discovered that their tastes were diametrically opposed. Although Jonson praised his poem 'Forth Feasting', his censure of Drummond's verses was 'that they were all good . . . save that they smelled too much of the Schools' (*Conv.*, ll. 94–6). Whereas Drummond was a disciple of Petrarch, Jonson 'cursed Petrarch for redacting verses to sonnets' (l. 51). Drummond accounted Daniel second to none 'for sweetness in rhyming' and judged Drayton's *Polyolbion* 'one of the smoothest poems I have seen in English', but Jonson dismissed Daniel as 'no poet' (l. 22) and reported that Drayton 'feared him, and he esteemed not of him' (l. 142). Finally, while Jonson considered John Donne 'the first poet in the world in some things' (ll. 101–2), Drummond disliked his metaphysical style and rated him as inferior to Sidney and Alexander, though he conceded that he was best at 'Anacreontics'.[55] These differences provide the context for Drummond's 'character' of his guest, in which he struggles to maintain his objectivity:

> He is a great lover and praiser of himself, a contemner and scorner of others, given rather to lose a friend than a jest, jealous of every word and action of those about him (especially after drink, which is one of the elements in which he liveth), a dissembler of ill parts which reign in him, a bragger of some good that he wanteth, thinketh nothing well but what either he himself or some of his friends and countrymen hath said or done, he is passionately kind and angry, careless either to gain or keep, vindictive, but, if he be well answered, at himself. (ll. 682–91)

Despite his reservations, however, Drummond was too diplomatic to offend such a well-placed celebrity; writing Jonson after he left, he asked to be put 'in the calendar of those that love you' and reported, 'I have heard from court, that the late mask was not so approved of the King, as in former times, and that your absence was regret[t]ed'.[56] Jonson had revealed to him that 'he hath intention to write a fisher or pastoral play, and set the stage of it in the Lomond Lake' and that 'he is to write his foot pilgrimage hither, and to call it a discovery' (ll. 407–8, 411–12). In the exchange of correspondence that followed Drummond helpfully provided information for both projects, which had already caught the interest of King James.

Jonson left Scotland on 25 January 1619, returning once again to a changing political scene. On 2 March Queen Anne died; the dissolution of her household left a vacuum that was filled by the family of George Villiers. Now Marquis of Buckingham and Lord Admiral, Villiers was the dominant figure at the late Jacobean court, having broken the power of the Howards, asserted his independence from the lords that promoted him and driven off other youthful rivals. More actively involved in government than James' other favourites, Buckingham worked for reform in the royal household and the navy, but he also centralised patronage, demanding total commitment from his clients and opposing any faction unwilling to co-exist with him. His many relatives shared in his bounty, benefiting from marriages, titles, appointments and monopolies.[57] Less haughty than Carr, he affirmed his dependence on the King, whose preoccupation with his newly ennobled favourite explains why Jonson's masques in this period are rituals in which James contemplates the glories of his creation as his creatures express their devotion to him. Thus in *News from the New World* (January 1620) the Herald introduces the masquers to him as 'a race of your own, formed, animated, lightened and heightened by you' (ll. 274–5), while in *Pan's Anniversary* (19 June 1620, James' birthday) the masquers' descent is followed by a 'hymn' beginning, 'Pan is our all, by him we breathe, we live, / We move, we are' (ll. 170–1). It is unclear whether the impetus for such rhetoric came from James or Buckingham, but Jonson's function here is not so much to instruct the court as to celebrate the mysteries of royal favour.

There is no better index of Jonson's changing role than his masque *The Gypsies Metamorphosed*, written for Buckingham's entertainment of the King at Burley-on-the-Hill on 3 August 1621. So well-received that it was repeated again on 5 August at Belvoir Castle and in September at Windsor Palace, it cast Buckingham and six of his relatives or close associates as gypsies who tell the fortunes of the King and the assembled guests, dance with country folk whose pockets they seem to pick, and then reappear in their own persons

for speeches and songs of homage to James. From a modern
perspective the portrayal of the Buckingham clan as a troop of
thieving gypsies resonates with the ironic awareness that they were
enriched with grants and monopolies at the country's expense, and
Jonson's fiction has accordingly been read as covert criticism.[58] His
concept, however, was not original, but offers yet another instance
of his adaptation of a previous model, in this case an entertainment
quite possibly written by Thomas Campion for presentation to
James at Brougham Castle in August 1617. Only its songs survive,
but their lyrics indicate that it, too, featured singers costumed as
gypsies, an anti-masque of clownish lovers and a song of prophecy
praising James.[59] Blending thieves' cant lifted from Dekker's
Lanthorn and Candlelight with the zesty roguery attributed to
gypsies in Middleton's *More Dissemblers Besides Women* (c. 1615),
Jonson embellished the basic elements of Campion's masque into an
artful bit of coterie theatre, full of private jokes and salty humour, to
highlight Buckingham's skills as a performer and present him to the
King (and at Windsor to the court at large) as a grateful client.

A revisionist reading of the masque, in fact, has argued that
potential ironies in the gypsy motif are carefully contained by
Buckingham's submission to James, whose 'high bounty' he
acknowledges as the source of his own fortune (ll. 323–40).[60]
Despite their entry with stolen poultry and their seeming robbery of
the rustics, the Buckinghamites prove 'most restorative gypsies'
when the Patrico's legerdemain reveals that the clown's lost
treasures have merely shifted places. Metamorphosed back into
their own shapes at the end, they show themselves 'true men' by
lauding the King's virtues. In the Windsor version their fortune-
telling, which had previously been given over to playful flattery of
the ladies present, is directed to familiar praise of the King's chief
officers. Whether this should be taken as Buckingham's effort to
gain support after indirect attacks on him in the Parliament of 1621
or as Jonson's own humanist advice, the fortunes stress the
importance of integrity, concern for public welfare and nobility
based on goodness. Jonson's personal judgement can perhaps be
seen in their individual shadings – his praise of Pembroke's skill
with the sword and the pen, for example, is much more substantial
than the joking about the Marquis of Hamilton's wenching. Any
oblique instruction, however, is a minor part of the masque. Its jests
are not subversive, but calculated to appeal to the King's earthy
sense of humour. Both 'The Ballad of Cock-Lorel', a scatological just-

so story of how the Derbyshire peak came to be known as Devil's Arse, and 'The Blessing of the King's Senses' in the Windsor version contain satire on various 'estates', yet as Martin Butler points out, it is satire 'adapted to the outlook of a king who was hostile to the growth of the London world of fashion and anxious about collisions of interest between metropolitan power and royal authority'.[61] 'The Blessing of the King's Senses' charms him against such personal dislikes as women in masculine clothes, noisy lawyers, pork and tobacco. Buckingham and Jonson knew how to put their master into a good mood.

Buckingham paid Jonson one hundred pounds for *The Gypsies Metamorphosed*; it pleased the King so much that he was also granted the reversion to the office of the Master of the Revels and was rumoured (falsely) to have had his pension increased.[62] The masque's widespread popularity in court circles is attested by the many surviving manuscript copies of the fortunes and 'The Ballad of Cock-Lorel'.[63] However, a parody of 'The Blessing of the King's Senses' that was also widely circulated shows how little Jonson's masque represented the mood of the country at large. Written from a militantly Protestant point of view, the parody attacks 'jests prophane and flatterers' tongues', bribery, social injustice and James' Spanish-orientated foreign policy, and it condemns Buckingham as a Ganymede 'whose whorish breath hath power to lead / His excellence which way he lists'.[64] Like the Germanicans' asides while Tiberius is eulogised in *Sejanus*, it exposes realities that Jonson glosses over. He was now a much tamer writer than the one who protested in 1603/4 against powerful favourites, the manipulation of senates and the suppression of dissent. Ironically, his earlier attack on corrupt sycophants inspired opposition to Buckingham even though Jonson was increasingly identified in the public eye with the extravagant court he served. Another anonymous ballad from 1621 calls Buckingham a Sejanus while prophesying sarcastically that

> When the Banqueting House is finished quite,
> Then James 'Sir King-o' we will call,
> And poet Ben brave masques shall write,
> And the subsidy shall pay for all.[65]

Though he would continue to criticise courtly manners in his poems and plays, to many readers the edge of his satire had been blunted by his royal pension and his acceptance of Buckingham's patronage.

10

The Beleaguered Muse

The Gypsies Metamorphosed was the last real triumph of Jonson's career. In the course of the 1620s and early 1630s he would receive the adulation of his literary 'sons' in 'the Tribe of Ben', but in general the years from his fiftieth birthday in June 1622 to his death in 1637 were filled with difficulties. At court his position was threatened first by the ageing King's hyper-sensitivity to public criticism and then by the change in cultural styles following the accession of Charles and Henrietta Maria. Though he continued writing into the mid-1630s, still showing flashes of his old inventiveness, satiric wit and lyric grace, the literary methods that produced his great middle plays were no longer effective. His ongoing dispute with Inigo Jones, now securely established as one of Charles' chief artistic advisors, lost him masque commissions and contributed to his eclipse. Never one to take rejection gracefully, Jonson responded to these artistic slights with agressive scorn or fantasies of retribution, straining old friendships and inviting new quarrels with his critics. His artistic difficulties were compounded by such personal crises as fire, illness and mounting debts. The themes of his later works – the superiority of spiritual to physical love, the opposition between a corrupt peace and honour in war, the nature of true valour and friendship, and Stoic resolution in the face of death and misfortune – reflect both his adjustment to the new attitudes of the Caroline court and his efforts to resolve long-standing inner conflicts aggravated by his declining circumstances.

The year 1623 was particularly trying. While his prestige was signalled by the prominence of his commendatory poem in the Shakespeare First Folio, he found himself out of favour at court, and he lost his literary manuscripts in a fire that ravaged his study. To this last bit of adversity we owe 'An Execration upon Vulcan', the god of fire (*Und.* XLIII), a witty diatribe of over two hundred lines venting his frustration and ending with the amusing curse, 'Pox on thee, Vulcan' (l. 213). The works-in-progress he lists as destroyed include an unfinished play (perhaps an early version of *The Staple of*

News), drafts of his *English Grammar* and his translation of Horace's *Art of Poetry* (with a commentary on its relation to Aristotle's *Poetics*), the account in verse of his journey to Scotland, a translation of Barclay's allegorical romance *Argenis* (undertaken at King James' command and already entered on the Stationers' Register on 2 October) and a nearly completed narrative of the reign of King Henry V. Jonson offers these as partial evidence of his 'mastery in the arts', though he admits in 'An Execration' that they were not sufficient to form a literary corpus or 'body' (ll. 87–8). Still, David Riggs' judgement that he had become 'an important man writing unimportant literature' is unnecessarily severe, for his activities as a scholarly man of letters helped to validate the status of poetry.[1] His lost commentary on Horace with its 'Apology for *Bartholomew Fair*' would surely have been a major contribution to English criticism. His *English Grammar*, later rewritten in parallel Latin and English versions and perhaps occasioned by his service as an assistant lecturer in rhetoric at Gresham College, proves him a thoughtful student of English phonology and syntax.[2] Along with the 'epic poem entitled *Herologia*, of the worthies of his country, roused by fame' mentioned to Drummond in 1619 (*Conv.*, ll. 1–2), his narrative of Henry V was apparently a serious effort to compete with Samuel Daniel and Michael Drayton in their own genres. The reference to a lost play shows, too, that he had not completely abandoned writing for the stage.

Jonson's complaints against Vulcan's injustice in 'An Execration' allow for amusing satire on the shape poems and chivalric romances he despised, but they also betray the satirist's anxiety about overstepping limits: 'Did I', he asks in self-justification, 'Itch to defame the state? Or brand the times? / And myself most, in some self-boasting rhymes?' (ll. 23–6). Though he expected his readers to answer in the negative, his old friend George Chapman viewed the 'Execration' itself as a 'self-boasting rhyme'. In an 'Invective' of his own he attacked Ben for claiming to be 'most-great-most-learned-witty most / Of all the kingdom'.[3] His charge that a true genius would be able to transcend losses (see ll. 91–3) is harshly unsympathetic to the discouragement Jonson must have felt at the waste of so much creative energy. Chapman may have been irritated by Jonson's resentment of Inigo Jones, with whom Chapman was friendly, but he was no doubt also stung by Jonson's habitual air of superiority, documented in the marginal criticisms he penned in his copy of Chapman's translation, *The Whole Works of Homer, Prince of Poets* (1616).[4]

It was Jonson's feud with another writer, George Wither, that precipitated his troubles over *Time Vindicated to Himself and His Honours*, produced on 6 January 1622/3. One of the school of Spenserian poets influenced by the tradition of Protestant apocalypticism, Wither had been imprisoned in 1614 for his satire *Abuses Stripped and Whipped* and again in 1621 for criticism of the King's overtures toward Spain. Jonson was not automatically hostile to the Spenserian poets: he had written commendatory poems to Christopher Brooke's *The Ghost of Richard the Third* (1614) and William Browne's *Britannia's Pastorals. The Second Book* (1616), and he may privately have approved of their protests against court corruption and the abuse of power.[5] Wither, however, earned Jonson's contempt for his flaccid, sing-song couplets, his flagrant appeal to a mass audience (he boasted that *Wither's Motto* [1621] sold over thirty thousand copies), and his pretension to be the Juvenal of the times. Since Wither was in disfavour, he may have seemed to be a safe target, but Jonson's clever parody of his verse only angered the King, who had tried unsuccessfully to suppress debate about 'matters of state'. The newsletter writer John Chamberlain reported, 'Ben Jonson they say is like to hear of it on both sides of the head [that is, to lose his ears for libel] for personating George Wither, a poet or poetaster as he terms him, as hunting after fame by being a Chronomastix or whipper of the time, which is become so tender an argument that it must not be touched either in jest or earnest'.[6] The incident illustrates once again Jonson's irrepressible satiric impulse and the quirky nature of Jacobean censorship.

Jonson's argument proved 'tender' because James was under increasing pressure from militant Protestants in Parliament to abandon his plans for a Spanish marriage and to send troops to the defence of his son-in-law the Elector Palatine, defeated and forced into exile by Hapsburg powers after accepting the throne of Bavaria from its Protestant subjects in 1618. Eager to play the role of peacemaker in Europe by marrying Charles to a Catholic princess, James was unwilling to take England into a land war it could not afford, but his caution was viewed as a betrayal of the faith by zealous Calvinists. Jonson, who told Drummond he was 'for any religion, as being versed in both' (*Conv.*, l. 692), had little sympathy with Protestant militancy, though his aggressive temperament and pride in his own soldiering led him to regard military valour highly.

His conflicted attitudes thus made it possible for him to shift his position without a complete loss of integrity as court policy altered during the 1620s.

One reason for the opposition's jibes at 'poet Ben' quoted at the end of the last chapter may have been that his 'brave masques' glorified the King's pacifism. As Graham Parry notes, 'the firm images of Roman authority' in *The Masque of Augurs* (6 January and 5/6 May 1622), written to celebrate the completion of Inigo Jones' classically inspired Banqueting House at Whitehall, 'ratified James' policy of non-intervention', while *Time Vindicated* urges the masquers to substitute the pleasures of the chase for military pursuits: 'Turn hunters then / ... But not of men' (ll. 420–2).[7] James' role in knitting 'the wished peace of Europe' is also a theme of *Underwoods* XLVIII, 'The Dedication of the King's New Cellar. To Bacchus', and in 'An Execration' Vulcan's patronage of weapons and explosives makes him unwelcome at the Jacobean court (see ll. 197–212).

Although James maintained hopes of resolving the European crisis diplomatically, the return of Prince Charles and Buckingham from Spain without the Infanta occasioned widespread public rejoicing and shifted policy toward diversionary attacks against Spain and a French match for Charles.[8] Jonson's reluctant acceptance of a more war-like policy, perhaps influenced by his connection with the Earl of Pembroke (one of the leading Protestant lords), is evidenced in *Underwoods* XLVII, 'An Epistle answering to One that Asked to Be Sealed of the Tribe of Ben'. Written sometime in the autumn of 1623, it expresses his indifference to current events in Europe but concedes that 'if for honour, we must draw the sword, / And force back that, which will not be restored', he will volunteer 'To live, or fall, a carcass in the cause' (ll. 39–42). Traces of popular anti-Spanish sentiment are evident in his references to Charles' escape from the sirens of Celtiberia in *Neptune's Triumph for the Return of Albion*, intended for performance on Twelfth Night 1624. Because of objections from the Spanish ambassador, it was never staged but revised the following year as *The Fortunate Isles and Their Union*, with new allusions to the projected marriage of Charles and Princess Henrietta Maria of France. 'A Speech according to Horace' (*Und.* XLIV), written after the defeats of English-backed forces in the Low Countries in 1625, is an ironic comment on the decline of English heroism, heaping mock praise on the citizen-soldiers of the Honourable Artillery Company of London, but directing its most biting criticism toward England's 'tempestuous grandlings' – the nobility who have fallen away from their traditional leadership 'in politic and militar' affairs' (ll. 60, 64). Jonson's satire on these 'carcasses of honour' – mere 'tailor's blocks, / Covered with tissue' – anticipates the disillusioned tone of 'An Epistle to a Friend, to Persuade Him to the Wars' (*Und.* XV), a powerful diatribe against the vices of 'soft peace' that was written, or at least revised, in 1629. Its pessimistic vision of a corrupted society may be partly a reaction to the failure of the English expedition to the Isle of Rhé, which Jonson had supported two years earlier when endorsing Drayton's *The Battle of Agincourt* as 'a catechism to fight'.[9]

Despite their political orientation, a recurring subtext in many of these works from the mid-1620s is Jonson's conflict with Inigo Jones, which broke out again when Jonson was excluded from planning for the Infanta's reception in June 1623. Ill-feeling between them had apparently festered since Jonson satirised Jones in his *Epigrams* (see above, Chapter 7), and their frequent collaboration on court masques served only to increase their professional rivalry and personal dislike. According to a passage in Selden's *Table Talk*, the puppet-master Lantern Leatherhead in *Bartholomew Fair* was either originally named Inigo Lanthorn or understood by Jonson's friends to be a portrait of Jones, the intended effect being to belittle his expertise in the theatrical and scenic arts.[10] Jonson stopped mentioning him in the printed texts of his masques, and 'he said to Prince Charles . . . that when he wanted words to express the greatest villain in the world, he would call him an Inigo' (*Conv.*, ll. 479–81).

Deciding who is the injured and who the innocent party in this quarrel is impossible, for both antagonists accuse each other of egotism and back-stabbing. In a manuscript poem 'To His False Friend Mr. Ben Jonson', Jones charges him with ingratitude and with railing at men when he was drunk.[11] This old accusation, made previously by Marston and Dekker in the Poet's War, is not without truth, as Jonson himself indirectly admits in his revelations to Drummond: 'Jones having accused him for naming him, behind his back, a fool: he denied it; but, says he, "I said he was an arrant knave, and I avouch it"' (*Conv.*, ll. 482–4). Jones mocks Jonson's imitations of the classics ('The good's translation, but the ill's thine own') and complains that hearing Jonson's repeated boasts about his journey to Scotland made him 'as tired as thou could'st be to go' (ll. 22, 30). In 'An Epistle answering to One that Asked to Be Sealed of the Tribe of Ben' (*Und.* XLVII), Jonson turns Jones' accusation of false friendship back on him, contrasting 'square, well-tagged, and permanent' friendships (this is Jonson the ex-bricklayer speaking) with those that are 'built with canvas, paper, and false lights / As are the glorious scenes, at the great sights' (ll. 64–6).[12] In an even bolder move he satirises his collaborator under the person of the Cook in the antimasque of *Neptune's Triumph*, ridiculing claims for cookery/architecture as an inclusive discipline that draws on all the arts and sciences: 'He is an architect, an inginer, / A soldier, a physician, a philosopher, / A general mathematician!' (ll. 77–9).[13] Jonson's anti-masque was never acted, but he incorporated the Cook's part into Act III of *The Staple of News* a few years later.

Jonson was threatened by Jones' claim to comprehensive artistry because he himself craved recognition as a defence against his inner anxieties. Needing to compensate for his lack of formal education and for the social handicap of his past as a bricklayer, he sought to achieve through his works a vindictive triumph that would confirm his merit absolutely.[14] The intensity of his ambition is evidenced by his statement to Drummond that 'in his merry humour he was wont to name himself The Poet' (*Conv.*, ll. 662–3). In his middle years, as we have seen, he was able to live up to this idealised self-image by transforming dramatic paradigms borrowed from the popular theatre into highly ironic structures, enriching them with many different elements assimilated from earlier classical or Elizabethan treatments of their subjects and invariably giving a new twist to well-worn romance or morality conventions. Even when he did not meet with popular success, he at least had the inner confidence that his plays had surpassed his models, ancient and modern. As his powers of synthesis failed, however, he reacted defensively to criticism, lashing out angrily at competitors and friends who refused to acknowledge his pre-eminence and assailing his audience for their failure to appreciate his art, though it no longer met the high standard he had earlier set for himself.

In *The Staple of News* Jonson continued his practice of elaborating on English dramatic models by incorporating classical materials and contemporary satire. Praised by Richard James, Sir Robert Cotton's librarian, as one of Jonson's 'rich mosaic works inlaid by art / And curious industry with every part / And choice of all the ancients', it combines topical satire on the emerging news industry, a prodigal-son plot with a twist of intrigue and an allegorical representation of wealth derived from Aristophanes, Lucian and the English moralities.[15] Once again Jonson attempts to extract the quintessence from previous versions of his theme (in this case the right use of riches as contrasted with prodigality and miserliness), but he is no longer able to assimilate his various materials into a coherent whole.

Some of the play's problems are due to its divided focus on wealth and on news. The 'staple' or commercial office where news is registered and sold should be the play's magnetic centre, but since it is only one of many contenders to attract Pecunia (or money), it cannot play as pivotal a role as do the alchemist's shop or Bartholomew Fair in their respective plays. Like the projected office of dependences (that is, quarrels awaiting settlement) and the register for cosmetics ridiculed in *The Devil Is an Ass* (see III.iv and v), it satirises the Jacobean tendency to organise economic activity in licensed monopolies. Its master Cymbal opposes the printing of news on the grounds that then 'it leaves . . . to be news' (I.v.48), but the arrangement of the office and the many references to printers like Nathaniel Butter and Thomas Archer indicate that it is in fact a caricature both of the commercial syndicate formed in 1622 to publish newsbooks and of Matthew de Quester's newly-established post office, where letters were registered for delivery overseas.[16]

Jonson's satire on the news industry is partially recycled from his masque *News from the New World Discovered in the Moon* (1620), in which the anti-masque is introduced by a debate between a Printer, a Chronicler and a Factor (or private newsletter writer). The Factor's disclosure that he has 'friends of all ranks and religions, for which . . . I have my Puritan news, my Protestant news and my Pontifical news' (ll. 36–9) links the rage for news to public anxiety about the progress of the religious wars on the continent. The satiric strategy here, as in *The Staple of News* where Cymbal's office records such improbabilities as the election of the King of Spain to the Papacy (see III.ii.21), is to discredit the popular newsbooks that fuelled demands for English intervention abroad by implying that current news reports were merely wild rumours or old fictions recycled by profiteering printers. Like the opposition between true Fame and the Curious (grotesquely depicted as the Eyed, the Eared and the Nosed) in *Time Vindicated to Himself and His Honours*, the satire in *News from the New World* and *The Staple of News* supported King James' ban on public discussions of foreign policy.[17] It was, however, easy for Jonson to accept such matters as 'mysteries of state' beyond the reach of common understanding because his Erasmian humanism was grounded in Platonic distinctions between the few and the many, truth and ignorance (the basis, as suggested in Chapter 7, of his satire on the Puritans). Always alert to gullibility and self-delusion, he found the public's eagerness for news reports of doubtful authenticity to be an inviting target for ridicule.

The satire on the Staple, however, remains tangential to the main plot, in which Penniboy Junior, a young prodigal just come into his inheritance, and his uncle Penniboy Senior, an old miser, vie for control of Aurelia Clara Pecunia, the Infanta of the Mines. In the fashion of Jonson's early comedies, their actions find a choric commentator in Junior's father, Penniboy Canter, disguised as a beggar after staging his own death like the father in the old play *The London Prodigal*. Jonson was also indebted to the old morality of *Liberality and Prodigality*, where Liberality's role as a mean between the youthful Prodigality and the usurer Tenacity parallels the three-fold division of the Penniboys. The allegorical figure of Pecunia, attended by figures like Mortgage, Wax, Statute and Band and confined strictly by Penniboy Senior, may owe its inspiration to the treatment of Riches in Lucian's *Timon, or The Misanthrope* and to Aristophanes' *Plutus*. Penniboy Senior ('a notable tough rascal') is vividly conceived – so vividly that his uncharitable nastiness makes the mad trial of his dogs, modelled on that of Philocleon in Aristophanes' *The Wasps*, more disgusting than its Greek prototype. His antisocial nature finds its just punishment in the mockery of the Jeerers, themselves the object of Jonson's criticism for their 'buffoon license' (V.vi.10), but his supposed conversion in the play's last scene is no more persuasive than the equally improbable transformation of the miserly Sordido in *Every Man out of His Humour*.

The play's main satiric agent is Penniboy Canter, who reveals his true identity as the Jeerers and Penniboy Junior revel wildly with Pecunia at the end of Act IV. Jonson gives an interesting twist to the plot at this point: he frustrates the scheme by the shifty lawyer Picklock to cheat Penniboy Canter out of the trust of his estate by making Penniboy Junior bring forth a hidden witness to Picklock's villainy. Canter's vulnerability to fraud betrays less self-right-eousness than Jonson's earlier authority-figures; as Douglas M. Lanier observes, the son is needed to teach his father 'the potentially reforming power of guile in a world of disguises'.[18] The dramatic effect of this plotting and counter-plotting, however, is largely undercut by Jonson's failure to reveal Picklock's intentions early enough to generate suspense, just as Canter's attack on the arcane jargon of heraldry, medicine, soldiering, poetry and politics (see

IV.iv) is not sufficiently based on the Jeerers' own speech. The intrigue and linguistic pretension that make Jonson's best plays such brilliant theatrical vehicles are simply not given full enough scope here to overcome the topicality of the satire.

The Staple of News was performed in February 1626, shortly after the coronation of Charles I, who had acceded to the throne at his father's death in March 1625.[19] Though Charles felt some sense of obligation toward Jonson, the new reign was not to prove so auspicious for Ben as the old had been. Shyer and more fastidious than his father, Charles immediately reformed the household regulations, restricting access to his person and introducing a more ceremonious order than existed under James, whose broad sense of humour had been more receptive to Jonson's comic vein.[20] Charles' marriage in May 1625 to Henrietta Maria shifted court taste toward the pastoral fictions and neo-Platonic love theory in fashion at the French court; during the first five years of the reign the customary Twelfth Night masque was replaced by plays employing illusionistic scenery and acted by the Queen and her attendants. Only one masque from 1626–30 seems to have been an elaborate affair; none of the texts was published.[21] The trend away from the fully-staged masque may have been encouraged by the low state of the treasury, already drained by the Jacobean deficit and further depleted by foreign wars and Charles' art purchases.[22]

In the late 1620s, then, Jonson was a court poet without a function and perhaps also without regular pay. Surviving records show that he was in the habit of borrowing money against his pension and that he was regularly in debt. In 1628 his financial position was improved considerably by his appointment as London City Chronologer on the death of his old rival Thomas Middleton. After his gibes at the gulf between 'aldermanity' on the one hand and 'urbanity' and 'humanity' on the other (see *Staple of News*, Third Intermean, ll. 7–10), his selection for a post requiring him to 'collect and set down all memorable acts of this City' comes as a surprise; it was most likely owing to court influence, for it is hard to imagine the Court of Aldermen freely choosing a poet so disdainful of their role.[23]

The year 1628 saw Jonson involved in the aftermath of another event symptomatic of the political turmoil of the time – the assassination of the Duke of Buckingham by John Felton, a discontented sailor, on 23 August. His wealth and many offices, his suspected Catholicism, his involvement in monopolies, and the failures of his expeditions to Cadiz in 1626 and to the Isle of Rhé in

1627 made Buckingham, the Lord Admiral, the focus of discontent in the country. The Commons repeatedly attempted to force his dismissal as the cost of voting supply, and the Earl of Pembroke encouraged its efforts to impeach him until fears of foreign invasion in late 1626 led to his reconciliation with the Duke.[24] Jonson's friends Cotton and Selden, however, continued to be involved in opposition. Cotton's *History of Henry the Third*, published in 1627, indirectly criticised Charles through the analogy of a ruler misled by powerful favourites. Selden read charges against Buckingham in the Parliament of 1626, represented one of the defendants in the Five Knights' Case and researched precedents denying royal powers in 1628.[25]

Jonson had used his influence with Buckingham to intercede for Selden in 1618 when his *History of Tithes* had incurred King James' displeasure, but Ben had been no lover of Parliament (see Epigram XXIV), and he was still satirising Sir Edward Coke in 1625/6.[26] Nevertheless, he must have had mixed feelings about the political turmoil of the late 1620s. In a passage in his *Discoveries* elaborated from Lipsius' treatise *On Politics* he seems to allude to Charles' choice of ministers and his policy of forced loans:

He is an ill prince, that . . . makes his exchequer a receipt for the spoils of those he governs. No, let him keep his own, not affect his subjects'; strive rather to be called just, than powerful. . . Sell no honours, nor give them hastily; but bestow them with council, and for reward . . . But above all, the prince is to remember that when the great day of account comes, which neither magistrate nor prince can shun, there will be required of him a reckoning for those whom he hath trusted; as for himself. (ll. 1562–5; 1579–89)

This may simply be conventional advice in the mirror for magistrates tradition, but it is noteworthy that Cotton, at whose house he was a frequent visitor, thought him capable of writing a poem in praise of Buckingham's assassin. He was examined (and exonerated) by Attorney-General Sir Robert Heath about the piece, which he ascribed to his friend Zouch Townley, yet the evidence of his continuing friendship with opponents of Buckingham indicates how conflicted his situation as a court poet had become.[27]

The strain of this tumultuous period and his examination by Sir Robert Heath may well have contributed to the paralysing stroke

Jonson experienced late in 1628. Hereafter he seems to have been confined to his quarters in Westminster, 'in the house under which you pass as you go out of the church yard into the old palace'.[28] In his 'To the Right Honourable, the Lord High Treasurer of England. An Epistle Mendicant. 1631' (*Und.* LXXI), he portrays himself as 'a bedrid wit', besieged by 'Disease, the enemy, and his engineers, / Wants' (ll. 15, 4–5). The Dean and Chapter of Westminster contributed five pounds to him 'in his sickness and want' on 19 January 1629; his Chaucerian appeal, 'The Humble Petition of Poor Ben to the Best of Monarchs, Masters, Men, King Charles' (*Und.* LXXVI), resulted in the increase of his pension to one hundred pounds a year and the annual grant of a barrel of canary wine from the King's cellar.[29] When the latter was not immediately forthcoming, Jonson wrote 'An Epigram. To the Household. 1630' (*Und.* LXVIII), in which he reminded Charles' officers that the King's fame was dependent on his poetry. Charles was later instrumental in restoring Jonson's wages as City Chronologer, suspended in November 1631 by the Court of Aldermen because he had failed to fulfil any of the duties of the post.[30] Though paid irregularly, these two pensions protected him from physical need in his old age, but his carelessness about getting and spending kept him in straitened circumstances. George Morley, the Bishop of Winchester, reported, 'his pension (so much as came in) was given to a woman that governed him, with whom he lived and died near the Abbey in Westminster. . . . Neither he nor she took much care for next week and would be sure not to want wine, of which he usually took too much before he went to bed, if not oftener and sooner'.[31]

At the time of Jonson's stroke he must have been near completion of his comedy *The New Inn, or The Light Heart* (licensed 19 January 1629), which received a disastrous reception when performed by the King's Men at Blackfriars. Published in 1631 'as it was never acted, but most negligently play'd, by some, the King's servants, and more squeamishly beheld, and censured by others, the King's subjects', *The New Inn* is in several respects a notable departure from Jonson's usual mode of comical satire. It is, first of all, a 'family romance' like Shakespeare's last plays, in which, as David Riggs points out, Jonson atones for his own fragmented family life by depicting the reunion of Lord Frampul with his wife and daughters after years of separation.[32] Secondly, it offers a real hero in the middle-aged Lovel, subordinating Jonson's customary satire to the happy ending foreshadowed by the play's sub-title.

Like the Spanish inn in John Fletcher's *Love's Pilgrimage*, with which Jonson's play shares some one-hundred lines of dialogue, The Light Heart is both the scene of fraud and a place of chance encounters, but Jonson also develops its symbolic value as a theatre of the world.[33] Its host, Goodstock (really the disguised Lord Frampul) imagines human life as a play and sits 'at ease here i' mine inn' to view 'the throng of humours / And dispositions that come jostling in / And out still' (I.iii.132–6). Though the pretentious humours of Sir Glorious Tipto and the tailor's wife Pinnacia Stuff, who impersonates a countess, are purged in the fashion of Jonson's early comedies, play-acting is now also seen as a mode of discovery, especially for Lady Frances Frampul, who happens to visit her father's inn with her friends on a lark. Under the guidance of her chambermaid Prudence, elevated for a day as sovereign over the mock-judicial Court of Love, the romantic hopes of the principal characters are brought to fulfilment. Jonson may have imitated this motif from Massinger's play *The Parliament of Love* (1624), but whereas Massinger's parliament is the device by which his characters' follies and misdeeds are exposed or punished, Jonson's becomes the medium by which they realise their true feelings or identities. Sentenced to award Lovel kisses for his discourses on love and valour, Frances comes to love him indeed, though Jonson creates some dramatic suspense about whether her declarations of affection are real or feigned. The Host's boy Frank, dressed as a girl and married in jest to Lord Beaufort, proves to be the lost Laetitia she represents, and Pru's convincing performance as mistress of the day's sports demonstrates the manners and virtue that prove her worthy – in Jonson's humanist fantasy – to marry the young Lord Latimer.

As a piece directed toward the elite auditory of the Caroline private theatre and undoubtedly written in hopes of a court performance, *The New Inn* both flatters and challenges its audience's values through its presentation of Lovel, described in 'The Persons of the Play' as 'a complete gentleman, a soldier, and a scholar' (l. 6).[34] His discourse on love (III.ii.56–198) is based on Ficino's commentary on Plato's *Symposium* and counterpointed (as in Bembo's analogous discourse on love in Castiglione's *The Book of the Courtier*) by the comical sensuality of the young Lord Beaufort. Jonson had drawn on Ficino in composing *The Masque of Beauty* in 1608; his return to his theories in 1628 was undoubtedly influenced by Henrietta Maria's delight in Honoré D'Urfé's neo-Platonic romance *Astrée* and perhaps also by his young friend and patron Sir Kenelm Digby, whose *Loose Fantasies* (composed in the summer of 1628) defended his passionate attraction to Venetia Stanley as a union of two souls. Once viewed as a satire, Lovel's discourse has more recently been accepted as dramatically persuasive. Unlike some varieties of court neo-Platonism, however, Lovel's leads to marriage rather than chaste friendship, transforming Frances from a wilful lady with a multitude of Platonic 'servants' to one who eagerly seeks his proposal.[35]

While Lovel's first discourse elevates love from merely sensual gratification to a meeting of minds based on knowledge, benevolence and friendship, his second challenges the audience's assumptions about personal valour. As in Jonson's 'An Epigram. To William, Earl of Newcastle' (*Und.* LIX), where Spanish styles of fencing that teach men 'To hit in angles, and to clash with time' are contrasted with 'the mettled fire' of Newcastle's lightning-quick swordplay, Lovel's dexterity is contrasted with the bluster of Sir Glorious Tipto, an admirer of the Spanish duellists Don Lewis and Carranza.[36] Yet in both the epigram to Newcastle and Lovel's discourse, Jonson further distinguishes between mere 'daring' and true valour, which (following Seneca's *On Anger* and *On Constancy*) he redefines as Stoic fortitude – the ability to endure with equanimity 'poverty, restraint, captivity, / Banishment, loss of children, long disease' (IV.iv.106–7).

Jonson is once again playing his preferred role as instructor of manners, judging superficial social codes against enduring virtues. However, Jonson's portrait of Lovel, who is described as old enough to be Frances Frampul's father, can also be seen as an effort to adjust his values to his own changing circumstances. The youthful fighter who boasted of combating military enemies and fellow actors was now a mature man to whom physical daring seemed less glorious as he came to face 'poverty . . . loss of children, long disease'. The virile seducer offering secret pleasures to other men's wives had become the corpulent, ageing wooer content with kisses and affirming language and truth to be the qualities that give the lover 'weight and fashion' (*Und.* II, 1, l. 12). Lovel's discourses may have appealed to the sensibilites of Charles and Henrietta Maria and exalted patrons like Digby and Newcastle into models for the times, but like many of his cavalier heroes Lovel is also a version of Jonson's ideal self, here adjusted to a mature perspective.[37]

Jonson is more frequently identified with the figure of Good-stock/Lord Frampul, the genial commentator on the human comedy whose reconciliation with his family may well be an atonement for Jonson's own separations and wanderings. The surprising discoveries and reunions which take up the play's last moments are also a belated homage to Shakespeare, against whose romantic mode of comedy Jonson had habitually positioned his own satiric realism. Even in his commendatory poem to the 1623 First Folio, 'To the Memory of My Beloved, the Author Mr. William Shakespeare: And What He Hath Left Us' (*M.P.* XV), he found it necessary to make Shakespeare over into his own ideal image of the Horatian poet. Privately convinced that 'Shakespeare wanted [that is, lacked] art' and that despite his 'excellent fancy; brave notions, and gentle expressions . . . he flowed with that facility, that sometime it was necessary he should be stopped', he nevertheless publicly praised his old rival as an exponent of laboured revision whose 'well-turned, and true-filed lines' show that 'a good poet's made, as well as born'.[38] His use of Shakespeare to exalt his own ideal of polished art would be turned against him in 1632 by Dudley Digges, who anticipates the Bardolatry of later centuries by praising Shakespeare as a poet 'born, not made' and belittling Jonson's 'tedious (though well laboured)' tragedies.[39] What Jonson never fully appreciated, of course, is that romance has its own art. The elements on which Shakespeare's happy endings depend – the sense of wonder, the themes of time's healing power and the grace that makes forgiveness and reconciliation possible – are all missing from his own mechanical manipulation of romance formulas in *The New Inn*, where the senior Lady Frampul is changed from a comical Irish nurse and reunited with her lord merely by removing her eye patch and altering her accent.

Whether the Blackfriars' audience was puzzled by its mixture of dramatic modes or offended by its prologue, which attributed any potential criticism to their 'sick palates', *The New Inn* met with such a hostile reception that it was quickly withdrawn from production. In the octavo edition of 1631 Jonson retorted with his famous 'Ode to Himself', attacking his fashionable spectators for 'swinish taste' that favoured 'some mouldy tale, / Like *Pericles*' over 'the best ordered meal' of his own comic cookery. Humiliated by the recent theatrical successes of his former servant Richard Brome, he vowed to withdraw from the stage entirely.[40] Once again his rage at his audience showed that he was incapable of the Stoic calm he repeatedly idealised, and his outburst prompted replies from both friends and enemies. Owen Felltham condemned his efforts 'to rail men into approbation' and complained of his declining wit. Thomas Carew conceded the justice of the latter charge, but reassured him that 'Thy laboured works shall live when Time devours / Th'abortive offspring of their [his critics'] hours'. Thomas Randolph, 'I.C.' and R. Goodwin echoed his own ode.[41]

Jonson's admirers were to prove an important source of support as he came under repeated attack in his later years. By the late 1620s the original company of Mermaid wits had given way to new associates who shared in drinking sessions at the Apollo Room of the Devil and St. Dunstan Tavern or in the 'lyric feasts' at 'the *Sun*, / The *Dog*, the triple *Tun*' described by Robert Herrick in his 'Ode' to Jonson.[42] In addition to Herrick and his contemporary Thomas May (the translator of Lucan and Virgil), this later fellowship was composed of many youthful friends and disciples like Thomas Carew, Sir Lucius Cary (later Viscount Falkland), James Howell, Joseph Rutter (a dependent of Sir Kenelm Digby), Thomas Randolph, William Cartwright and Jasper Mayne (the last three being graduates of Jonson's old school, Westminster). Though most did not aspire to be professional poets, all could versify; many wrote plays. Impressed by his 'full style' and 'strong wit', they modelled their poetry upon his and were flattered to be accepted into his company. Falkland's 'Epistle to His Noble Father, Mr. Jonson' compares his awe at first being in Jonson's presence to that of a fearful fox approaching a lion, while Randolph's 'A Gratulatory to Mr. Ben. Jonson for His Adopting of Him to Be His Son' describes the confidence gained from Ben's approval.[43]

Precisely when Jonson started formally inducting his young followers into 'the Tribe of Ben' and adopting them as his 'sons' is not clear. In the mid-1620s the Apollo Room gave a certain mystique to the fellowship, with its verses in praise of wine above the entrance, its bust of Apollo and its Latin rules for conduct.[44] Though John Chamberlain speaks of it as 'lately built' in June 1624, an inscription by one 'Richard Butcher gent.' in a copy of Michael Drayton's *Poems* (1619) was 'written . . . in the poet's hall called Apollo' on 30 November 1620.[45] Moreover, Drayton's ode 'The Sacrifice to Apollo' (1619) predates Jonson's *Convivial Laws* in describing 'learn'd meetings' closed to 'the profane vulgar', poetic recitations, good-natured jesting and 'flagons filled with sparkling wine'. Butcher's description of himself as 'once his son adopted' suggests that Drayton may have been the original priest of Apollo and 'father' of the company, commanding his sons to contribute ten shillings apiece toward 'sack and smoke'. If Drayton was 'at jealousies' with Jonson, as the latter told Drummond, it may have been because Jonson, with his strong sense of rivalry, appropriated for himself rituals developed by Drayton or turned a common poetic fellowship into a vehicle for self-glorification. To his credit, Jonson did attempt in 1627 to bridge the rift between them with his generous poem of tribute, 'The Vision of Ben Jonson, on the Muses of His Friend M. Drayton' (*M.P.* XVIII).

Nevertheless, the desire to dazzle youthful admirers with his learning and accomplishments was clearly a motive behind Jonson's gatherings with his 'sons'. Falkland says that at first he thought Jonson proud, though he came to feel his pride was justifiable.[46] James Howell reports in a letter to Sir Thomas Hawkins: 'I was invited yesterday to a solemn supper by B. J. . . . There was good company, excellent cheer, choice wines, and jovial welcome; one thing intervened which almost spoiled the relish of the rest, that B. began to engross all the discourse, to vapour extremely of himself, and by vilifying others to magnify his own muse'.[47] While 'An Epistle answering to One that Asked to Be Sealed of the Tribe of Ben' (*Und.* XLVII) requests the addressee to 'give me faith, who know / Myself a little' (ll. 75–6), Jonson rarely perceived how his egotism struck others. Presenting himself in the best light, 'An Epistle' contrasts his tested friendships with the fellowship of those that 'live in the wild anarchy of drink' and 'will jest / On all souls that are absent' (ll. 10, 16–17), yet the line between the 'rhymes and riots' he condemns in others and the revelry of the Tribe of Ben must sometimes have been hard to draw. From a writer boasting of self-knowledge one would like to see more poems like 'An Epistle to a Friend' (*Und.* XXXVII), where he confesses that he sometimes failed to live up to his ideal of friendship.

The most memorable product of Jonson's relationship with his 'sons' is his Pindaric ode 'To the Immortal Memory and Friendship of that Noble Pair, Sir Lucius Cary and Sir H. Morison' (*Und.* LXX), written to console young Cary after Morison's death in August 1629. An illustration of his powers of synthesis at their best, the ode fuses materials from Pindar, Horace, Seneca, Pliny and Cicero into a meditation nicely calculated to address Cary's grief.[48] Picking up Senecan themes that Cary had sounded briefly in his own elegy on his friend's death, Jonson argues that despite Morison's short life 'All offices were done / By him, so ample, full, and round' that 'His life was of humanity the sphere' (ll. 48–9, 52), and he contrasts the pair's friendship, founded on 'simple love of greatness, and of good', to that based on profit or vain pleasures (ll. 102–5).[49] Cary's wish to join Morison in death is tactfully denied by equating the two of them to Castor and Pollux, whose 'fate doth so alternate the design, / Whilst that in heaven, this light on earth must shine' (ll. 95–6). Technically the poem is a virtuoso performance, sustaining the intricate verse pattern of 'turn', 'counter-turn' and 'stand' for twelve stanzas and placing key terms or images, such as the 'lily of a day' in line sixty-nine, strategically at short lines. Moreover, it neatly links Jonson's Horatian aesthetic to his Senecan philosophy through the metaphor of life as poetry: 'her measures are, how well / Each syllabe answered, and was formed, how fair' (ll. 63–4). The Cary–Morison ode is a mature restatement of Jonson's views on life and art and proof that his poetic skills were still formidable despite his recent stroke.

In his 'Ode to Himself' Jonson promised to devote his talents in the future to praising King Charles, and *Underwoods* does include nine lyrics written to the King and Queen on special occasions. None of these is impressive enough to cause the 'flesh-quake' in his listeners that he fantasised in his ode, but they illustrate the challenge of writing court panegyric when the public is hostile. Composed just after Charles' conflict with Parliament reached its crisis, 'An Epigram. To Our Great and Good K[ing] Charles on His Anniversary Day. 1629' (*Und.* LXIV) condemns Britain's ingratitude and exalts the King as an example of faith and morality. 'An Ode, or Song, by All the Muses: In Celebration of Her Majesty's Birthday, 1630' (*Und.* LXVII) attempts to stir up 'public joy' but acknowledges the silent church-bells of her Protestant subjects, who conspicuously celebrated Queen Elizabeth's accession one day later in defiance of Henrietta Maria's Catholicism. In a happier mood, Jonson's last two court masques, *Love's Triumph through Callipolis* (9 January 1631) and *Chloridia* (22 February), honoured the blossoming love of the King and Queen following the death of Buckingham. The first of these, danced by the King and his attendants, figured the royal pair as emblems of heroic love and beauty; the entrance of the masquers drives out the anti-masque of 'depraved lovers' from 'the suburbs or skirts of Callipolis' as Charles had recently attempted to reform London and its environs.[50] *Chloridia* was danced by Henrietta Maria as 'Chloris the queen of flowers' in a setting whose nature imagery is reminiscent of Catholic devotional painting associated with the Virgin.[51] The climactic appearance of Fame, attended by Poesy,

History, Architecture and Sculpture, may have been forced on Jonson by Inigo Jones, who was also responsible for the masque's elaborate changes of scenery and perhaps for the eight different entries of anti-masquers as well.[52] No longer the dominant partner in their collaboration, the bed-ridden poet felt his role as co-ordinator of the masque's various elements threatened by Jones' emphasis on spectacular scenic effects.

Though he had renounced the theatre after the failure of *The New Inn*, Jonson wrote two more plays. With characteristic self-consciousness about the shaping of his public career, he presented the first of these, *The Magnetic Lady, or Humours Reconciled* (licensed 20 September 1632) as the work of an author 'now near the close or shutting up of his circle' (Ind., l. 89). His attempt at artistic closure, however, was hardly a triumphant return to the humours comedy that won him celebrity in the *Every Man* plays. While his characters form a panorama of genteel society, they tend with few exceptions to be pale shadows of his earlier satiric types. Like Fastidious Brisk in *Every Man out of His Humour*, the courtly Sir Diaphonous Silkworm is more concerned about harm to his clothes than to his person and prefers to talk about valour rather than to fight. The garrulity of the Puritanical nurse Dame Polish is reminiscent of Lady Politic Would-Be and introduces some amusing allusions to Arminianism that got Jonson and the King's Men in trouble.[53] Sir Moth Interest, in a new variation on the usurious citizen, propounds the witty paradox that avarice is a virtue (see II.vi); his attack of apoplexy in III.v prompts Doctor Rut's clever prescription for the purgation of his purse. For the most part, however, the traits of the various humours are only described by Jonson's surrogate, the scholarly gallant Master Compass, not represented mimetically, and the characters lack the 'energy of dullness' seen in Jonson's earlier creations.

The main interest of *The Magnetic Lady* lies in its plot concerning the marriage of Placentia Steel, whose dowry of sixteen thousand pounds makes her the play's 'centre attractive'. Following Renaissance commentary on the nature of comic plotting, Jonson neatly observes the divisions between the *protasis* (exposition), *epitasis* (complication), *catastasis* (sudden turn) and *catastrophe* (or conclusion). The contention among the various suitors for Placentia produces a surprising crisis in Act III, where the assault of Compass's brother Captain Ironside on Sir Diaphonous Silkworm accidentally reveals Placentia to be pregnant by inducing her labour.

The discovery by Compass that Placentia had been switched at birth with Pleasance, now her waiting-woman, leads to further manoeuvring in which he secretly marries Pleasance, thereby gaining the inheritance. Compass 'reconciles' the humours in the play primarily by finding ways to buy off some of his rivals, while his resolution in facing down others places him in the long line of opportunistic gallants whose lack of scruples guarantees success in the amoral world of Jonsonian comedy.

Despite its well-developed intrigue and surprising reversals, *The Magnetic Lady* was 'not liked' by the audience and was subsequently attacked in verse by Alexander Gill, son of a London schoolmaster whom Jonson had previously satirised.[54] As did so many of Jonson's enemies, he taunted Ben with his bricklaying, charging that 'Thou better know'st a groundsill for to lay, / Than lay the plot or groundwork of a play' (*M.P.* CXXII, ll. 3–4). Quick to exploit Gill's own past, Jonson retorted with verses alluding to his prosecution in Star Chamber. In the same confident spirit that Martial dismisses his victims, he derides him as 'A rogue by statute, censured to be whipped, / Cropped, branded, slit, neck-stocked; go, you are stripped' ('Ben Jonson's Answer', ll. 15–16).

Jonson's belligerence also aggravated continuing tensions with Inigo Jones, who had been highly offended when Ben put his own name first on the title-page of *Love's Triumph through Callipolis* (published in early 1631). His demand for top billing stimulated Jonson's 'An Expostulation with Inigo Jones' (*M. P.* CXVIII), which attacks both his character and his advocacy of architecture as a liberal rather than a mechanical art.[55] Belittling Jones' efforts to exalt 'design' over his own poetic invention, he heaps irony on his claims that 'Painting and carpentry are the soul of masque!' and dismisses 'his feat / Of lantern-lerry' (Jones' brilliant lighting effects) as mere 'shop-philosophy' (ll. 50, 70–4). His satire evoked a friendly warning from James Howell, who wrote, 'I heard you censured lately at court, that you have lighted too foul upon Sir Inigo, and that you write with a porcupine's quill dipped in too much gall'.[56] Jonson, however, tried to make his quarrel public in his comedy, *A Tale of a Tub*, licensed 7 May 1633 for performance by Queen Henrietta Maria's Men on condition that 'Vitru[vius] Hoop's part' (named after the Roman architect Jones admired) and 'the motion of the tub' (the concluding puppet play) be 'wholly struck out'.[57] Vitruvius Hoop has disappeared from the text, but his place has been taken in the printed version by the joiner In-and-In Medlay, an '*Architecto-*

nicus professor', who stages the concluding 'masque' – actually a shadow-play – recounting Squire Tub's adventures. Like the Inigo of 'An Expostulation', Medlay is a 'dominus-do-all': 'He will join with no man. . . . He must be sole inventor' (V.ii.35–7). Even more banal than the puppet play in *Bartholomew Fair*, Medlay's show reduces Jones' stagecraft to the level of absurdity. Jonson got his revenge by putting it in print even though it could not be played.

Whether *A Tale of a Tub* is an early work revised in order to satirise Jones or whether it was newly written has been something of a puzzle. Set in Finsbury-hundred in the reign of Queen Mary or the early years of Queen Elizabeth, its intrigue plot centres on the pursuit of the country beauty Audrey Turf by the tile-maker John Clay, Squire Tub of Totten Court, Justice Preamble of Marylebone and Lady Tub's usher Pol-Martin, who finally wins her. To the Oxford editors the play's simple characters and representation of rural life placed it early in Jonson's canon, but recently it has been taken as a late product of Caroline nostalgia for the Elizabethan era.[58] Yet as Martin Butler points out, Tobias Turf the High Constable of Kentish Town and his under-officers, 'the wisest heads o' the hundred', are made to look ridiculous as they speculate about the identity of 'Zin [for 'St.'] Valentine' (one of 'the nine deadly Sims', according to To-Pan the Tinker) and debate whether poetry goes on feet. The play's evocation of village life in a pre-Puritan past, Butler argues, is not meant to compare the Stuarts unfavourably with their predecessors; rather, its vision of local authority caught in conflict between neighbourliness and duty is intended to promulgate 'ideas of deference and political passivity which reinforce . . . other kinds of political persuasion emanating from the court' in the Caroline period.[59]

Jonson's dramatisation of rural sports in his late works may have been encouraged by William, Earl of Newcastle, known to him since 1617, when Jonson wrote the epitaph for his father Sir Charles Cavendish (*M.P.* XXVII). For Newcastle, one of his most dependable Caroline patrons, he devised three shows: *The Entertainment at Blackfriars* (1624), honouring Prince Charles' attendance at the christening of his son; *The King's Entertainment at Welbeck* (31 May 1633), for his feast of Charles on his journey to Scotland; and *Love's Welcome at Bolsover* (30 July 1634), for his entertainment of Charles and Henrietta Maria. The latter was neatly calculated to highlight the splendours of Bolsover: its opening song, 'When Were the Senses in Such Order Placed', reflects the decor of the banqueting hall, painted with lunettes depicting the five senses; the concluding show of Eros and Anteros, honouring the mutual love of the royal couple, was staged in a garden featuring a statue of Venus.[60] Jonson also trusted to his patron's protection while taking one last dig at Inigo Jones, satirised as Coronell Vitruvius, a surveyor (Jones was Surveyor of the King's Works) who leads a dance of mechanics. These 'Musical, Arithmetical, Geometrical Gamesters' make comic sport of Jones' Palladian theories of architecture and its principles of 'number, weight and measure', straining the boundaries of licence as far as the occasion permitted.

Closer in spirit to the country revelry of *A Tale of a Tub* is *The King's Entertainment at Welbeck*, which featured a mock bride-ale and riding at the quintain like that used to entertain Queen Elizabeth at Kenilworth in 1575. Jonson had previously evoked the memory of that entertainment by introducing the figure of Captain Cox and his hobby horse into *The Masque of Owls*, actually performed at Kenilworth on 19 August 1624.[61] His portrayal of mummings and bride-ales, morris-dances and May-day festivities echoes the policies of James and Charles, who promoted traditional sports in the face of Puritan opposition. It would have been especially welcome to the Earl of Newcastle, for he later recommended such folk traditions to Charles II as diversions that 'will amuse the peoples' thoughts and keep them in harmless action which will free your Majesty from faction and rebellion'.[62]

That Newcastle was Lord-Lieutenant of Nottingham and Leicestershire and Lord Warden of Sherwood Forest may also have influenced the locale of Jonson's unfinished pastoral, *The Sad Shepherd*, set in Sherwood Forest where Robin Hood and Maid Marian plan to feast all the shepherds in the vale of Belvoir. The contemporary associations of Belvoir castle with witchcraft practised against the Earl of Rutland and his wife is perhaps echoed as well in the figure of Maudlin, the Witch of Papplewick. Because of her role and that of Alken, an old shepherd who is a surrogate for Jonson, *The Sad Shepherd* would appear to be a revision of an earlier work described to Drummond in 1619:

He hath a pastoral entitled *The May Lord*. His own name is Alkin, Ethra the Countess of Bedford's, Mogibell [is] Overbury, the old Countess of Suffolk an enchantress, other names are given to Somerset's lady, Pembroke, the Countess of Rutland, Lady Wroth.

In his first story, Alkin cometh in mending his broken pipe. Contrary to all other pastorals he bringeth the clowns making mirth and foolish sports. (*Conv.*, ll. 399–406)

The Sad Shepherd may also be a response to two recent pastorals by his 'sons' – Thomas Randolph's *Amyntas* and Joseph Rutter's *The Shepherds' Holiday* (both written before 1635) – but as he did in *The May Lord* Jonson rejects the Italianate tradition of court pastoral they follow and instead introduces recognisably English rustics speaking an imaginary quasi-Northern dialect. If *The Sad Shepherd*, like *The May Lord*, was intended as an allegory of Jonson's noble acquaintances, it is now undecipherable.[63] Its depiction of the love madness of Aeglamour, the sad shepherd, and his female counterpart, Amie, marks a new departure for Jonson, as does the uninhibited romanticism of the love scenes between Robin Hood and Maid Marian. Maudlin's malignant witchcraft is portrayed with the same authentic detail he employed in *The Masque of Queens*. The 'mirth and foolish sports' of the clowns that would apparently end this play like its predecessor are missing in the truncated version we possess, but its three acts demonstrate that even in his mid-sixties Jonson was capable of striking out in new directions with impressive results.

The Sad Shepherd is not the only work left unfinished at Jonson's death. The 'Arguments' of all five acts and two beginning scenes of a tragedy on *Mortimer his Fall* also survive, as does the miscellaneous collection of his reading notes called *Timber: or Discoveries*. As we pointed out in Chapter 3, these are passages assimilated from other writers, chosen because of their personal resonance or their application to the Jacobean context; the title indicates their function as raw materials for Jonson's art, in contrast to the living creations of *The Forest* and *Underwoods*. *Timber* at first seems a series of disconnected observations drawn from the classical moralists and Renaissance humanists. The longer fragments on statecraft, oratory and style that follow sound like unfinished essays: a section paraphrasing Quintilian's theories of education begins, 'It pleased your lordship of late, to ask my opinion, touching the education of your sons' (ll. 2024–6). The concluding sections on poets, poetry and dramatic fables show us what Jonson's lost commentary on Horace's *Art of Poetry* might have been like, though they are heavily indebted to Daniel Heinsius' treatises on tragedy and on Terence and Plautus.

Together with the late plays and masques, the poetic miscellany *Underwoods*, *The English Grammar* and Jonson's translation of *Horace his Art of Poetry*, these unfinished works were printed for the first time in the collected two-volume folio edition published post-humously in 1640. Jonson initiated this project by 1631, when *Bartholomew Fair*, *The Devil Is an Ass* and *The Staple of News* were printed in folio by John Beale for the bookseller Robert Allot. Beale's printing was slovenly, and Jonson, who had always taken unusual care with his texts, was extremely frustrated. 'My printer and I', he wrote to the Earl of Newcastle, 'shall afford subject enough for a tragi-comedy, for with his delays and vexation, I am almost become blind'.[64] He obtained some copies of these texts for presentation to his patrons, but Allot seems not to have sold the others, and it was Thomas Alchorne, not Allot, whom Jonson chose to publish *The New Inn*. Thereafter he seems to have reserved his works until a collected edition could be issued, meanwhile arranging his poems into the selection entitled *Underwoods*, a misnomer of sorts because it contains both early work not thought suitable for inclusion in his previous collections and later pieces of a stature equal to those in *The Forest*. Shortly before his death he gave his manuscripts to Sir Kenelm Digby, who sold them for forty pounds to Thomas Walkley, the publisher of the 1640 Folio.

Digby's service as Jonson's literary executor links him closely to Jonson in his last days. Their relationship was grounded in a mutual appreciation of Spenser (an undervalued influence in Jonson's later work), and in Digby's admiration for Jonson's verse, which he read aloud at the table of Lord Treasurer Weston, another patron of Jonson's later years.[65] Jonson had been a source of comfort to Digby after the death in 1633 of his wife Venetia, whom Jonson called his 'Muse'. A noted beauty who had been mistress to the Earl of Dorset in her youth, the reformed Venetia was such a pious and devoted wife that the grieving Digby went into seclusion for two years after her death. Jonson's 'Eupheme' sequence (*Und.* LXXXIV), only half complete, celebrated 'the fair fame left to posterity of that truly-noble lady'. Its Christian consolation, much different in spirit from that in the Cary–Morison ode, is of interest for what it reveals of Jonson's frame of mind in his late years. Though Bishop Morley, who visited him frequently, reports that he was 'much afflicted that he had prophaned the scripture in his plays and lamented it with horror', Jonson's 'Elegy on My Muse' (9) is a confident vision of the resurrection of the just – 'That great eternal holiday of rest, / To body, and soul!' (ll. 63–4).[66] In consoling Digby, he may have found some reassurance for his own melancholy anxieties.

The weary Jonson 'went / Himself to rest' on 16 August 1637. The man who had dissuaded William Drummond from poetry, 'for that she had beggared him, when he might have been a rich lawyer, physician, or merchant' (*Conv.*, ll. 637–9), did not leave much in the way of possessions – his whole estate was valued at eight pounds, eight shillings, ten pence.[67] He had, however, won the age's respect for his remarkable talents. On 17 August the herald Edward Walker reported in his diary, 'Died at Westminster Mr. Benjamin Jonson, the most famous, accurate, and learned poet of our age. . . . He was buried the next day following, being accompanied to his grave with all or the greatest part of the nobility and gentry then in the town'.[68] He is buried – upright – in the north aisle of the nave in Westminster Abbey. His grave is marked by a simple stone, engraved at the charge of a passer-by with the words, 'O Rare Ben Jonson'.[69]

Epilogue:
Sons

Jonson, Thomas Fuller reported, 'was not very happy in his children, and ... none lived to survive him'.[1] He did, however, leave an extrordinary literary progeny, the adopted 'Sons of Ben' described in the last chapter. Psychologically, they had replaced his own deceased children as the objects of nurture and friendship. Poetically, they completed what Douglas Lanier has called his 'self-presentational project' of rivalling the classic authors of antiquity. 'In order to "speak" poetic authority so that it might be seen', Lanier suggests, 'Jonson would have to both displace his textual fathers [that is, his classical models] and position the "brainchildren" that mark him as an originary father' – as a creative force of equal worth.[2] His success in doing so may be gauged from the memorial volume, *Jonsonus Virbius*, published in 1638, six months after his death at the instigation of his friend Brian Duppa, Bishop of Chichester. Though some of the thirty contributors to the volume were Oxford undergraduates eager to showcase their talents with a well-turned elegy, most were friends and 'sons' paying tribute to the figure whose encouragement inspired their own poetic efforts.[3] Again and again they apologise for their inadequacies and declare that Jonson's death robs the age of its wit.

Such hyperbolic judgements must not have been shared by all of their contemporaries, for the contributors are also concerned to defend Jonson against criticism, but the poems in *Jonsonus Virbius* reveal how his disciples conceived of his achievement. He appears as the reformer of the stage, whose work is distinguished by wit, judgement, learning and art (1:90), and as the 'great refiner of our poesy' (3:6), whose language is pure and metrically 'smooth, yet not weak' (17:123). The 'ethic lectures of his comedies' (1:116) are instructive, correcting the age's manners by whipping vice, yet sparing individuals (3:26) and laughing the audience into virtue (16:453). His Roman tragedies portray 'All the disorders of a tottering state' (1:124) in a style so effective that they will outlive Rome itself (8:56–7). Jonson, in fact, is viewed not only as the conduit by which the qualities of such classic authors as Pindar, Plautus, Seneca and Horace are assimilated into English (19:5–7), but also as a classic in his own right (24:87). Lord Falkland, Jasper Mayne and William

Cartwright all insist that Jonson's classical borrowings became his own (16:127–8) and that their essence was refined by his distillation (17:137) or, as Falkland put it, that 'his productions far exceed his notes' (1:102). His judgement led him to weigh each syllable (24:59); in turn, his works require careful attention. Shakespeare and Beaumont may be good company on a winter's night: 'But thou exact'st our best hour's industry; / We may *read* them; we ought to *study* thee (24:29–30).

This praise, which confirms T.S. Eliot's remark about a 'perfect conspiracy of approval' by downplaying such theatrical values as Jonson's skilful comic plotting and his delightful comic ironies, tells us as much about how Jonson wished to be seen and about the nature of the audience he attracted as it does about the qualities of his plays and poems.[4] In effect, the authors of *Jonsonus Virbius* took Jonson at face value as 'the first best judge in his own cause' (15:2), accepting his view of himself as a slow writer whose careful art aimed at true fame, not mere celebrity; as a satirist whose goal was to improve men's manners, not to lampoon individuals; and as a learned writer whose borrowings were creative assimilation, not plagiarism. At the same time it reminds us that 'the Jonsonian moment' was the product not only of Jonson's success in campaigning for the seriousness of his work, but also of the availability of an elite audience like that discussed in Chapter 4 – an audience of grammar-school or university-educated gentry, knowledgeable in the classics, valuing wit and learning and therefore responsive to the allusive, ironic mode of his satire and to his application of Roman wisdom to the conditions of early Stuart life.

As writers the 'Sons of Ben' helped to assure that the Jonsonian tradition remained one of the dominant strains of Stuart literature. The graceful simplicity of his lyrics, the dignified, but familiar mode of address in his Horatian epistles and the inventive stanza patterns of his odes set the pattern for much seventeenth-century poetry. Among his immediate circle of disciples it was Herrick, who openly offered prayers to 'St. Ben', and Carew, who took as much from Donne as from Jonson, who imitated his manner most closely. Carew's answer to his 'Ode to Himself' has been praised for mirroring Jonson's own stance in its balance of 'admiration and honesty, criticism and flattery'.[5] In his *Hesperides* Herrick would make Clerimont's song about female adornment in *Epicoene* the major source of inspiration for his lyrics on the 'sweet disorder' of his mistresses' clothes, and a number of his verse epistles borrow from Horace as filtered through Jonson. Both Carew and Herrick develop the *carpe diem* tradition of Volpone's song to Celia. They both praise country estates and rural life in the manner of 'To Penhurst' and the 'Epistle to Wroth'.

In taking so many different types of Jonson's verse as models for close imitation, Herrick and Carew testify to the potency of his literary example, but they also demonstrate that literary sons face difficulties of self-actualisation as great as those of biological sons. Despite his absent father, Jonson was keenly aware of the problems of rivalling paternal models. In his *Discoveries* he comments that 'Greatness of name, in the father, ofttimes helps not forth, but overwhelms the son: they stand too near one another. The shadow kills the growth' (ll. 510–13). Speaking of literary imitation, he cautions: 'One, though he be excellent, and the chief, is not to be imitated alone. For never no imitator, ever grew up to his author; likeness is always on this side truth' (ll. 1091–4). One index of Jonson's superiority was the great number of genres he mastered; poets like Herrick and Carew, however skilful for amateurs, could only hope to equal a small part of his achievement. Moreover, even a poem like Herrick's 'A Panegyric to Sir Lewis Pemberton', which imitates the details of 'To Penhurst' while praising Pemberton's hospitality as evidence of greatness rooted in goodness, seems a less impressive accomplishment than its Jonsonian model. Despite his artful reproduction of Jonson's manner, Herrick attempts no more than Jonson had already shown to be possible; by contrast, Jonson's creation of the country-house poem was an inventive cultural translation that introduced new themes to English poetry and required an innovative style to express them. Though his own praise of Penhurst draws heavily on Martial and Horace, it transforms the Roman villa of Martial III.1viii into a pattern for civilised living in which unstinting hospitality and the gift-exchange between landlord and tenant are only one aspect of more comprehensive familial, social and spiritual duties.[6]

Jonson's own imitators subtly alter his emphases just as he transformed his classical sources, but we often feel that such shifts result as much from failure to appreciate his example as they do from conscious revision of his outlook. One area of conscious difference between Jonson and his disciples was their greater emphasis on 'the happy life' as opposed to 'the good [or moral] life'.[7] Developing the Epicurean strain in Horace rather than his Stoic elements, the Cavalier poets stressed Epicurean hedonism as an antidote to earthly transience, as in Herrick's 'His Age, Dedicated to his Peculiar Friend Master John Weekes, under the Name of Posthumus'. Jonson may have encouraged this sentiment in his poetical drinking sessions at the Apollo Room and elsewhere, but it is not a theme that he takes up in his poetry. On the other hand, even when imitating forms such as the epigram of praise or the country-house poem, Jonson's 'sons' rarely achieve the distinctively Jonsonian voice – what Thomas M. Greene describes as 'a felt weight of personality, the plain, candid, blunt, but discriminating man, quick to size up, contemptuous of the ignorant or fraudulent . . . alert, brusque, a famous character'.[8] It is this voice that rescues his poetry from charges of toadyism and convinces us of the moral integrity of his praise. Carew commends the hierarchical seating at Wrest, and Herrick instructs the labourers of 'The Hock-Cart' in their duties to the Earl of Westmorland; Jonson celebrates the freedom that dispenses with degree in the Wroth household and judges the owners of Penshurst by their treatment of *him*, the bricklayer-turned-poet and self-knowing glutton.

In comedy also, Jonson's special combination of qualities proved difficult for his 'sons' to duplicate. Some, like William Cartwright, Jasper Mayne or the Earl of Newcastle, were amateur playwrights who produced only a few stage-plays. The most professional among them was Richard Brome, Jonson's former servant, who wrote some twenty plays before the theatres closed in 1642.[9] Brome assimilated motifs from a broad range of English playwrights – Shakespeare, Massinger, Beaumont and Fletcher, Middleton – but the shadow of Jonson on his work looms large. Not surprisingly, Brome's imitation seems most creative when it is least obvious. *The Weeding of the Covent Garden* (1632, revived 1641/2), for example, derives its title from the efforts of Justice Cockbrain, an uninspired copy of Justice Overdo from *Bartholomew Fair*, to root out disreputable occupants of the fashionable new development, and it includes a young Puritan, Gabriel, who proves as hypocritical as Jonson's Anabaptists but lacks the misdirected zeal that makes them ridiculous. The main blocking character, Gabriel's father Crosswill, has a 'humour' of contradiction that opens him to comical manipulation by his other children and is politically significant as an analogue to King Charles' wilful personal rule, but he is an isolated case. Although there is considerable knavery in Covent Garden, it never becomes the universal scene of human folly that is Jonson's Fair.[10]

Rather more successful, both as Jonsonian imitation and as comedy, is Brome's *The Sparagus Garden* (1635), which earned one thousand pounds for the managers of the Salisbury Court Theatre. Somewhat like the pig booth of *Bartholomew Fair*, the London resort after which Brome's play is named is shown to lure guests with asparagus (a recently imported delicacy), wine and private rooms for illicit affairs, but exploits its clients' desires by overcharging. Its owners are in league with Moneylacks, a Jonsonian rogue who also bilks the gullible Tim Hoyden, a clown aspiring to gentility in the manner of the foolish Sogliardo of *Every Man out of His Humour*. Moneylacks' instructions to Hoyden on courtly forms of address rework the tedious challenge at courtship from Act Five of *Cynthia's Revels* into an effective comic scene, and Brome makes Hoyden's folly more absurd than that of Jonson's gulls because he literally submits to bleeding to remove his clownish blood. Brome's two main blocking characters, Touchwood and Striker, are modelled partly on the antagonistic seniors Hoard and Lucre of Middleton's *A Trick to Catch the Old One*, yet they have some of the snarling nastiness of Pennyboy Senior from Jonson's *The Staple of News*, and they are tricked by the young wits of the play in an intricate deception much as Morose is outmanoeuvred in *Epicoene*. Despite an effective plot and fine comic scenes, however, *The Sparagus Garden* seems a thinner play than Jonson's best, lacking the crowded scene and the rich mixture of jargon in *The Alchemist* and *Bartholomew Fair* and falling somewhere between two different Jonsonian models. For a comedy of humour, it does not develop its clever young gallants into the ironic commentators on affected folly of *Epicoene* and the two *Every Man* plays. For a rogue comedy, it is missing the virtuoso manipulation of multiple gulls that pushes the tricksters of *Volpone* and *The Alchemist* beyond their limits as their plots spiral out of control. However, Brome brings the play to a close in a spirit of reconciliation like that which concludes *Every Man in His Humour* and *Bartholomew Fair*, making up in comic geniality what he lacks in satiric intensity.

One further difference distinguishes Brome from his old master – his attitude toward his audience and his art. Whereas Jonson told his audience that their failure to appreciate his work showed their deficiencies, not his, Brome adopted a more humble stance. In the Prologue to *The Sparagus Garden* he speaks as one 'that his wonted modesty retains / And never set a price upon his brains / Above your judgements' (ll. 1–3).[11] To those who find Jonson arrogant, Brome's humility may be refreshing, but it is the product of a lower self-estimate and lower aspirations. Jonson aimed to be not simply a good playwright and poet, but an extraordinary one. His intense ambitions, wide-ranging talent and deliberate art raised his best works above those of his contemporaries, defining new standards of artistic excellence and challenging other writers to grow up to them. It is this achievement that makes him so rare.

Suggestions for Further Reading

As noted in the Preface, the authoritative source for Jonson's life and works is the eleven-volume, old-spelling edition by C. H. Herford and Percy and Evelyn Simpson (Oxford, 1925–52). The editions that I have chosen to cite (see the Preface) offer more compact, modernised texts. A selection of Jonson's works with helpful annotation is also available in the Oxford Authors series (ed. Ian Donaldson, 1985) and in *The Selected Plays of Ben Jonson*, ed. Johanna Procter and Martin Butler, 2 vols. (Cambridge, 1989). Serious students may wish to consult the detailed notes and introductions to individual plays in such series as the Revels Plays and the Yale Ben Jonson.

The critical literature on Jonson has grown so rapidly in recent years and the notes to this volume are already so inclusive that the following suggestions are confined primarily to a selection of recent book-length studies. For detailed bibliography, see D. Heyward Brock, *Ben Jonson: A Quadricentennial Bibliography, 1947–1972* (Metuchen, NJ, 1974); J. B. Bamborough, 'Jonson and Chapman', in Stanley Wells (ed.), *English Drama (Excluding Shakespeare): Select Bibliographical Guides* (Oxford, 1975) and Walter D. Lehrman, Dolores J. Sarafinski, and Elizabeth Savage, SSJ, *The Plays of Ben Jonson: A Reference Guide* (Boston, 1980).

Among books that consider Jonson's work as a whole, J. B. Bamborough, *Ben Jonson* (London, 1970) and Richard Dutton, *Ben Jonson: To the First Folio* (Cambridge, 1983) offer sound introductory readings. George Parfitt, *Ben Jonson: Public Poet and Private Man* (London, 1976) treats various aspects of his personality, artistic development, classicism and social thought, while Katharine Eisaman Maus, *Ben Jonson and the Roman Frame of Mind* (Princeton, 1984) focuses on his use of the Roman moralists. A thematic approach is taken by Alexander Leggatt, *Ben Jonson: His Vision and His Art* (London, 1981) and, more narrowly, by Robert Wiltenberg, *Ben Jonson and Self-Love: The Subtlest Maze of All* (Columbia, Mo, 1990). Rosalind Miles, *Ben Jonson: His Craft and Art* (London, 1990) attempts a critical assessment of Jonson's whole canon. *A Celebration of Ben Jonson*, ed. William Blissett and others (Toronto, 1973) and *Ben Jonson: Quadricentennial Essays* (*Studies in the Literary Imagination*, VI:1 [April 1973]) contain essays of major importance.

Earlier modern criticism of the plays is sampled in Jonas A. Barish (ed.), *Ben Jonson: A Collection of Critical Essays* (Englewood Cliffs, NJ, 1963) and in two Macmillan Casebooks: *Jonson: 'Volpone'*, ed. Jonas A. Barish (London, 1972) and *Jonson: 'Every Man in his Humour' and 'The Alchemist'*, ed. R. V. Holdsworth (London, 1978). Among studies of the plays, Gabrielle Bernhard Jackson's *Vision and Judgment in Ben Jonson's Drama* (New Haven, Conn., 1968) illuminates Jonson's dramatic method. His satiric mode is stressed in Alvin Kernan, *The Cankered Muse: Satire of the English Renaissance* (New Haven, 1959). Three studies that use Jonson's language or imagery as the entry to broader insights are Edward B. Partridge, *The Broken Compass: A Study of the Major Comedies of Ben Jonson* (London, 1958); Jonas A. Barish, *Ben Jonson and the Language of Prose Comedy* (Cambridge, Mass., 1960), and L. A. Beaurline, *Jonson and Elizabethan Comedy: Essays in Dramatic Rhetoric* (San Marino, Calif., 1978). Ian Donaldson's *The World Upside Down: English Comedy from Jonson to Fielding* (Oxford, 1970) contains excellent chapters on *Epicoene* and *Bartholomew Fair*. In *Jonson's Moral Comedy* (Evanston, Ill., 1971) Alan Dessen reads Jonson's major comedies as sophisticated adaptations of the estates morality tradition, while Douglas Duncan's *Ben Jonson and the Lucianic Tradition* (Cambridge, 1979) views them as examples of audience entrapment. Their readings of *Volpone* should be compared with that of Robert Jones, *Engagement with Knavery* (Durham, NC, 1986). Anne Barton's *Ben Jonson: Dramatist* (Cambridge, 1984) traces Jonson's dramatic development in relation to the Elizabethan theatre, with particular insight into his late plays. In *Ben Jonson's Parodic Strategy: Literary Imperialism in the Comedies* (Cambridge, Mass., 1987), Robert N. Watson organises many perceptive insights about role-playing by Jonson's characters around the doubtful thesis that they, and not Jonson himself, are imitating conventional theatrical roles. George E. Rowe's *Distinguishing Jonson: Imitation, Rivalry, and the Direction of a Dramatic Career* (Lincoln, Nebr., 1988) relates Jonson's own impulse to rivalry to competition among his characters.

Studies exploring Jonson's relationships with Shakespeare and other playwrights include: Arthur C. Kirsch, *Jacobean Dramatic Perspectives* (Charlottesville, Va., 1972); Ian Donaldson (ed.), *Jonson and Shakespeare* (London, 1983); E. A. J. Honigmann (ed.), *Shakespeare and His Contemporaries: Essays in Comparison* (Manchester, 1986); Russ McDonald, *Shakespeare & Jonson: Jonson & Shakespeare* (Lincoln, Nebr., 1988) and James Shapiro, *Rival Playwrights: Marlowe, Jonson, Shakespeare* (New York, 1989).

Discussion of Jonsonian comedy as a variety of 'City Comedy' may be found in Brian Gibbons, *Jacobean City Comedy* (London, 1968; rev. 1980); Alexander Leggatt, *Citizen Comedy in the Age of Shakespeare* (Toronto, 1973); Gail Kern Paster, *The Idea of the City in the Age of Shakespeare* (Athens, Ga., 1985); and Theodore B. Leinwand, *The City Staged: Jacobean Comedy, 1603–1613* (Madison, Wis., 1986). London allusions are explained in Fran C. Chalfant, *Ben Jonson's London: A Jacobean Placename Dictionary* (Athens, Ga., 1978). The issue of Jonson's attitude toward emerging capitalism raised in L. C. Knights' pioneering study, *Drama & Society in the Age of Jonson* (London, 1937), has recently been reformulated by critics influenced by Bakhtin and Cultural Materialism. Their views are considered in Jonathan Haynes, *The Social Relations of Jonson's Theater* (Cambridge, 1992). A Bakhtinian introduction to Jonson's drama is Peter Womack, *Ben Jonson* (Oxford, 1986). For *Bartholomew Fair* see Peter Stallybras and Allon White, *The Politics and Poetics of Transgression* (Ithaca, NY, 1986). Such issues as social mobility and the rise of commodification are linked to feminist readings of *Epicoene* in Mary Beth Rose, *The Expense of Spirit: Love and Sexuality in English Renaissance Drama* (Ithaca, NY, 1988) and Karen Newman, *Fashioning Femininity and English Renaissance Drama* (Chicago, 1991).

For Jonson's masques, see W. Todd Furniss, 'Ben Jonson's Masques', in *Three Studies in the Renaissance: Sidney, Jonson, Milton* (New Haven, Conn., 1958); John C. Meagher, *Method and Meaning in Jonson's Masques* (South Bend, Ind., 1966); Stephen Orgel, *The Jonsonian Masque* (Cambridge, Mass.,

1965) and *The Illusion of Power: Political Theater in the English Renaissance* (Berkeley, Calif., 1975); D. J. Gordon, *The Renaissance Imagination*, ed. Stephen Orgel (Berkeley, Calif., 1975); David Lindley (ed.), *The Court Masque* (Manchester, 1984); Jerzy Limon, *The Masque of Stuart Culture* (Newark, Del., 1990); and, for the Jonson's Caroline masques, Erica Veevers, *Images of Love and Religion: Queen Henrietta Maria and Court Entertainments* (Cambridge, 1989). Inigo Jones' designs can be found in Stephen Orgel and Roy Strong (eds), *Inigo Jones: The Theatre of the Stuart Court*, 2 vols. (London, 1973). Mary Chan's *Music in the Theatre of Ben Jonson* (Oxford, 1980) treats both the masques and the plays.

Solid readings of Jonson's poetry can be found in Richard S. Peterson, *Imitation and Praise in the Poems of Ben Jonson* (New Haven, Conn., 1981) and Sara J. van den Berg, *The Action of Ben Jonson's Poetry* (Newark, Del., 1987). It also figures largely in Earl Miner's *The Cavalier Mode from Jonson to Cotton* (Princeton, 1971) and in Claude J. Summers and Ted-Larry Pebworth, *Classic and Cavalier: Essays on Jonson and the Sons of Ben* (Pittsburgh, 1982). Robert C. Evans, *Ben Jonson and the Poetics of Patronage* (Lewisburg, Pa., 1989) and Michael McCanles, *Jonsonian Discriminations: The Humanist Poet and the Praise of True Nobility* (Toronto, 1992) consider his poems of praise in the context of patronage. Don E. Wayne, *Penshurst: The Semiotics of Place and the Poetics of History* (Madison, Wis., 1984) offers a cultural materialist reading of 'To Penshurst'.

More broadly, Jonson's views on history and politics have been considered by Isabel Rivers, *The Poetry of Conservatism 1600–1745: A Study of Poets and Public Affairs from Jonson to Pope* (Cambridge, 1973); Philip Edwards, *Threshold of a Nation: A Study in English and Irish Drama* (Cambridge, 1979); David Norbrook, *Poetry and Politics in the English Renaissance* (London, 1984) Leah S. Marcus, *The Politics of Mirth: Jonson, Herrick, Milton, Marvell, and the Defense of Old Holiday Pastimes* (Chicago, 1986); and Achsah Guibbory, *The Map of Time: Seventeenth-Century English Literature and Ideas of Pattern in History* (Urbana, Ill., 1986). Jonson's works are related to their court setting by Graham Parry, *The Golden Age Restor'd: The Culture of the Stuart Court, 1603–42* (New York, 1981) and R. Malcolm Smuts, *Court Culture and the Origins of a Royalist Tradition in Early Stuart England* (Philadelphia, 1987). J. R. Mulryne and Margaret Shewring (eds), *Theatre and Government under the Early Stuarts* (Cambridge, 1993) contains essays by Graham Parry and Martin Butler on the politics of Jonson's masques and by Richard Dutton on Jonson's relation to the Master of the Revels. On censorship, see Annabel Patterson, *Censorship and Interpretation: The Conditions of Reading and Writing in Early Modern England* (Madison, Wis., 1984); Richard Dutton, *Mastering the Revels: The Regulation and Censorship of English Renaissance Drama* (London, 1991) and Richard Burt, *Licensed by Authority: Ben Jonson and the Discourses of Censorship* (Ithaca, NY, 1993). His relation to the Elizabethan literary system and his modes of publication have been treated in Richard Helgerson, *Self-Crowned Laureates: Spenser, Jonson, Milton and the Literary System* (Berkeley, Calif., 1983); Timothy Murray, *Theatrical Legitimation: Allegories of Genius in Seventeenth–Century England and France* (Oxford, 1987); Martin Elsky, *Authorizing Words: Speech, Writing and Print in the English Renaissance* (Ithaca, NY, 1989) and Jennifer

Brady and W. H. Herendeen (eds), *Ben Jonson's 1616 Folio* (Newark, Del., 1991).

For Jonson's reputation, see vol. XI of Herford and Simpson, *Ben Jonson*; G. E. Bentley, *Shakespeare and Jonson: Their Reputations in the Seventeenth Century Compared*, 2 vols. (Chicago, 1945) and D. H. Craig, *Ben Jonson: The Critical Heritage 1599–1798* (London, 1990). For stage history, see R. G. Noyes, *Ben Jonson on the English Stage 1660–1776* (Cambridge, Mass., 1935) and Ejner J. Jensen, *Ben Jonson's Comedies on the Modern Stage* (Ann Arbor, Mich., 1985).

Notes

Preface

1. *Ben Jonson: His Vision and His Art* (London, 1981) p. 200.

Chapter 1

1. The evidence is reviewed by Rosalind Miles, *Ben Jonson: His Life and Work* (London, 1986) pp. 280–2.
2. *The History of the Worthies of England* (London: 1662), 'Westminster', p. 243.
3. See J. B. Bamborough, 'The Early Life of Ben Jonson', *Times Literary Supplement*, 8 April 1960, p. 225. At this time the link between Brett and Jonson is purely circumstantial; it is always possible that there was yet another bricklayer living in Hartshorn Lane and married to Jonson's mother; however, the conjunction between Brett's association with Hartshorn Lane and his work at Lincoln's Inn makes him a very probable candidate.
4. For this and the other records in this paragraph, see Thomas Mason (ed.) *A Register of Baptisms, Marriages, and Burials in the Parish of St. Martin in the Fields . . . from 1550 to 1619*, Publications of the Harleian Society, vol. XXV (London: 1898). Robert Brett's son John named his first child, born on 23 August 1612, Rebecca, possibly after his mother.
5. Guildhall MS 3043 (unfolioed).
6. Drummond's ambiguous wording has been taken by some to mean that Camden paid Jonson's tuition; I assume the parenthetical addition to mean only that Camden was his schoolmaster.
7. See Kenneth Charlton, *Education in Renaissance England* (London, 1965) pp. 116–18.
8. See Charlton, *Education in Renaissance England*, pp. 41–85; and Joan Simon, *Education and Society in Tudor England* (Cambridge, 1966) pp. 102–23.
9. See Arthur F. Leach (ed.), *Educational Charters and Documents: 598 to 1909* (Cambridge, 1911) pp. 497–525.
10. Leach, p. 511.
11. See C. H. Herford, Percy and Evelyn Simpson (eds), *Ben Jonson*, 11 vols. (Oxford, 1925–52), vol. I, p. 3. Hereafter this title is referred to as Herford and Simpson, *BJ*.
12. No one could be elected a Queen's scholar without having been at the school one year, nor be admitted without being seven years old. See Leach, *Educational Charters*, p. 501. Herford and Simpson (*BJ*, vol. I, p. 6) suggest that Jonson left Westminster in 1588, aged sixteen – a date that sorts poorly with their assumption that he finished only the fourth form.

13. See Herford and Simpson, *BJ*, vol. VIII, p. 547, and vol. XI, p. 207–8.
14. For the possibility that he spent some time at college, see ch. 2.
15. See E. K. Chambers, *The Elizabethan Stage*, 4 vols. (Oxford, 1923) vol. II, pp. 72–3. This title is hereafter referred to as Chambers, *ES*.
16. *Plays*, vol. IV, p. 321.
17. Cicero, *Letters to His Friends*, trans. W. Glynn Williams, Loeb ed. (London, 1927–9) vol. I, p. 393.
18. See J. K. Sowards (ed.), *Literary and Educational Writings 3*, Collected Works of Erasmus, vol. 25 (Toronto, 1985) pp. 83, 96.
19. See Robert C. Evans, 'Jonson's Copy of Seneca', *Comparative Drama*, XXV (1991) pp. 257–92.
20. For a translation, see John Brinsley, *Cato Translated Grammatically* (London, 1612).
21. John Sargeaunt, *Annals of Westminster School* (London, 1898) p. 45.
22. *Imitation and Praise in the Poems of Ben Jonson* (New Haven, Conn., 1981) p. 61.
23. *Britain*, trans. Philemon Holland (London, 1610) p. v, italics reversed.
24. *Institutio Oratoria*, trans. H. E. Butler, Loeb ed. (London, 1920) vol. I, p. 271.
25. Herford and Simpson, *BJ*, vol. IV, p. 4.

Chapter 2

1. *Worthies*, 'Westminster', p. 243. In his 'Funeral Elegy' on Jonson, John Taylor the Water-Poet also records that Jonson was recalled from his university studies by his step-father the bricklayer, but since he says that Jonson's father died when Ben was seventeen, his account is not totally trustworthy. See Herford and Simpson, *BJ*, vol. XI, pp. 424–5.
2. Oliver Lawson Dick (ed.), *Aubrey's Brief Lives*, (1949; repr., Ann Arbor, Mich., 1962) p. 177.
3. There is no trace in the surviving records of the Tylers and Bricklayers Company of the Thomas Brett 'le Bricklayer' mentioned in the Lincoln's Inn accounts, so it is difficult to ascertain his relationship to Robert Brett or to Jonson. See Mark Eccles, 'Jonson's Marriage', *Review of English Studies*, XII (1936) pp. 263–4.
4. See David Norbrook, *Poetry and Politics in the English Renaissance* (London, 1984) pp. 175–6.
5. See the *Report on the Manuscripts of Lord De L'Isle & Dudley*, Historical Manuscripts Commission, vol. II (London, 1934) pp. 104, 130, 131–2, 226.
6. See Eccles, 'Jonson's Marriage', pp. 258–61.
7. For the average marriage age, see Steve Rappaport, *Worlds within Worlds: Structures of Life in Sixteenth-Century London* (Cambridge, 1989) p. 327.
8. There was a 'Maria Johnson' baptised at St. Martin-in-the-Fields on 1 February 1595, but there is no evidence to connect her to Jonson. For his poem, see Ann Lauinger, ' "It makes the father, lesse, to rue":

Resistance to Consolation in Jonson's "On my first Daughter"', *Studies in Philology*, LXXXVI (1989) pp. 219–34.

9. See Mary Edmond, 'Pembroke's Men', *Review of English Studies*, New Series, XXV (1974) pp. 135–6; and Mark Eccles, 'Ben Jonson, "Citizen and Bricklayer"', *Notes and Queries*, New Series, XXXV (1988) pp. 445–6. Edmond and Eccles make a case for Jonson's possible admission into the company in 1594 on the doubtful basis of unexplained marginal notations in the Quarterage Book. The quarter-age payments in 1611 are particularly interesting because they come much later than Jonson can reasonably be assumed to have worked as a bricklayer. Possibly he kept his membership in good standing because it provided burial benefits for himself and his wife or because it allowed him formally to apprentice his servants.

10. See Rappaport, *Worlds within Worlds*, pp. 29–36, 236–7, 291–4.

11. See the company's Book of Ordinances, Guildhall MS 4321A; Walter George Bell, *A Short History of the Worshipful Company of Tylers and Bricklayers of the City of London* (London, 1938) pp. 28–32; George Unwin, *The Gilds and Companies of London*, 2nd ed. (London, 1925) pp. 214–16, 267–92; and David M. Bergeron, *English Civic Pageantry, 1558–1642)* (Columbia, SC, 1971) pp. 123–39.

12. His satire on Munday was added later; see Herford and Simpson, vol. IX, pp. 308–9.

13. *Brief Lives*, p. 177. Aubrey's reliability is called into question by his accompanying note that Jonson 'killed Mr. Marlowe, the Poet', whom he confuses with the actor Gabriel Spencer. See ch. 3.

14. *The Dramatic Works of Thomas Dekker*, ed. Fredson Bowers, 4 vols. (Cambridge, 1953–61) vol. I, p. 351.

15. For a recent review of evidence concerning the company, see Karl P. Wentersdorf, 'The Origin and Personnel of the Pembroke Company', *Theatre Research International*, V (1979) pp. 45–68, which corrects Mary Edmond's assumption that Jonson was a member of the troupe in 1592. Jonson's acting is discussed by Fredson Thayer Bowers, 'Ben Jonson the Actor', *Studies in Philology*, XXXIV (1937) pp. 392–406.

16. For Nashe's allusion to 'the merry cobler's cut in that witty play of *The Case Is Altered*', see *The Works of Thomas Nashe*, ed. Ronald B. McKerrow, 5 vols. (1903–10; repr. Oxford, 1958) vol. III, p. 220.

17. Ibid., vol. III, p. 254.

18. Ibid., pp. 257–8.

19. See Charles Nicholl, *A Cup of News: The Life of Thomas Nashe* (London, 1984) pp. 244–5.

20. For the documents, see Chambers, *ES*, vol. III, pp. 321–3.

21. See Mark Eccles, 'Jonson and the Spies', *Review of English Studies*, XIII (1937) pp. 385–91.

22. Nashe, *Works*, ed. McKerrow, vol. III, p. 154.

23. Stephen S. Hilliard, *The Singularity of Thomas Nashe* (Lincoln, Nebr., 1986) pp. 2–3, 9.

24. Nashe, *Works*, ed. McKerrow, vol. III, p. 324; Jonson, *Plays*, vol. III, p. xiv.

25. Herford and Simpson, *BJ*, vol. I, p. 194; see Nicholl, *A Cup of News*, p. 249.

26. For the amalgamation of the two companies, see Chambers, *ES*, vol. II, pp. 151–6.

27. See Herford and Simpson, *BJ*, vol. IX, pp. 168, 185–6 and vol. XI, pp. 307–8. For speculation about the content of the Scot's tragedy, see James Shapiro, 'The Scot's Tragedy and the Politics of Popular Drama', *English Literary Renaissance*, XXIII (1993) 428–49.

28. See G. E. Bentley, *The Profession of Dramatist in Shakespeare's Time, 1590–1642* (Princeton, 1971) pp. 111–26.

29. See Herford and Simpson, *BJ*, vol. XI, p. 362.

30. *Plays*, vol. I, pp. 181 and 183; for Jonson's manipulation of his image in the Folio, see ch. 9.

31. *EMO*, Grex, III.vi (*Plays*, I, p. 350). For Jonson's indebtedness to Elizabethan dramatic forms, see Charles Read Baskervill, *English Elements in Jonson's Early Comedy* (1911, repr., New York, 1967); Alan C. Dessen, *Jonson's Moral Comedy* (Evanston, Ill., 1971); Alexander Leggatt, *Citizen Comedy in the Age of Shakespeare* (Toronto, 1973); Brian Gibbons, *Jacobean City Comedy*, 2nd edn. (London, 1980); Anne Barton, *Ben Jonson: Dramatist* (Cambridge, 1984); and Jonathan Haynes, *The Social Relations of Jonson's Theater* (Cambridge, 1992).

32. See W. David Kay, 'Ben Jonson and Elizabethan Dramatic Convention', *Journal of Modern Philology*, LXXVIII (1978–9) pp. 18–28; and Robert N. Watson, *Ben Jonson's Parodic Strategy: Literary Imperialism in the Comedies* (Cambridge, Mass., 1987).

33. See Barton, *Ben Jonson: Dramatist*, pp. 35–44; and Russ McDonald, *Shakespeare & Jonson: Jonson & Shakespeare* (Lincoln, Nebr., 1988) pp. 17–30.

34. See John Jacob Enck, 'The Case Is Altered: Initial Comedy of Humours', *Studies in Philology*, L (1952) pp. 195–214.

35. See W. David Kay, 'The Shaping of Ben Jonson's Career: A Reexamination of Facts and Problems', *Modern Philology*, LXVII (1970–71) p. 228.

36. For the reader's convenience, I give the more familiar names from the 1616 Folio version in parentheses after those from the 1601 Quarto in the first references to each character; citations are to the parallel-text edition of J. W. Lever (Lincoln, Nebr., 1971).

37. For specific parallels, see Baskervill, *English Elements*, pp. 34–75 and 107–43.

38. See Alvin B. Kernan, *The Plot of Satire* (New Haven, 1965) pp. 4–6.

39. See I.i.188–298. All references to Shakespeare's works are to *The Riverside Shakespeare*, ed. G. Blakemore Evans (Boston, 1974).

40. See Douglas Duncan, *Ben Jonson and the Lucianic Tradition* (Cambridge, 1979) pp. 125–7; and John Scott Colley, 'Opinion, Poetry, and Folly in *Every Man in His Humor*', *South Atlantic Bulletin*, XXXIX (1974) pp. 10–21.

41. *Elizabethan Critical Essays*, ed. G. Gregory Smith, 2 vols. (Oxford, 1904) vol. I, p. 176.

Chapter 3

1. Reprinted with English translation in John Cordy Jeaffreson (ed.), *Middlesex County Records*, vol. I (London, 1886) pp. xxxviii–xlii.
2. R. A. Foakes and R. T. Rickert (eds), *Henslowe's Diary* (Cambridge, 1961) p. 286.
3. See Gerald Eades Bentley (ed.), *The Seventeenth-Century Stage* (Chicago, 1968) p. 15.
4. His indictment is reprinted in Jeaffreson, *Middlesex County Records*, pp. xlv–xlvii.
5. For Lipsius, study of the church fathers and ancient and ecclesiastical history (subjects in which Jonson was well-read) only confirmed his view of Protestantism as a dangerous innovation. See Jason Lewis Saunders, *Justus Lipsius: The Philosophy of Renaissance Stoicism* (New York, 1955) p. 35; and W. David Kay, 'Jonson, Erasmus, and Religious Controversy: *Discoveries*, Lines 1046–1062', *English Language Notes*, XVII (1979) pp. 108–12.
6. See Theodore Stroud, 'Ben Jonson and Father Thomas Wright', *English Literary History*, XIV (1947) pp. 274–82. Wright's work was completed in October 1598.
7. William Webster Newbold (ed.), *The Passions of the Mind in General* (New York, 1986) p. 164.
8. See Eccles, 'Jonson's Marriage', p. 267.
9. See Eccles, 'Citizen and Bricklayer', p. 445; Eccles corrects Herford and Simpson's misdating of the court record, reprinted in *BJ*, vol. XI, pp. 571–3.
10. See Bentley, *The Profession of Dramatist*, pp. 28, 53, 102–4. Jonson told Drummond that 'Of all his plays he never gained two hundred pounds' (*Conv.*, l. 586).
11. See Richard Helgerson, *Self-Crowned Laureates: Spenser, Jonson, Milton, and the Literary System* (Berkeley, Calif., 1983) pp. 144–53.
12. See David McPherson, 'Ben Jonson's Library and Marginalia: An Annotated Catalogue', *Studies in Philology*, LXXI, no. 5 (December, 1974), pp. 1–103; and Robert C. Evans, 'Ben Jonson's Library and Marginalia: New Evidence from the Folger Collection', *Philological Quarterly*, LXVI (1987) pp. 521–8.
13. *Art of Poetry*, ll. 128–130, from Horace, *Satires, Epistles and Ars Poetica*, trans. H. Rushton Fairclough, Loeb edn. (London, 1929) p. 461.
14. *Ben Jonson: Public Poet and Private Man* (London, 1976) p. 35.
15. Smith (ed.) *Elizabethan Critical Essays*, vol. II, p. 316.
16. *Imitation and Praise*, p. 5. See also Thomas M. Greene, *The Light in Troy: Imitation and Discovery in Renaissance Poetry* (New Haven, Conn., 1982) pp. 264–93.
17. See George E. Rowe, *Distinguishing Jonson: Imitation, Rivalry, and the Direction of a Dramatic Career* (Lincoln, Nebr., 1988) pp. 1–37.
18. See *Conv.*, ll. 31–6, 217; and T. K. Whipple, *Martial and the English Epigram from Sir Thomas Wyatt to Ben Jonson* (1925; repr., New York, 1970) pp. 384–406.

19. The title-page states that the 1600 edition contained 'more than hath been publically spoken or acted'. It is therefore possible that the Induction and Grex had been expanded in the printed version, though the claim may refer merely to the addition of the prose 'characters' of the dramatis personae.
20. See Herford and Simpson, *BJ*, vol. IX, p. 396.
21. See ch. 8 below.
22. Quoted in D.J. Palmer's excellent essay on 'The Verse Epistle' in *Metaphysical Poetry*, Stratford-upon-Avon Studies 11 (London, 1970) p. 76.
23. See J.R. Barker, 'A Pendant to Drummond of Hawthornden's *Conversations*', *Review of English Studies*, New Series, XVI (1965) pp. 284–8.
24. For Jonson's strategies, see Robert C. Evans, *Ben Jonson and the Poetics of Patronage* (Lewisburg, Pa., 1989) pp. 39–48; however, where Evans sees Jonson as stimulating competiton among his patrons, I see him claiming familiarity with the Bedford circle.
25. *Art of Poetry*, ll. 240–2. Jonson's own translation 'I can out of known gear, a fable frame' (l. 349) indicates that he viewed these lines as advice on creating plots, but since Horace is here describing the stylistic norms that he followed in his epistles and satires and that Jonson imitates, we may take the passage as a stylistic prescription also.
26. Palmer, 'Verse Epistle', p. 93, quoting Jonson's 'Epistle to Selden' (*Und.* XIV), l. 60.
27. See Herford and Simpson, *BJ*, vol. VIII, p. 364. Jonson states in the 'Epistle to Rutland' that he had 'already used some happy hours / To her [the Countess of Bedford's] remembrance' (ll. 74–5). His title creates more of a classical air by employing the Greek *'enthousiastikè'*.
28. Carol Maddison, *Apollo and the Nine: A History of the Ode* (Baltimore, 1960) p. 295; see also D. S. J. Parsons, 'The Odes of Drayton and Jonson', *Queen's Quarterly* LXXV (1968) pp. 675–84.
29. J. William Hebel (ed.), *The Works of Michael Drayton*, 5 vols. (Oxford, 1961) vol. II, p. 347.
30. See Bernard H. Newdigate, *Michael Drayton and His Circle* (Oxford, 1961) pp. 56–69.

Chapter 4

1. See Helgerson, *Self-Crowned Laureates*, pp. 101–44.
2. Kevin Sharpe, *Sir Robert Cotton 1558–1631: History and Politics in Early Modern England* (Oxford, 1979) p. 203.
3. See Sharpe, *Sir Robert Cotton*, pp. 196–203. Martin and Davies were at odds after Davies' attack on Martin in the dining hall of the Middle Temple in 1598, and Jonson took Martin's side: see Robert Krueger (ed.), *The Poems of Sir John Davies* (Oxford, 1975) pp. xxxii-vi.
4. Jonson addressed poems to several eminent persons who had been 'benchers' on the ruling bodies of their houses in the 1590s – Francis Bacon at Gray's Inn, Edward Coke at the Inner Temple and Thomas

Egerton at Lincoln's Inn, but there is no evidence to link him to them in 1599.

5. See Herford and Simpson, *BJ*, vol. XI, pp. 274–8.
6. *Brief Lives*, p. 169.
7. Quoted in R. C. Bald, *John Donne: A Life* (Oxford, 1970) p. 72.
8. See Robert Parker Sorlien (ed.), *The Diary of John Manningham of the Middle Temple 1602–1603* (Hanover, NH, 1976) pp. 1–10.
9. *The Third University of England* (London, 1615) p. 988, as printed with John Stow, *The Annals, or General Chronicle of England* (London, 1615); and Bald, *John Donne: A Life*, p. 62. For the Inns of Court as a social and educational milieu, see Wilfrid R. Prest, *The Inns of Court under Elizabeth I and the Early Stuarts: 1590–1640* (London, 1972) pp. 137–73.
10. Walton's 'Life', reprinted in *Devotions upon Emergent Occasions, together with Death's Duel* (Ann Arbor, Mich., 1959) p. xxxi.
11. *Middle Temple Records*, vol. I, p. 318, quoted in Philip J. Finkelpearl, *John Marston of the Middle Temple: An Elizabethan Dramatist in His Social Setting* (Cambridge, Mass., 1969) p. 47, which also offers an excellent discussion of literary life and revels at the Inns.
12. Finkelpearl, *John Marston of the Middle Temple*, p. 73. See also M. C. Bradbrook, 'London Pageantry and Lawyer's Theater in the Early Seventeenth Century', in Peter Erickson and Coppelia Kahn (eds), *Shakespeare's 'Rough Magic': Renaissance Essays in Honor of C. L. Barber* (Newark, Del., 1985) pp. 256–62.
13. See Richard A. McCabe, 'Elizabethan Satire and the Bishops' Ban of 1599', *Yearbook of English Studies*, XI (1981) pp. 188–94.
14. James Burbage had originally built the theatre in Blackfriars in 1596 but had been prevented from operating it by a petition from the residents. See Chambers, *ES*, vol. II, p. 503–4, and vol. IV, pp. 319–20.
15. Edward B. Partridge, 'Ben Jonson: The Makings of the Dramatist (1596–1602)', in John Russell Brown and Bernard Harris (eds), *Elizabethan Theatre* (London, 1966) p. 229.
16. Compare Horace's laughter at himself in Satires II.iii and II.vii.
17. See Hoyt H. Hudson (ed.), *Directions for Speech and Style* (Princeton, NJ, 1935) p. 7.
18. Arnold Davenport (ed.), *The Poems of John Marston* (Liverpool, 1961) p. 67.
19. Ll. 6–8, *Poems*, p. 77.
20. *Brief Lives*, p. 178.
21. *Ben Jonson: A Life*, p. 262. For Jonson's satire on clothes as a false sign of nobility, see Michael McCanles, *Jonsonian Discriminations: The Humanist Poet and the Praise of True Nobility* (Toronto, 1992) pp. 102–25.
22. See John Carey, *John Donne: Life, Mind and Art*, rev. edn. (London, 1990) pp. 56–7.
23. *Self-Crowned Laureates*, p. 136.
24. See Arthur F. Marotti, *John Donne, Coterie Poet* (Madison, Wis., 1986) p. 38.
25. Ibid., p. 39.
26. Similar stories about the silencing of Chester are told by Nashe and Aubrey; see Herford and Simpson, *BJ*, vol. IX, pp. 405–6.

27. For the effect of Jonson's original ending, see Frank Kerins, 'The Crafty Enchaunter: Ironic Satires and Jonson's *Every Man Out of His Humour*', *Renaissance Drama*, New Series, XIV (1983) pp. 125–50; see also William Blissett, 'The Oddness of *Every Man out of His Humour*', *Elizabethan Theatre*, XII (1986) pp. 157– 79.

28. There is some doubt about the date of the Third Quarto; see Herford and Simpson, *BJ*, vol. III, pp. 409–11.

29. For Jonson's independence from the London theatre companies and the uniqueness of his publication patterns, see Bentley, *The Profession of Dramatist*, pp. 288–91. For his treatment of plays as literary texts, see Joseph Loewenstein, 'The Script in the Marketplace', *Representations*, XII (1985) pp. 101–14; and Timothy Murray, *Theatrical Legitimation: Allegories of Genius in Seventeenth-Century England and France* (Oxford, 1987), especially ch. 3.

30. Herford and Simpson, *BJ*, vol. III, p. 604, ll. 31–2.

31. See Richard Dutton, *Mastering the Revels: The Regulation and Censorship of English Renaissance Drama* (London, 1991) pp. 110–12.

32. See W. A. Armstrong, 'The Audience of the Elizabethan Private Theatres', *Review of English Studies*, New Series, X (1959) pp. 234–49; Andrew Gurr, *Playgoing in Shakespeare's London* (Cambridge, 1987) pp. 59–79; and Richard Levin, 'The Two-Audience Theory of English Renaissance Drama', *Shakespeare Studies*, XVIII (1986) pp. 251–75.

33. See Robert Wiltenburg, *Ben Jonson and Self-love: The Subtlest Maze of All* (Columbia, Mo., 1990) pp. 6–15.

34. See W. David Kay, 'Jonson and Elizabethan Dramatic Convention', pp. 19–20; and Michael Shapiro, *Children of the Revels: The Boy Companies of Shakespeare's Time and Their Plays* (New York, 1977) pp. 186–7.

35. The disclaimer in V.i (Folio version) replaces Jonson's distinction in the Quarto edition between 'exact courtiers' and those who are merely their 'zanies'; see the textual notes to Herford and Simpson, *BJ*, vol. IV, pp. 17–22 and 68.

36. See Donne's epistle to Wotton from court, 20 July 1598, and its predecessor in Milgate (ed.), *Satires, Epigrams, and Verse Letters*, pp. 71–74 and Milgate's note, pp. 225–6.

37. For Jonson's praise of Stoic withdrawal in general, see Thomas R. Greene, 'Ben Jonson and the Centered Self', *Studies in English Literature*, X (1970) pp. 325–48; for the problems it created for his own role as satirist, see Robert Jones, 'The Satirist's Retirement in Jonson's "Apologetical Dialogue"', *English Literary History*, XXXIV (1967) pp. 447–67.

38. This incident, like other passages in the Folio version, may either be an answer to Marston's ridicule of Jonson-Crites, discussed below, or an element of the original play that Jonson later removed because Marston's satire made it embarrassing.

39. Michael Shapiro (*Children of the Revels*, pp. 72–3) views this as a form of subtle flattery.

40. Induction to *What You Will*, l. 56. Citations for Marston's plays are to Arthur Henry Bullen (ed.), *The Works*, 3 vols. (London, 1887; repr. 1970).

41. The most influential of the early studies is Roscoe A. Small, *The Stage Quarrel between Ben Jonson and the So-Called Poetasters* (Breslau, 1899); an important corrective is Ralph W. Berringer, 'Jonson's *Cynthia's Revels* and the War of the Theatres', *Philological Quarterly*, XXII (1943) pp. 1–22. In *Tudor Drama and Politics: A Critical Approach to Topical Meaning* (Cambridge, Mass., 1968) pp. 279–88, David Bevington emphasises contrasting views of authority in the public and private theatres, rather than personalities, as the basis of the conflict.

42. The argument for viewing Chrisoganus and Posthaste as portraits of Jonson and Munday has been revived by James P. Bednarz, 'Representing Jonson: *Histriomastix* and the Origin of the Poets' War', *Huntington Library Quarterly*, LIV (1991), pp. 1–30. For Jonson's lampoon of Munday, perhaps inserted when *The Case is Altered* was revived by the Children of the Chapel, see Herford and Simpson, *BJ*, vol. IX, pp. 308–9; and David Mann, 'Sir Oliver Owlet's Men: Fact or Fiction', *Huntington Library Quarterly*, LIV (1991) pp. 301–11. Munday's activity as a pursuivant involved in spying on Catholics for Richard Topcliffe would have given Jonson an additional motive for satirising him.

43. See *EMO*, III.iv.5–35 and the notes in Herford & Simpson, *BJ*, vol. IX, pp. 449–50. Bednarz (pp. 27–8, n. 12) shows that Jonson's satire must have been present in the stage version, not added later in the Quarto text.

44. See Finkelpearl, *John Marston of the Middle Temple*, pp. 163–4.

45. Gurr (*Playgoing*, pp. 153–9) suggests that Shakespeare's company occupied a middle position in the opposition between public and private theatre repertories.

46. See *Satires*, I.i.20, iv.14,21 and x.78–9.

47. See Herford and Simpson, *BJ*, vol. IX, p. 535 and Davenport, *Poems*, pp. 223–6.

48. Compare also IV.iii.99–106 with Horace's *Satires*, I.iv.33–8.

49. See Herford and Simpson, *BJ*, vol. IX, pp. 558–9 and vol. IV, p. 193.

50. A Privy Council directive to the Middlesex magistrates of 10 May 1601, occasioned by a production at the Curtain, indicates that the libel laws were understood to have been violated if 'gentlemen of good desert and quality' were represented even in an 'obscure manner, but yet in such sort as all the hearers may take notice both of the matter and the persons that are meant thereby'; see Chambers, *ES*, vol. IV, p. 332; and Dutton, *Mastering the Revels*, pp. 138–9.

51. See Helgerson, *Self-Crowned Laureates*, pp. 110–12; and Marotti, *John Donne: Coterie Poet*, p. 26.

52. See Katharine Eisaman Maus, *Ben Jonson and the Roman Frame of Mind* (Princeton, New Jersey, 1984) pp. 10–11; Robert B. Pierce, 'Ben Jonson's Horace and Horace's Ben Jonson', *Studies in Philology*, 78 (1981) pp. 20–31; and Joanna Martindale, 'The Best Master of Virtue and Wisdom: The Horace of Ben Jonson and His Heirs', in Charles Martindale and David Hopkins (eds), *Horace Made New: Horatian Influences on British Writing from the Renaissance to the Twentieth Century* (Cambridge, 1993) pp. 50–68.

53. Dekker's allusions are fully explicated by Cyrus Hoy, *Introductions, Notes, and Commentaries to Texts in 'The Dramatic Works of Thomas Dekker'* Edited by Fredson Bowers, 4 vols. (Cambridge, 1980) vol. I, pp. 179–309.
54. 'Jonson, *Satiromastix*, and the Poetomachia: A Patronage Perspective', *Iowa State Journal of Research*, 60, no. 3 (February 1986) p. 373; see also Kathleen E. McLuskie, 'The Poets' Royal Exchange: Patronage and Commerce in Early Modern Drama', *Yearbook of English Studies*, XXI (1991) pp. 53–62.
55. For Jonson's contradictory poses, see Jones, 'The Satirist's Retirement', pp. 447–67.
56. J. B. Leishman (ed.), *The Three Parnassus Plays (1958–1601)* (London, 1949) p. 337.
57. See Leishman, ibid, pp. 369–71.
58. Dedication 'To the World', ll. 18–22.
59. Quoted in Herford and Simpson, *BJ*, vol. XI, p. 374; see also the excerpt from Henry Chettle's *England's Mourning Garment* in Jesse Franklin Bradley and Joseph Quincy Adams (eds), *The Jonson Allusion-Book: A Collection of Allusions to Ben Jonson from 1597 to 1700* (New Haven, Conn., 1922) p. 35.

Chapter 5

1. *Diary*, p. 187.
2. *Plays*, vol. II, p. 234.
3. *Henslowe's Diary*, pp. 182, 203.
4. See Barton, *Ben Jonson: Dramatist*, pp. 13–28.
5. Compare Donne's vision of his wife with a dead child in her arms, Bald, *John Donne: A Life*, p. 252.
6. See J. Z. Kronenfeld, 'The Father Found: Consolation Achieved through Love in Ben Jonson's "On My First Sonne"', *Studies in Philology*, LXXV (1978) pp. 64–83; G. W. Pigman III, 'Suppressed Grief in Jonson's Funeral Poetry', *English Literary Renaissance*, XIII (1983) pp. 203–20; H. W. Matalene, 'Patriarchal Fatherhood in Ben Jonson's Epigram 45', in David G. Allen and Robert A. White (eds), *Traditions and Innovations: Essays on British Literature of the Middle Ages and the Renaissance* (Newark, Del., 1990) pp. 102–12; and Joshua Scodel, 'Genre and Occasion in Jonson's 'On My First Sonne"', *Studies in Philology*, LXXXVI (1989) pp. 235–59.
7. *Diary*, p. 209.
8. See Jenny Wormald, 'James VI and I: Two Kings or One?', *History*, LXVIII (1983) pp. 188–209; and Maurice Lee, jun., *Great Britain's Solomon: James VI and I in His Three Kingdoms* (Urbana, Ill., 1990) pp. 63–92.
9. Norman Egbert MacLure (ed.), *The Letters of John Chamberlain*, 2 vols. (Philadelphia, 1939) vol. I, p. 192.
10. *Dramatic Works*, vol. II, p. 255.
11. John Palmer, *Ben Jonson* (New York, 1934) p. 41.
12. See James D. Garrison, *Dryden and the Tradition of Panegyric* (Berkeley, Calif., 1975) pp. 92–3.

13. Quoted by J. E. Neale, 'The Elizabethan Political Scene', in *Essays in Elizabethan History* (London, 1958) p. 79.
14. See Maurice Lee, jun. (ed.), *Dudley Carleton to John Chamberlain, 1603–1624: Jacobean Letters* New Brunswick, NJ, 1972) p. 39.
15. See Carey, *John Donne*, pp. 2–4.
16. See Edmund Bolton's commendatory poem, Herford and Simpson, *BJ*, vol. XI, p. 317.
17. Herford and Simpson, *BJ*, vol. IV, 329–31.
18. See Herford and Simpson, *BJ*, vol. XI, p. 312; and Dutton, *Mastering the Revels*, pp. 10–14, 164.
19. 'To the Readers', ll. 15–17.
20. See Lawrence Michel (ed.), *The Tragedy of Philotas by Samiel Daniel* (New Haven, Conn., 1949) pp. 36–66; F. J. Levy, 'Hayward, Daniel and the Beginnings of Politic History in England', *Huntington Library Quarterly*, L (1987) pp. 1–34; and Dutton, *Mastering the Revels*, pp. 119–23, 165–71.
21. From Justus Lipsius' dedicatory epistle to his edition of Tacitus, as translated by Edmund Bohun from Degory Wheare, *The Method and Order of Reading Both Civil and Ecclesiastical Histories* (London, 1685), p. 105.
22. See J. H. M. Salmon, 'Seneca and Tacitus in Jacobean England', *Journal of the History of Ideas*, L(1989) pp. 199–225; Alan T. Bradford, 'Stuart Absolutism and the "Utility" of Tacitus', *Huntington Library Quarterly* 46 (1983) pp. 127–55; and David Womersley, 'Sir Henry Savile's Translation of Tacitus and the Political Interpretation of Elizabethan Texts', *Review of English Studies*, New Series, XLII (1991) pp. 313–42.
23. *The End of Nero and the Beginning of Galba. Four Books of the Histories of Cornelius Tacitus* (London, 1591) sig. 3.
24. See Margaret Dowling, 'Sir John Hayward's Troubles over His *Life of Henry IV*', *The Library*, 4th Series, XI (1930–31), pp. 212–24; and S. L. Goldberg, 'Sir John Hayward, "Politic" Historian', *Review of English Studies*, New Series, VI (1955) pp. 233–44; and Levy, 'Hayward, Daniel, and . . . Politic History in England', pp. 15–21.
25. London, 1688, Sig. b1 and b1ᵛ·
26. Ralegh, quoted by F. J. Levy, *Tudor Historical Thought* (San Marino, Calif., 1967) p. 292.
27. 'To the Readers', ll. 24–5.
28. Herford and Simpson, *BJ*, vol. IV, p. 353.
29. *Censorship and Interpretation: The Conditions of Writing and Reading in Early Modern England* (Madison, Wis., 1984) p. 44.
30. See Kenneth C. Schelhase, *Tacitus in Renaissance Political Thought* (Chicago, 1976); Mark Morford, 'Tacitean *Prudentia* and the Doctrines of Justus Lipsius', in T. J. Luce and A. J. Woodman (eds), *Tacitus and the Tacitean Tradition* (Princeton, 1993) pp. 129–51; and Ronald Mellor, *Tacitus* (London, 1993) pp. 87–111.
31. See Daniel C. Boughner, *The Devil's Disciple: Ben Jonson's Debt to Machiavelli* (New York, 1968) pp. 89–112.
32. Likewise, Jonson's satire on the 'ripe statesmen' of 'The New Cry' (Epigram XCII), who carry Tacitus' works about with them to bolster their seeming intelligence of court intrigues and foreign plots, is

consistent with his general ridicule of affectation in all its forms and does not, in my view, constitute any change in his attitude toward Tacitus.

33. See his edition of *Sejanus* for The Revels Plays (Manchester, 1990) pp. 16–22.
34. *Works*, vol. II, p. 493, lines 511–12; see the notes in vol. V, p. 179.
35. See Matthew H. Wikander, ' "Queasy to Be Touched": The World of Ben Jonson's *Sejanus*', *Journal of English and Germanic Philology*, LXXIX (1980) pp. 345–57.
36. 'The Sources, Text, and Readers of *Sejanus*: Jonson's "Integrity in the Story" ', *Studies in Philology*, LXXV (1978) p. 192.
37. See also *Discoveries*, ll. 1494–7; for the possible influence of Hooker on Jonson, see Joseph John Kelly, 'Ben Jonson's Politics', *Renaissance and Reformation*, New Series, VII (1983) pp. 192–215.
38. Jonson reinforces Lepidus' dramatic credibility in Act V by showing him to have a shrewder insight into Tiberius' plots than Arruntius.
39. Gainsford, as quoted in Salmon, 'Seneca and Tacitus', p. 218; Rudolph Kirk (ed.), *Two Bookes of Constancie Written in Latine by Justus Lipsius*, trans. Sir John Stradling (New Brunswick, N J, 1939) p. 127.
40. Compare Lipsius' sentiment, 'Let who so list stand aloft on the slippery height of the court; as for me, I will fill my self with pleasant ease and in an obscure place will take the benefit of quiet leisure' (*Six Books of Politics or Civil Doctrine*, trans. William Jones [London, 1594] p. 58).
41. See R. Malcolm Smuts, *Court Culture and the Origins of a Royalist Tradition in Early Stuart England* (Philadelphia, 1987) p. 81.
42. For Marston, see Herford and Simpson, *BJ*, vol I, p. 192; a letter of Chapman to the Lord Chamberlain, reprinted by Bertram Dobell in the *Athenaeum*, 30 March 1901, states: 'Of all the oversights for which I suffer, none repents me so much as that our unhappy book was presented without your Lordship's allowance, for which we can plead nothing by way of pardon but your person so far removed from our required attendance, our play so much importun'd, and our clear opinions that nothing it contain'd could worthily be held offensive' (p. 403).
43. James gave grants of eighty-eight thousand pounds to Scotsmen in the first seven years of his reign, fifteen thousand of it in the first few months; see Lawrence Stone, *The Crisis of the Aristocracy: 1558–1641* (Oxford, 1965) p. 416.
44. For the suggestion that Murray believed his brother touched by an indirect allusion to the Gentlemen of the Bedchamber, see Albert H. Tricomi, *Anticourt Drama in England 1603–1642* (Charlottesville, Va., 1989) pp. 32–3; ambassadorial reports detailing ridicule of James in the theatre, at times with Queen Anne in attendance, are quoted by Chambers, *ES*, vol. I, p. 325.
45. The reference to Scots in Virginia was eliminated by resetting two pages of type, and blank spaces in the text suggest that other passages glancing at court corruption were also altered; see Janet Clare, '*Art Made Tongue-Tied by Authority': Elizabethan and Jacobean Dramatic Censorship* (Manchester, 1990) pp. 122–4; and Dutton, *Mastering the*

Revels, pp. 171–9. Chapman's letter of submission to King James pleads as an excuse that the 'chief offences are but two clauses, and both of them not our own' (Dobell, 'Newly Discovered Documents', p. 403).

46. Herford and Simpson, *BJ*, vol I, p. 195.
47. Chapman wrote a second letter to Suffolk, soliciting 'the propagation of your most noble favours to our present freedom. And the rather since we hear from the Lord d'Aubigny that his Highness hath remitted one of us wholly to your Lordship's favour and that the other had still your Lordship's passing noble remembrance for his joint liberty, which his Highness' self would not be displeased to allow' (Dobell, p. 403).
48. Herford and Simpson, *BJ*, vol. XI, p. 578; for Roe see Alvaro Ribeiro, 'Sir John Roe: Ben Jonson's Friend', *Review of English Studies*, New Series, XXIV (1973) pp. 153–64. Roe had been Percy's lieutenant during his service in Ireland.
49. Herford and Simpson, *BJ*, vol. I, pp. 196 and 203.
50. Herford and Simpson, *BJ*, vol. I, p. 202.
51. Herford and Simpson, *BJ*, vol. I, pp. 220–3.
52. Bodleian MS. Selden Supra 108, f. 65^v

Chapter 6

1. See Barbara Kiefer Lewalski, *Writing Women in Jacobean England* (Cambridge, Mass., 1993) pp. 15–43; and Leeds Barroll, 'The Court of the First Stuart Queen', in Linda Levy Peck (ed.), *The Mental World of the Jacobean Court* (Cambridge, 1991) pp. 191–208.
2. Jonson told Drummond that 'Sir John Roe loved him; and when they two were ushered by my Lord Suffolk from a masque, Roe wrote a moral epistle to him, which began "That next to plays, the court and the state were the best. God threateneth kings, kings lords, and lords do us" ' (*Conv.* ll. 145–50). The text of the epistle (reprinted in Herford and Simpson, *BJ*, vol. XI, p. 371) actually begins 'The state and men's affairs are the best plays / Next yours'; it is dated 6 January 1604, the date of a 'Scots' Masque' that consisted of a simple sword dance. On the basis of Roe's reference to 'the Queen's masque' Joseph Loewenstein argues cogently that he alludes to *The Vision of the Twelve Goddesses*; see his essay 'Printing and "The Multitudinous Presse"; The Contentious Texts of Jonson's Masques', in Jennifer Brady and W. H. Herendeen (eds), *Ben Jonson's 1616 Folio* (Newark, Del., 1991) pp. 170–2.
3. Richard Dutton (ed.), *Jacobean and Caroline Masques*, Nottingham Drama Texts, vol. 1 (Nottingham, 1981) p. 4. For the background of their disagreement, see John Peacock, 'Ben Jonson's Masques and Italian Culture', in J. R. Mulryne and Margaret Shewring (eds), *Theatre of the English and Italian Renaissance* (New York, 1991) pp. 73–93.
4. Dutton, *Masques*, vol. 1, p. 4. Jonson's boastful classicism produced a strong counter-reaction in this period. His objections to Dekker's choice in *The Magnificent Entertainment* of a woman to present his guardian spirit or Genius (usually male in classical poetry) led to the criticism quoted above in ch. 4, and after the *Eastward Ho* incident

Marston used his dedication to *Sophonisba* to sneer at those who 'transcribe authors, quote authorities, and translate Latin prose orations into blank verse' (Herford and Simpson, *BJ*, vol. XI, p. 374).

5. Dutton, *Masques*, vol. 1, p. 7.

6. Ibid., pp. 4, 8.

7. Ibid., pp. 7–8.

8. Ibid., p. 102, from the preface to *Tethys' Festival* (performed 5 June 1610), which is an embittered attack on Jonson's theory of the masque, his pride and his boasting about his fidelity to antiquity. Dutton (p. 99) questions whether the choice of Daniel for the *Tethys' Festival* commission might not reflect some disaffection with Jonson's work on Queen Anne's part; for a possible explanation, see below, ch. 8.

9. See Stephen Orgel, *The Illusion of Power: Political Theater in the English Renaissance* (Berkeley, Calif., 1975).

10. See Suzanne Gossett, '"Man-maid, begone": Women in Masques', *English Literary Renaissance*, XVIII (1988) pp. 96–113; Margaret Maurer, 'Reading Ben Jonson's *Queens*', in Sheila Fisher and Janet E. Halley (eds), *Seeking the Woman in Late Medieval and Renaissance Writings: Essays in Feminist Contextual Criticism* (Knoxville, Tenn., 1989) pp. 233–63; Stephen Orgel, 'Jonson and the Amazons', in Elizabeth D. Harvey and Katharine Eisaman Maus (eds), *Soliciting Interpretation: Literary Theory and Seventeenth-Century English Poetry* (Chicago, 1990) pp. 119–39; and Eugene R. Cunnar, '(En)gendering Architectural Poetics in Jonson's *Masque of Queens*', *Lit*, IV (1993) pp. 145–60. For a similar analysis of domestic interplay between the King and Queen, see Hardin Aasand, '"To blanch an Ethiop, and revive a corse": Queen Anne and *The Masque of Blackness*', *Studies in English Literature*, XXXII (1992) pp. 271–85.

11. In stressing defensive arms, Jonson was probably influenced by Sir Robert Cotton, who at the urging of King James, wrote a tract to Prince Henry 'inciting him to affect arms more than peace'. See Sharpe, *Sir Robert Cotton*, pp. 120, 227–8.

12. These lines are overlooked by Norman Council in his 'Ben Jonson, Inigo Jones, and the Transformation of Tudor Chivalry', *English Literary History*, XLVII (1980) pp. 259–75; and by J. W. Williamson, *The Myth of the Conqueror, Prince Henry Stuart: A Study of 17th Century Personation* (New York, 1978) pp. 80–95. For a balanced reading, see John Peacock, 'Jonson and Jones Collaborate on *Prince Henry's Barriers*', *Word and Image*, III (1987) pp. 172–94.

13. See John C. Meagher, *Method and Meaning in Jonson's Masques* (Notre Dame, Ind., 1966) pp. 57–124.

14. D. J. Gordon, *The Renaissance Imagination*, ed. Stephen Orgel (Berkeley, Calif., 1980) p. 154.

15. See Stone, *Crisis of the Aristocracy*, p. 665.

16. Described by Dudley Carleton, *Jacobean Letters*, pp. 66–7.

17. See D. J. Gordon, 'Hymenaei: Ben Jonson's Masque of Union', *The Renaissance Imagination*, pp. 157–84.

18. At *The Masque of Blackness* the previous year, the crowd had overturned the refreshment table and one lady was detained for public fornication.

See the letters by Dudley Carleton in Herford and Simpson, *BJ*, vol. X, pp. 448–9.
19. See Allardyce Nicoll, 'Court Hieroglyphicks', *Stuart Masques and the Renaissance Stage* (London, 1938) pp. 154–91; and D. J. Gordon, 'Roles and Mysteries', *The Renaissance Imagination*, pp. 3–23.
20. See Anne Cline Kelly, 'The Challenge of the Impossible: Ben Jonson's *Masque of Blackness*', *College Language Association Journal*, XX (1977) pp. 341–55.
21. *Jacobean Letters*, p. 68.
22. Herford and Simpson, *BJ*, vol. VII, p. 91.
23. See Elizabeth T. Jordan, 'Inigo Jones and the Architecture of Poetry', *Renaissance Quarterly*, XLIV (1991) pp. 280–92; and D. J. Gordon, 'Poet and Architect: The Intellectual Setting of the Quarrel between Ben Jonson and Inigo Jones', *The Renaissance Imagination*, pp. 77–101.
24. Herford and Simpson, *BJ*, vol. VII, pp. 77–9.
25. For the distinctive nature of Jonson's masque texts, see Timothy Murray, *Theatrical Legitimation*, pp. 83–93; Loewenstein, 'Printing and "The Multitudinous Presse"', pp. 168–91; and S. Musgrove, '"Edified by the margent": Dramaturgical Evidence in Jonson's Masques', *Parergon*, New Series, III (1985) pp. 163–72.
26. See John Pory's description of the masque in Herford and Simpson, *BJ*, vol. X, p. 466. Pory's account suggests that the *machina versatilis* used in this case may have been more primitive than is usually assumed.
27. Jonson states in the 1616 Folio that *Volpone* was first performed in 1605, but he seems here to be using Old Style dating, as he may also have done in the case of *Sejanus*, for the text's reference to a whale seen at Woolwich corresponds to a similar reference in Stow's *Annals* for January of 1606. Its performance at Oxford and Cambridge would have been probable during the plague-ridden summer of 1606, suggesting that the date of 11 February 1607 in the preface to the Quarto is a calendar date. Jonson's dating would seem to be more inconsistent than has been suggested by W. W. Greg, 'The Riddle of Jonson's Chronology', *The Library*, 4th Series, VI (1925–6) pp. 340–7.
28. Ovid makes a similar distinction between plays and poems at *Poetaster*, I.ii.54–8, and Jonson defends *Sejanus* against objections that it is not a 'true poem' in his preface 'To the Readers', l. 5.
29. See Linda Levy Peck, *Court Patronage and Corruption in Early Stuart England* (Boston, 1990) pp. 12–20.
30. *Brief Lives*, p. 291. See Robert C. Evans, 'Thomas Sutton: Ben Jonson's *Volpone*?', *Philological Quarterly*, LXVIII (1989) pp. 295–313; and Margaret Hotine, 'Ben Jonson, Volpone, and Charterhouse', *Notes and Queries*, New Series, XXXVIII (1991) pp. 79–81.
31. *Brief Lives*, p. 170.
32. Eumolpus and his party are told, 'Any man you meet in that town you may be certain belongs to one of two classes: the makers of wills and those who pursue the makers of wills. . . . In short, sirs, you are going to a place . . . in which you will see only two things: the bodies of those who are eaten, and the carrion crows who eat them', *The Satyricon*, trans. William Arrowsmith (New York, 1959) p. 126.

33. See Brian Parker, 'Jonson's Venice', in Mulryne and Shewring (eds), *Theatre of the English and Italian Renaissance*, pp. 95–112; and David C. McPherson, *Shakespeare, Jonson, and the Myth of Venice* (Newark, Del., 1992) pp. 90–116.

34. Jonson's various sources are admirably surveyed and reproduced in R. B. Parker's edition for The Revels Plays (Manchester, 1983) pp. 11–29, 312–33.

35. *Ben Jonson: Public Poet and Private Man*, p. 116.

36. III.ii.10–12, Standish Henning (ed.), (Lincoln, Nebr., 1965).

37. Most discussions of *Michaelmas Term* assume that it is an imitation of *Volpone*; this assumption has been supported by uncertainty about the dating of both plays and by the belief that Jonson generally ignored Elizabethan drama. However, recent editors have favoured an earlier date for Middleton's play, and Jonson's use of it as a pattern would be entirely consistent with his practice of improving on popular dramatic models. For the date of *Michaelmas Term*, see the editions of Richard Levin (Lincoln, Nebr., 1966) pp. x–xi, and George R. Price, (The Hague, 1976) pp. 12–15.

38. For Middleton's problems in passing moral judgement on his trickster heroes, see Leggatt, *Citizen Comedy*, pp. 70–4.

39. See John S. Weld, 'Christian Comedy: *Volpone*', *Studies in Philology*, LI (1954) pp. 172–93.

40. For a reading that stresses the audience's detachment from Volpone, see Robert Jones, *Engagement with Knavery: Point of View in Richard III, The Jew of Malta, Volpone, and The Revenger's Tragedy* (Durham, NC, 1986) pp. 99–121.

41. For a fuller discussion see Kay, 'Ben Jonson and Elizabethan Dramatic Convention', pp. 22–7.

42. 'Jonson and the Loathed Stage', in William Blissett, Julian Patrick and R. W. Van Fossen (eds.), *A Celebration of Ben Jonson* (Toronto, 1973) pp. 27–53.

43. See Stephen J. Greenblatt, 'The False Ending in *Volpone*', *Journal of English and Germanic Philology*, LXXV (1976) pp. 90–104.

Chapter 7

1. Herford and Simpson, *BJ*, vol. V, p. 21n. For problems with the date, see ch. 6.

2. Jonson is referred to as 'armiger' [entitled to bear heraldic arms] in the indictment against him for recusancy on 9 January 1605/6. See Herford and Simpson, *BJ*, vol. XI, p. 579.

3. Ibid., vol. I, p. 221.

4. Drummond's ambiguous wording is 'To me he read the preface of his *Art of Poesy*, upon Horace *Art of Poesy*, where he hath an apology of a play of his, *St. Bartholomee's Fair* . . . . There is an epigram of Sir Edward Herbert's before it, the he said he had done in my Lord Aubigny's house ten years since anno 1604' (*Conv.*, ll. 71–6). The preface and apology are lost.

5. See Eccles, 'Jonson's Marriage', pp. 268–70. Riggs (*Ben Jonson: A Life*, p. 369, n. 14) and Eccles prefer a late date for Jonson's five years with D'Aubigny, but if Jonson were living with him from 1614 to 1619 Aubigny would surely figure more largely in the dedications to the 1616 Folio. See Herford and Simpson, *BJ*, vol. I, pp. 232–3, and vol. XI, pp. 576–7 and 580.

6. *Ben Jonson: A Life*, p. 140.

7. For new evidence that the songs to Celia drew on neo-Latin poetry, see Stella P. Revard, 'Classicism and Neo-Classicism in Jonson's *Epigrammes* and *The Forrest*', in Brady and Herendeen (eds), *Ben Jonson's 1616 Folio*, pp. 155–60.

8. Newbold (ed.), *The Passions of the Mind in General*, pp. 157–8.

9. Translated from his Latin note in a copy of Persius presented to Sir John Roe in 1605; see Herford and Simpson, *BJ*, vol. VIII, p. 663.

10. See D. H. Rawlinson, 'Ben Jonson on Friendship', *English*, XXXIX (1980) pp. 203–17; and Stanley Fish, 'Authors-Readers: Jonson's Community of the Same', *Representations*, VII (Summer 1984) pp. 26–58.

11. Camden also listed Jonson among the 'most pregnant wits of these our times' in the 1605 edition of his *Remains concerning Britain*. See Bradley and Adams (eds), *The Jonson Allusion-Book*, p. 33.

12. For Northampton's employment of Cotton and Jonson's friend Edmund Bolton, see Linda Levy Peck, *Northampton: Patronage and Policy at the Court of James I* (London, 1982) pp. 101–21.

13. See the entry on Selden in the *Dictionary of National Biography*, p. 1157.

14. Herford and Simpson, *BJ*, vol. XI, pp. 383–4. Selden's praise is generous, considering that he later believed writing verse to be appropriate for a gentleman only in youth. See Samuel Harvey Reynolds (ed.), *The Table Talk of John Selden* (Oxford, 1892) p. 135.

15. See Parker (ed.), *Volpone*, p. 77; Bolton's wording echoes Jonson's motto, discussed above in ch. 3.

16. See 'To My Well-accomplished Friend, Mr. Ben Jonson' by John Davies of Hereford (Herford and Simpson, *BJ*, vol. XI, p. 379). Davies criticises those who accuse Jonson of envy for having 'corrupted hearts', but wishes that his own poetry were good enough for Jonson to envy.

17. See *M.P.* V and XII; Jonson's use of refining as a metaphor for Chapman's translation of Hesiod would later be used by Thomas Cartwright in praising Jonson's imitation; see Herford and Simpson, *BJ*, vol. XI, p. 458.

18. Herford and Simpson, *BJ*, vol. XI, pp. 376.

19. Jonson's praise of Beaumont here should be compared with Richard Brome's testimony in his poem on John Fletcher that Jonson '(proud to call him *Son*) / In friendly envy swore, he had out-done / *His very self*' (*Comedies and Tragedies. Written by Francis Beaumont and John Fletcher* [London, 1647] sig. g1). See also Rowe, *Distinguishing Jonson*, pp. 22–32.

20. For Roe, see below. Sir Edward Herbert's epigram for Jonson's translation of Horace was eventually printed in the 1640 edition; see *Conv.*, l. 73, and Herford and Simpson, *BJ*, vol. XI, p. 352. Jonson reciprocated with Epigram CVI. For Goodyer, see Epigrams LXXXV and LXXXVI.

21. Jonson told Drummond that 'Overbury was first his friend, then turned his mortal enemy' (*Conv.*, ll. 160–1). For his relation to the Overbury circle, see James E. Savage (ed.), *The 'Conceited Newes' of Sir Thomas Overbury and His Friends* (Gainesville, Fl., 1968) pp. xxvi–xxxix. For Rudyerd, see Epigrams CXXI–III.
22. See Ribeiro, 'Sir John Roe: Ben Jonson's Friend', pp. 153–64; Roe's poems are reprinted in H. J. C. Grierson (ed.), *The Poems of John Donne*, 2 vols. (Oxford, 1912) vol. I, pp. 400–17.
23. The second of these suggests the interesting possibility that Jonson was conversant with contemporary Spanish poetry. See Walter Holzinger, 'Garcilaso's Sonnet XVI in Poems by Gutierre de Cetina, Miguel de Barrios and Ben Jonson', *Hispanofila*, LXXII (1981) pp. 13–18; and Jennifer Brady, 'Jonson's Elegies of the Plague Years', *Dalhousie Review*, LXV (1985) pp. 208–30.
24. See Michael Strachan, *The Life and Adventures of Thomas Coryate* (Oxford, 1962) pp. 144–48, and 'The Mermaid Tavern Club: A New Discovery', *History Today*, XVII (1967) 533–8.
25. See I. A. Shapiro, 'The "Mermaid Club"', *Modern Language Review*, XLV (1950) pp. 6–17; and Annabel Patterson, 'All Donne', in Harvey and Maus (eds), *Soliciting Interpretation*, pp. 37–67.
26. See Menna Prestwich, *Cranfield: Politics and Profits under the Early Stuarts* (Oxford, 1966) pp. 61–106, where Jonson's satire is quoted extensively to illustrate the dealings of Ingram and Cranfield, but little evidence of his connection with them is offered.
27. 'I did your commandment with Mr. Johnson; both our interests in him needed not to have been employed in it. There was nothing obnoxious but the very name, and he hath changed that. If upon having read it before to divers, it should be spoken that that person was concerned in it, he sees not how Mr. Holland will be excused in it, for he protests that no hearer but Mr. Holland apprehended it so.' Edmund Gosse, *The Life and Letters of John Donne*, 2 vols. (1899; repr. Gloucester, Mass., 1959) vol. II, p. 16.
28. Jonson seems to have continued the attack in Epigram CXXIX, 'To Mime', where Jones' mimicry is compared to that of other Jacobean jesters, including 'thine own Coriat'.
29. *The Action of Ben Jonson's Poetry* (Newark, Del., 1987) pp. 52–62.
30. Jonson's manservant at this time may have been Richard Brome, mentioned in the Induction to *Bartholomew Fair* (1614), l. 7. Brome became a playwright himself, and since Jonson speaks of him later as serving his time in a 'prenticeship' (*M.P.* XXI, l. 10) it is possible that he was formerly apprenticed to Jonson through the Tylers and Bricklayers Company, in which Jonson maintained his dues at least through 1611.
31. *The Life of Edward Earl of Clarendon . . . Written By Himself*, 2 vols. (Oxford, 1857) vol. I, p. 26. This classical ideal, communicated both by Plutarch and by Athenaeus, re-emerged at the end of the sixteenth century in part due to to the educational influence of Erasmus, six of whose *Colloquies* describe *convivia* or feasts.
32. Ibid., p. 28.
33. *Table Talk*, ed. Reynolds, p. 71.

34. A corrected text of Alexander Brome's English translation of Jonson's Latin is printed by Herford and Simpson, *BJ*, vol. XI, pp. 360–61. See also ibid., pp. 294–300; and Katherine A. Esdaile, 'Ben Jonson and the Devil Tavern', *Essays and Studies by Members of the English Association*, XXIX (1943) pp. 93–100. For a fuller discussion of the Apollo Club, see ch. 10 below.

35. Quoted by Helen Peters (ed.), *Paradoxes and Problems* (Oxford, 1989) p. xxvi.

36. For suggestions about the identity of the two adventurers, see Ian Donaldson (ed.), *Ben Jonson*, The Oxford Authors (Oxford, 1985) p. 668; and Peter E. Medine, 'Object and Intent in Jonson's "Famous Voyage"', *Studies in English Literature*, XV (1975) pp. 97–110.

37. *Coryat's Crudities*, 2 vols. (Glasgow, 1905) vol. I, pp. 16–17, 18.

38. See Herford and Simpson, *BJ*, vol. IX, 208–9. Field had contributed a commendatory poem that was pasted in some copies of the *Volpone* Quarto; see ibid., vol. V, p. 4 and vol. XI, pp. 322–3.

39. See Shapiro, *Children of the Revels*, pp. 82–90; and W. David Kay, 'Jonson's Urbane Gallants: Humanistic Contexts for *Epicoene*', *Huntington Library Quarterly*, XXXIX (1976) pp. 251–66. For emphasis on the flaws of the wits, see Rowe, *Distinguishing Jonson*, pp. 112–24; and Diana Benet, '"The Master-Wit is the Master-fool": Jonson, *Epicoene*, and the Moralists', *Renaissance Drama*, New Series, XVI (1985) pp. 121–39.

40. II.iii.96. Dauphine's reply that 'the noble Sidney lives by his' points out the utility of poetic fame, a theme that Jonson sounds repeatedly in this period. For Donne's uneasiness with his reputation as a poet, see above, ch. 4.

41. Marotti, *John Donne: Coterie Poet*, pp. 69–70.

42. See William W. E. Slights, '*Epicoene* and the Prose Paradox', *Philological Quarterly*, XLIX (1970) pp. 178–87; and John Ferns, 'Ovid, Juvenal, and "The Silent Woman": A Reconsideration', *Modern Language Review*, LVI (1970) pp. 248–53.

43. *Epicoene* seems to have got Jonson into difficulty again with the authorities, this time over a brief allusion to the involvement of Stephano Janiculo, the pretended Prince of Moldavia, with Lady Arabella Stuart, King James' cousin. Jonson's claim in the Folio dedication to Sir Francis Stuart that 'there is not a line, or syllable in it changed from the simplicity of the first copy' is a retrospective attempt to defend his innocence. See Dutton, *Mastering the Revels*, pp. 188–9.

44. Like Tom Otter, Selden spoke of wives as 'clogs'; see Reynolds (ed.), *Table Talk*, p. 194. For Donne's misogyny, see Achsah Guibbory, '"Oh Let Mee Not Serve So": The Politics of Love in Donne's *Elegies*', *English Literary History*, LVII (1990) pp. 811–33. The strongest manifestation of Jonson's misogyny is Epigram LXXXIII, 'To a Friend'. See Katherine Usher Henderson and Barbara F. McManus, *Half Humankind: Contexts and Texts of the Controversy about Women in England, 1540–1640* (Urbana, Ill., 1985) pp. 119–23; and Linda Woodbridge, *Women and the English Renaissance: Literature and the Nature of Womankind, 1540–1620* (Urbana,

Ill., 1986), *passim*. For a recent feminist reading of *Epicoene*, see Mary Beth Rose, *The Expense of Spirit: Love and Sexuality in English Renaissance Drama* (Ithaca, NY, 1988) pp. 50–64.

45. See Natalie Zemon Davis, *Society and Culture in Early Modern France* (Stanford, California, 1975) p. 135.

46. See L. G. Salingar, 'Farce and Fashion in *The Silent Woman'*, *Essays and Studies by Members of the English Association*, XX (1967) pp. 29–46; and Emrys Jones, 'The First West End Comedy', *Proceedings of the British Academy*, LXVIII (1982) pp. 215–58; and P. K. Ayers 'Dreams of the City: The Urban and the Urbane in Jonson's *Epicoene'*, *Philogical Quarterly*, LVI (1987) pp. 73–86. In *Fashioning Femininity and English Renaissance Drama* (Chicago, 1991) pp. 129–43, Karen Newman argues that commodification in the play is linked to female extravagance, but this is not strictly the case: Sir Amorous La Foole's boasts about the gold jerkin he wore when knighted in Ireland (I.iv.55–7) and Sir John Daw is eager to 'buy titles' of books he does not read (I.ii.70).

47. For the moral nature of Jonson's realism, see Richard Dutton, 'The Significance of Jonson's Revision of *Every Man in His Humour'*, *Modern Language Review*, LXIX (1974) pp. 241–9. Jonson's use of London references for satiric purposes is discussed by Fran C. Chalfant, *Ben Jonson's London: A Jacobean Placename Dictionary* (Athens, Ga., 1978) pp. 3–28.

48. See Dessen, *Jonson's Moral Comedy*, pp. 105–37.

49. *Brief Lives*, p. 90. For Dee's career, see Peter J. French, *John Dee: The World of an Elizabethan Magus* (London, 1972).

50. See Keith Thomas, *Religion and the Decline of Magic* (New York, 1971).

51. A. L. Rowse, *Sex and Society in Shakespeare's Age: Simon Forman the Astrologer* (New York, 1974) p. 294.

52. Arthur Edward Waite (ed.), *The Hermetic and Alchemical Writings of . . . Paracelsus the Great*, 2 vols. (Berkeley, California, 1976) vol. I, pp. 20–21. For Jonson's use of specific alchemical treatises, see Edgar Hill Duncan, 'Jonson's Use of Arnald of Villa Nova's *Rosarium'*, *Philological Quarterly*, XXI (1942) pp. 435–8, and 'Jonson's *Alchemist* and the Literature of Alchemy', *PMLA*, 61 (1946) pp. 699–710; Supriya Chaudhuri, 'Jason's Fleece: The Source of Sir Epicure Mammon's Allegory', *Review of English Studies*, XXXV (1984) pp. 71–3; and the notes in Herford and Simpson, *BJ*, vol. X.

53. See 'The Jests of George and the Barber' and 'A Jest of George Going to Oxford' in *Shakespeare Jest-books*, ed. W. Carew Hazlitt, 2 vols. (London, 1864) vol. II, pp. 271–7, 297–302.

54. See Cheryl Lynn Ross, 'The Plague of *The Alchemist'*, *Renaissance Quarterly*, XLI (1988) pp. 439–58; and Jonathan Haynes, *Social Relations of Jonson's Theater*, pp. 99–118.

55. Rogers was related to Donne's father-in-law Sir George More; see Joseph T. McCullen, jun., *Studia Neophilologica*, XXIII (1951) pp. 87–95. Phillips' nickname is mentioned in K. M. Briggs, *The Anatomy of Puck: An Examination of Fairy Beliefs among Shakespeare's Contemporaries and Successors* (London, 1959) p. 108. See also Gamini Salgado, *The Elizabethan Underworld* (London, 1977).

56. The congregation had acquired the right to call its own pastors. See Brian Burch, 'The Parish of St. Anne's Blackfriars, London, to 1665', *Guildhall Miscellany*, III (1969–70) pp. 1–54.
57. See John S. Mebane, *Renaissance Magic and the Return of the Golden Age: The Occult Tradition and Marlowe, Jonson, and Shakespeare*, (Lincoln, Nebr., 1989) pp. 137–55; Gerard H. Cox, 'Apocalyptic Projection and the Comic Plot of *The Alchemist*', *English Literary Renaissance*, XIII (1983) pp. 70–87; Robert M. Schuler, 'Jonson's Alchemists, Epicures, and Puritans', *Medieval and Renaissance Drama in English*, II (1985) pp. 171–208; and Jeanette D. Ferreira-Ross, 'Jonson's Satire of Puritanism in *The Alchemist*', *Sydney Studies in English*, XVII (1991–2) pp. 22–42.
58. See Geoffrey Tillotson, '*Othello* and *The Alchemist* at Oxford', *The Times Literary Supplement*, 20 July 1933, p. 404. Jonson's satire on Puritans did not please the conservative Henry Jackson of Corpus Christi College, who complained that it prophaned the scriptures, a charge that was to give Jonson considerable anxiety in his later years (see ch. 10 below). Thomas Carew considered *The Alchemist* to be Jonson's 'Zenith'; see Herford and Simpson, *BJ*, vol. XI, p. 335. For the play's early stage history, see ibid., vol. IX, pp. 223–6.
59. Reprinted in *Plays*, vol. III, p. 229.
60. Herford and Simpson, *BJ*, vol. XI, pp. 488 and 453. Further evidence of popular rejection is perhaps to be found in the title-page motto in the 1612 Quarto, a quotation from Horace to the effect that Jonson does not labour so that the crowd might admire him but is content with a few readers.
61. See Gurr, *Playgoing*, pp. 162–9.

Chapter 8

1. For play dedications, see Loewenstein, 'The Script in the Marketplace', p. 109, n. 33. For Jonson's role in the shift from patronage to print, see J. W. Saunders, 'The Social Situation of Seventeenth-Century Poetry', in Malcolm Bradbury and David Palmer (eds), *Metaphysical Poetry* (London, 1970) pp. 237–59; Richard Dutton, 'Ben Jonson and the Master of the Revels', in J. R. Mulryne and Margaret Shewring (eds), *Theatre and Government under the Early Stuarts* (Cambridge, 1993) pp. 1–28; and Arthur F. Marotti, 'Patronage, Poetry, and Print', *Yearbook of English Studies*, XXI (1991) pp. 1–26.
2. No record of his dealings with publishers survives, but his unpublished literary manuscripts were sold by his literary executor, Sir Kenelm Digby, to Thomas Walkley for forty pounds, a relatively modest sum considering that they included three plays, a number of masques, the *Underwoods*, and the translation of Horace's *Art of Poetry*; see Herford and Simpson, *BJ*, vol. IX, pp. 100–1.
3. Herford and Simpson, *BJ*, vol. VIII, p. 662.
4. *Plays*, vol. II, p. xi; and *Epig.* LXV, ll. 13–14.
5. 'Ben Jonson and the Court', in Christopher Ricks (ed.), *English Poetry and Prose 1540–1674*, rev. edn. (London, 1986), p. 122.

6. A. J. Smith (ed.), *John Donne: The Complete English Poems* (Harmondsworth, 1977) p. 158.
7. See Frank Whigham, 'The Rhetoric of Elizabethan Suitors' Letters', *PMLA*, XCVI (1981) pp. 864–82; and Evans, *Ben Jonson and the Poetics of Patronage*.
8. Herford and Simpson, *BJ*, vol. XI, pp. 587. For Jonson's ability to suit the humour of the royal couple, see Riggs, *Ben Jonson: A Life*, pp. 112–3.
9. For the influence of Seneca and tension between concepts of patronage as a gift exchange, see Peck, *Court Patronage and Corruption*, pp. 12–20; and McCanles, *Jonsonian Discriminations*, pp. 182–9.
10. 'Authors–Readers: Jonson's Community of the Same', *Representations*, VII (Summer 1984) p. 56.
11. From Jonson's praise of Pembroke in *The Gypsies Metamorphosed*, l. 541.
12. See P. J. Croft (ed.), *The Poems of Robert Sidney* (Oxford, 1984); Josephine A. Roberts (ed.), *The Poems of Lady Mary Wroth* (Baton Rouge, La. 1983); and Gaby E. Onderwyzer (ed.), *Poems Written by the Right Honourable William Earl of Pembroke*, Augustan Reprint Society, no. 79 (Los Angeles, Calif., 1959). Jonson did not care for sonnets, which he compared to the Procrustean bed (see *Conv.*, ll. 51–3); like Lady Wroth and Sir Philip Sidney, however, he did write pastoral drama.
13. For the polycentric nature of the Jacobean court, see Kevin Sharpe, 'Faction at the Early Stuart Court', *History Today*, XXXIII (1983), pp. 39–46; Neil Cuddy, 'The Revival of the Entourage: the Bedchamber of James I, 1603–1625', in David Starkey (ed.), *The English Court: From the Wars of the Roses to the Civil War* (London, 1987) pp. 173–225; Malcolm Smuts, 'Cultural Diversity and Cultural Change at the Court of James I', in Peck (ed.), *Mental World of the Jacobean Court*, pp. 99–112; and Leeds Barroll, 'The Court of the First Stuart Queen', ibid., pp. 191–208.
14. See, for example, Evans' discussion of Jonson's epigram on Sir Henry Neville (*Epig.* CIX) in *Ben Jonson and the Poetics of Patronage*, pp. 80-2.
15. To William Jonson wrote, 'Neither am I or my cause so much unknown to your lordship, as it should drive me to seek a second means, or despair of this to your favour. You have ever been free and noble to me, and I doubt not the same proportion of your bounties, if I can but answer it with preservation of my virtue, and innocence', Herford and Simpson, *BJ*, vol. I, pp. 199–200. Jonson told Drummond that 'Every first day of the New Year he had £20 sent him from the Earl of Pembroke to buy books' (*Conv.*, ll. 311–12), but we do not know when Pembroke began doing so.
16. See ch. 10 below.
17. Chamberlain, *Letters*, I, 516–17.
18. See Herford and Simpson, *BJ*, vol, I, pp. 234–5; and Mark H. Curtis, *Oxford and Cambridge in Transition 1558–1642* (Oxford, 1959) p. 29.
19. Herford and Simpson, *BJ*, vol. I, p. 196.
20. See Robert Wiltenburg, ' "What need hast thou of me? or of my Muse": Jonson and Cecil, Politician and Poet', in Claude J. Summers and Ted-Larry Pebworth (eds), *'The Muses Common-Weale': Poetry and Politics in the Seventeenth Century* (Columbia, Miss., 1988) pp. 34–47.

21. See Riggs, *Ben Jonson: A Life*, pp. 175–6.
22. A line-by-line catalogue of Jonson's sources is provided in Appendix B of the edition by W. F. Bolton and Jane F. Gardner (Lincoln, Nebr., 1973) pp. 176–93; see also Joseph Allen Bryant, jun., 'Catiline and the Nature of Jonson's Tragic Fable', *PMLA*, LXIX (1954) pp. 265–77; and Philip J. Ayres, 'The Nature of Jonson's Roman History', *English Literary Renaissance*, XVI (1986) pp. 166–81.
23. The contribution of Felicius was first noted by Ellen M. T. Duffy, 'Ben Jonson's Debt to Renaissance Scholarship in *Sejanus* and *Catiline*', *Modern Language Review*, XLII (1947) pp. 24–6, which gives very brief citations to the Latin text. Felicius' work was translated by Thomas Paynell as *The Conspiracie of Lucius Catiline* (London, 1541; reprinted 1557). In considering whether Caesar and Crassus were involved in the conspiracy, Felicius acknowledges that 'Some say that all these things were feigned and blown abroad by their enemies and should in nowise be believed' (sig. C2ᵛ), but he speaks throughout as if they were, and he later adds, 'Nevertheless, Cicero in a certain oration, which after Crassus death came to light, writeth that M. Crassus was companion of the conspiracy' (sig. N4ᵛ). For Cicero's skill in persuading Curius and Fulvia, see Felicius, ch. IX.
24. See Michael J. Echeruo, 'The Conscience of Politics and Jonson's *Catiline*', *Studies in English Literature*, VI (1966) pp. 341–56; Michael J. Warren, 'Ben Jonson's *Catiline*: The Problem of Cicero', *Yearbook of English Studies*, III (1973) pp. 55–73; and Richard Dutton, *Ben Jonson: To the First Folio* (Cambridge, 1983) pp. 124–32. For a more positive reading see J. S. Lawry, 'Catiline and "the Sight of Rome in Us"', in P. A. Ramsey (ed.), *Rome in the Renaissance: The City and the Myth* (Binghamton, NY, 1982) pp. 395–407.
25. Felicius says that 'though he understood that this thing could not be brought to pass without great danger of his own life, yet so dearly loved he the common weal that he more esteemed the wealth public than his own life' (sig. Q4ᵛ).
26. Ll. 878–9; compare Felicius, Chapter XXII: 'Oh, the miserable estate of them that governed such common wealths, in the which he that is diligent is called wayward and hard to please; he that is negligent, dishonest; where he that is constant and just is called cruel and ungentle, and he that is merciful, fearful and dissolute; wherein is given no pardon to them that do amiss, and small praise to them that do well' (sig. M2ᵛ).
27. *Jonson's Romish Plot: A Study of 'Catiline' in its Historical Context* (Oxford, 1967).
28. DeLuna's suggestion that Jonson himself was represented by Curius founders on the latter's shallow character, and her argument for Jonson's involvement is undercut by new evidence about Sir John Roe discovered by Alva Ribeiro; see above, ch. 5, n. 48. Moreover, despite the fact that both Cethegus and Thomas Percy were violent hot-heads, De Luna's efforts to link each Gunpowder Plotter to one of the Catilinarian conspirators seem entirely arbitrary and unfounded.
29. See *Jonson's Romish Plot*, pp. 31–65.

30. Quoted by De Luna, p. 49.
31. See Neale, *Essays in Elizabethan History*, pp. 74–6; and Lawrence Stone, *Family and Fortune: Studies in Aristocratic Finance in the Sixteenth and Seventeenth Centuries* (Oxford, 1973) pp. 3–61.
32. See *Jonson's Romish Plot*, pp. 288–90.
33. Eric N. Lindquist, 'The Last Years of the First Earl of Salisbury, 1610–1612', *Albion*, XVIII (1986) pp. 23–41; and Pauline Croft, 'Robert Cecil and the Jacobean Court', in Peck (ed.), *Mental World of the Jacobean Court*, pp. 134–47.
34. *The History of the Rebellion and Civil Wars of England* (Oxford, 1839) p. 25a.
35. *Poems*, p. 33, ll. 3–4, 16–18.
36. Herford and Simpson, *BJ*, vol. VIII, p. 16; and A. L. Rowse, *Sir Walter Ralegh: His Family and Private Life* (New York, 1962) p. 290.
37. See James A. Riddell, 'The Arrangement of Ben Jonson's *Epigrammes*', *Studies in English Literature*, XXVII (1987) pp. 53–70; and Wiltenberg, *Ben Jonson and Self-Love*, p. 45–90
38. See David Wykes, 'Ben Jonson's "Chast Booke" – The *Epigrammes*', *Renaissance and Modern Studies*, XIII (1969) pp. 76–87; Edward Partridge, 'Jonson's *Epigrammes*: The Named and the Nameless', *Studies in the Literary Imagination*, VI (1973) pp. 153–98; Martin Elsky, 'Words, Things, and Names: Jonson's Poetry and Philosophical Grammar', in Summers and Pebworth (eds), *Classic and Cavalier*, pp. 91–104; and Richard Hillyer, 'In More than Name Only: Jonson's "To Sir Horace Vere"', *Modern Language Review*, LXXXV (1990) pp. 1–11.
39. For this reason, Stanley Fish has argued that 'representation is the line of work that Jonson's poems are almost never in', 'Authors–Readers: Jonson's Community of the Same', p. 34.
40. Peck, *Court Patronage and Corruption*, p. 27.
41. R. A. B. Mynors and D. F. S. Thomson (trans.), *The Correspondence of Erasmus*, Collected Works of Erasmus (Toronto, 1975) vol. 2, p. 81.
42. See Felicity Heal, 'The Crown, the Gentry and London: the Enforcement of Proclamation, 1596–1640', in Claire Cross, David Loades and J. J. Scarisbrick (eds), *Law and Government under the Tudors* (Cambridge, 1988) pp. 211–26.
43. See Norbrook, *Poetry and Politics*, p. 192; I find no evidence that Jonson encouraged Lady Wroth's extravagance.
44. For architectural parallels, see Alastair Fowler, *Conceitful Thought: The Interpretation of English Renaissance Poems* (Edinburgh, 1975) pp. 116–19; and William Alexander McClung, *The Country House in English Renaissance Poetry* (Berkeley, Calif., 1977) pp. 46–103.
45. See J. C. A. Rathmell, 'Jonson, Lord Lisle, and Penshurst', *English Literary Renaissance*, I (1971) pp. 250–60. For a contrary reading of Penshurst as a false sign of Sidney's family standing see Don Wayne, *Penshurst: The Semiotics of Place and the Poetics of History* (Madison, Wis., 1984) pp. 101–5. Wayne's view of the building as an attempt to 'valorise' the Sidney genealogy overlooks the fact that the Sidneys were a soldierly family and that Robert Sidney was the military governor of Flushing.

46. See Thomas M. Greene, 'Ben Jonson and the Centered Self', *Studies in English Literature*, X (1970) pp. 325–48; Isabel Rivers, *The Poetry of Conservatism: 1600–1745* (Cambridge, 1973) pp. 21–33; and Maus, *Ben Jonson and the Roman Frame of Mind*, pp. 3–46.
47. *Letters of John Chamberlain*, I, 470; for Lady Bedford's style of address see Herford and Simpson, *BJ*, vol. X, p. 34.
48. See Savage (ed.), *The 'Conceited Newes'*, pp. xxiii–xxviii; and Jongsook Lee, 'Biography into Poetry: Cecelia Boulstrode and Jonson's Epideictics', ch. 1 of *Ben Jonson's Poesis: A Literary Dialectic of Ideal and History* (Charlottesville, Va., 1989) pp. 5–16.
49. Herford and Simpson, *BJ*, vol. I, pp. 203–4
50. See Barbara K. Lewalski, *Writing Women in Jacobean England*, pp. 109–10, 120–2.
51. Herford and Simpson, *BJ*, vol. IX, p. 372.
52. See above, ch. 6, n. 8, and ch. 7, n. 43.
53. 'To the Countess of Bedford' ('T'have written then . . .'), l. 26; see Marotti, 'Donne, Lady Bedford, and the Poetry of Compliment', *John Donne, Coterie Poet*, pp. 202–32.
54. Herford and Simpson, *BJ*, vol. V, p. 289.
55. *Philip's Phoenix: Mary Sidney, Countess of Pembroke* (Oxford, 1990) pp. 106–7.
56. For the issue of whether or not she might have been Jonson's Celia, see Josephine A. Roberts (ed.), *The Poems of Lady Mary Wroth* (Baton Rouge, La., 1983) pp. 15–17.
57. See Savage (ed.), *The 'Conceited Newes'*, p. 57.
58. Herford and Simpson, *BJ*, vol. I, p. 53 and vol. III, p. 605; for Charis' name and mythological associations, see Richard S. Peterson, 'Virtue Reconciled to Pleasure: Jonson's "A Celebration of Charis"', *Studies in the Literary Imagination*, VI (1973) pp. 232–52.
59. See van den Berg, *Action of Ben Jonson's Poetry*, pp. 44–50; Ian Donaldson, 'Ben Jonson and the Story of Charis", *Sydney Studies in English*, XIII (1987–8) pp. 3–20; and McCanles, *Jonsonian Discriminations*, pp. 211–17.
60. The description of Charis is also echoed in 'An Elegy' (*Und.* XIX), cited above for its reference to an unworthy husband.
61. See the 'Proludium', *M.P.* CIX, ll. 1–2; and Raymond B. Waddington, '"A Celebration of Charis": Socratic Lover and Silenic Speaker', in Summers and Pebworth (eds), *Classic and Cavalier*, pp. 121–38.

Chapter 9

1. Ralegh's *History* was entered on the Stationer's Register in 1611 and printed in 1614. See John Racin, 'The Editions of Sir Walter Ralegh's *History of the World*,' *Studies in Bibliography*, XVII (1964) pp. 199–209.
2. Herford and Simpson, *BJ*, vol. I, pp. 65–6.
3. See Herford and Simpson, *BJ*, vol. XI, pp. 581–2.
4. See David McPherson, 'Ben Jonson Meets Daniel Heinsius, 1613', *English Language Notes*, XLIV (1976) pp. 105–9.

5. See David Lindley, 'Embarrassing Ben: The Masques for Frances Howard', *English Literary Renaissance*, XVI (1986) pp. 343–59. Lindley's *The Trials of Frances Howard: Fact and Fiction at the Court of King James* (London, 1993) offers a sympathetic defence of Lady Frances as a victim of Jacobean misogyny.
6. See Heather Dubrow, *A Happier Eden: The Politics of Marriage in the Stuart Epithalamium* (Ithaca, NY, 1990) pp. 178–200.
7. See P.R. Seddon, 'Robert Carr, Earl of Somerset', *Renaissance and Modern Studies*, XIV (1970) pp. 48–68.
8. Godfrey Goodman, *The Court of King James the First*, 2 vols. (London, 1839) vol. I, p. 225; see also Roger Lockyer, *Buckingham: The Life and Political Career of George Villiers, First Duke of Buckingham 1592–1628* (London, 1981) pp. 3–20.
9. *Letters*, vol. I, p. 561.
10. Chamberlain, *Letters*, vol. I, p. 570.
11. See John Orrell, 'The London Court Stage in the Savoy Correspondence, 1613–1675', *Theatre Research International*, New Series, IV (1979) pp. 83–4; and David Lindley and Martin Butler, 'Restoring Astraea: Jonson's Masque for the Fall of Somerset', forthcoming in *English Literary History*.
12. *Letters of King James VI & I*, ed. G. P. V. Akrigg (Berkeley, 1984) pp. 344–5.
13. See Herford and Simpson, *BJ*, vol. I, pp. 231–2.
14. Herford and Simpson, *BJ*, vol. VIII, p. 664.
15. See James K. Bracken, 'Books from William Stansby's Printing House, and Jonson's Folio of 1616', *The Library*, Sixth Series, X (1988) pp. 18–29; for dating, see Kevin J. Donovan, 'The Final Quires of the Jonson 1616 *Workes*: Headline Evidence', *Studies in Bibliography*, XL (1987) pp. 106–21.
16. Quoted from *Wits Recreations* (1640) by Herford and Simpson, *BJ*, vol. IX, p. 13.
17. For Horace, see *Epistles*, II.i.182–208, and *Ars Poetica*, ll. 89–98.
18. For the Folio's 'antitheatricality', see Murray, *Theatrical Legitimation*, pp. 64–93, which draws on concepts developed in Jonas Barish, *The Antitheatrical Prejudice* (Berkeley, Calif., 1981).
19. 'Ben Jonson and the Ideology of Authorship', in Brady and Herendeen (eds) *Ben Jonson's 1616 Folio*, p. 114.
20. See Frances Teague, 'Ben Jonson's Stagecraft in *Epicoene*', *Renaissance Drama*, New Series, IX (1978) pp. 175–92; and Joel H. Kaplan, 'Dramatic and Moral Energy in Ben Jonson's *Bartholomew Fair*', *Renaissance Drama*, New Series, III (1970) pp. 137–56.
21. See Alastair Fowler, 'The Silva Tradition in Jonson's *The Forest*', in Maynard Mack and George de Forest Lord (eds), *Poetic Traditions of the English Renaissance* (New Haven, Conn., 1982) pp. 163–80.
22. See W.H. Herendeen, 'A New Way to Pay Old Debts: Pretexts to the 1616 Folio', in Brady and Herendeen (eds), *Ben Jonson's 1616 Folio*, pp. 38–63; and Martin Butler, 'Jonson's Folio and the Poetics of Patronage', *Criticism*, XXXV (1993) pp. 377–90.

23. See, for example, Josephine Waters Bennett, *Measure for Measure as Royal Entertainment* (New York, 1966) and Henry N. Paul, *The Royal Play of Macbeth* (London, 1950) and for cautionary comments, Richard Dutton, *William Shakespeare: A Literary Life* (London, 1989) pp. 129–38.

24. John Aubrey reports that 'King James made him write against the Puritans, who began to be troublesome in his time' (*Lives*, p. 178), but his reference could apply to either *Bartholomew Fair* or *The Alchemist*. For parallels to the joke about 'Christ-tide' in the latter (III.ii.43), see James' *Letters*, ed. Akrigg, p. 237.

25. For staging, see the Yale edition by Eugene Waith (New Haven, 1963), Appendix II; and R. B. Parker, 'The Themes and Staging of *Bartholomew Fair*', *University of Toronto Quarterly*, XXXIX (1970) pp. 293–309.

26. Carnivalesque readings of the play are summarised in Jonathan Haynes, *The Social Relations of Jonson's Theatre* (Cambridge, 1992) pp. 119–38; for a corrective see Neil Rhodes, *Elizabethan Grotesque* (London, 1980) pp. 141–55, and Lorna Hutson, 'The Displacement of the Market in Jacobean City Comedy', *London Journal*, XIV (1989) pp. 3–16.

27. See Jonas A. Barish, '*Bartholomew Fair* and its Puppets', *Modern Language Quarterly*, XX (1959) pp. 3–17; James E. Robinson, 'Bartholomew Fair: Comedy of Vapors', *SEL: Studies in English Literature*, I (1961) pp. 65–80; and Jackson I. Cope, '*Bartholomew Fair* as Blasphemy', *Renaissance Drama*, New Series VIII (1965) pp. 127–52.

28. See Barish, *Prose Comedy*, pp. 197–204; and Keith Sturgess, *Jacobean Private Theatre* (London, 1987) p. 173; and Leah S. Marcus, *The Politics of Mirth: Jonson, Herrick, Milton, Marvell, and the Defense of Old Holiday Pastimes* (Chicago, 1986) p. 39.

29. Charles Howard McIlwain (ed.), *The Political Works of James I* (1918; repr. New York, 1965) p. 7.

30. Debora K. Shuger, 'Hypocrites and Puppets in *Bartholomew Fair*', *Modern Philology*, LXXXII (1984/5) pp. 70–3; Clifford Davidson, 'Judgement, Iconoclasm, and Anti-theatricalism in Jonson's *Bartholomew Fair*', *Papers on Language and Literature*, XXV (1989) pp. 349–63.

31. Marcus, *Politics of Mirth*, p. 13; for Overdo and James, see also Donaldson, *The World Upside Down*, pp. 46–77; and William Blissett, 'Your Majesty is Welcome to a Fair', *Elizabethan Theatre*, IV (1972) pp. 80–105.

32. David McPherson, 'The Origins of Overdo: A Study in Jonsonian Invention', *Modern Language Quarterly*, XXXVII (1976) pp. 221–33.

33. Gillian Manning, 'An Echo of King James in Jonson's *Bartholomew Fair*', *Notes and Queries*, New Series, XXXVI (1989) pp. 342–4.

34. *Political Works*, ed. McIlwain, p. 12.

35. See C. R. Baskervill, *English Elements*, pp. 13–14, and 'Some Parallels to *Bartholomew Fair*', *Modern Philology*, VI (1908/9) pp. 1–19.

36. Hoyt Hopewell Hudson (trans.), *The Praise of Folly* (1941; repr. New York, n.d.) p. 70; see also Douglas Duncan, *Ben Jonson and the Lucianic Tradition* (Cambridge, 1979) pp. 203–25; W. David Kay, '*Bartholomew Fair*: Ben Jonson in Praise of Folly', *English Literary Renaissance*, VI (1976) pp. 299–316, and 'Erasmus' Learned Joking: The Ironic Use of

Classical Wisdom in *The Praise of Folly*, *Texas Studies in Literature and Language*, XIX (1977) pp. 247–67.

37. Robert Ornstein, 'Shakespearian and Jonsonian Comedy', *Shakespeare Survey*, XXII (1969) p. 46; see also Dutton, *Ben Jonson*, pp. 168–71.

38. Bodleian MS Selden Supra 108, fol. 64–5.

39. Sturgess, *Jacobean Private Theatre*, pp. 172–4.

40. For Dekker's politics, see Marcus, *Politics of Mirth*, pp. 95–8, and Julia Gasper, *The Dragon and the Dove: The Plays of Thomas Dekker*, (Oxford, 1990) pp. 109–35; for Jonson's inversion of the tradition, see Dessen, *Jonson's Moral Comedy*, pp. 221–35.

41. *Political Works*, ed. McIlwain, p. 343. For a fuller discussion of the court-country opposition in Jonson's works of this period, see Marcus, *The Politics of Mirth*, pp. 64–139.

42. See Barton, *Ben Jonson, Dramatist*, pp. 219–36.

43. See G. L. Kittredge, 'King James I and *The Devil Is an Ass*', *Modern Philology*, IX (1911/12) pp. 195–209; Marcus, *The Politics of Mirth*, pp. 91–4; and Robert C. Evans, 'Contemporary Contexts of Jonson's *The Devil Is an Ass*', *Comparative Drama*, XXVI (1992) pp. 140–76.

44. See L. C. Knights, *Drama and Society*, (1937; repr. London, 1962) pp. 210–18; Joan Thirsk, *Economic Policy and Projects: The Development of a Consumer Society in Early Modern England* (Oxford, 1978) pp. 78–105; and J. W. Gough, *The Rise of the Entrepreneur* (London, 1969).

45. Ethel M. Portal, 'The Academ Roial of King James I', *Proceedings of the British Academy*, VII (1915–16), pp. 189–208.

46. See Enid Welsford, *The Court Masque: A Study in the Relationship between Poetry & the Revels* (1927; repr. New York, 1962) pp. 184–205.

47. See the payments for errands of the Prince's messenger to Jonson during December 1617, Herford and Simpson, *BJ*, vol. I, pp. 232–3; Marcus, *The Politics of Mirth*, pp. 121–4; and Kevin Sharpe, 'The Image of Virtue: The Court and Household of Charles I, 1625–1642', in Starkey (ed.), *The English Court*, pp. 226–60.

48. Text quoted from C. E. McGee (ed.), 'Cupid's Banishment: A Masque Presented to Her Majesty . . . May 4, 1617', *Renaissance Drama*, New Series, XIX (1988) pp. 227–64; the connection was first noted by Peter Walls, 'Jonson's Borrowing', *Theatre Notebook*, XXVIII (1974) pp. 80–1.

49. Reprinted in *A Book of Masques: In Honour of Allardyce Nicoll* (Cambridge, 1967), p. 233.

50. See Orgel, *The Jonsonian Masque*, pp. 147–85; Richard S. Peterson, 'The Iconography of Jonson's *Pleasure Reconciled to Virtue*', *Journal of Medieval and Renaissance Studies*, V (1975) pp. 123–62; Nathaniel Strout, 'Jonson's Jacobean Masques and the Moral Imagination', *Studies in English Literature*, XXVII (1987) pp. 233–47.

51. See Herford and Simpson, *BJ*, vol. X, pp. 576–7.

52. Bradley and Adams, *Jonson Allusion Book*, p. 100.

53. See Herford and Simpson, *BJ*, vol. I, pp. 233–4 and vol. XI, pp. 382–3.

54. See Robert H. MacDonald, *The Library of Drummond of Hawthornden* (Edinburgh, 1971) pp. 9–36.

55. For Drummond's opinions, see the 1711 edition of his *Works*, pp. 226–7 and 'A Letter on the True Nature of Poetry', in Robert H. MacDonald

(ed.), *William Drummond of Hawthornden: Poems and Prose* (Edinburgh, 1976) pp. 191–2.

56. Herford and Simpson, *BJ*, vol. I, p. 205.
57. See Lockyer, *Buckingham*, pp. 25–76.
58. See Dale B. J. Randall, *Jonson's Gypsies Unmasked: Background and Theme of The Gypsies Metamorphos'd* (Durham, NC, 1975).
59. See Ian Spink, 'Campion's Entertainment at Brougham Castle, 1617', in John H. Long (ed.), *Music in English Renaissance Drama* (Lexington, K Y, 1968) pp. 57–75; and R. T. Spence, 'A Royal Progress in the North: James I at Carlisle Castle and the Feast of Brougham, August 1617', *Northern History*, XXVII (1991) pp. 41–89.
60. See Martin Butler, '"We Are One Mans All"': Jonson's *The Gipsies Metamorphosed'*, *Yearbook of English Studies*, XXI (1991) pp. 253–73.
61. Butler, p. 262.
62. See Herford and Simpson, *BJ*, vol. I, p. 87 and vol. XI, p. 614.
63. See Herford and Simpson, *BJ*, vol. X, pp. 633–4; and W. W. Greg (ed.), *Jonson's Masque of Gipsies in the Burley, Belvoir, and Windsor Versions* (London, 1952) pp. 9–10.
64. Text from Historical Manuscripts Commission 9, *Calendar of the Manuscripts of the Most Honourable the Marquess of Salisbury*, Part XXIV (1976) pp. 252–3; see also C. F. Main, 'Ben Jonson and an Unknown Poet on the King's Senses', *Modern Language Notes*, LXXIV (1959) pp. 389–93.
65. Quoted by Richard Cust, 'News and Politics in Early Seventeenth-Century England', *Past and Present*, CXII (1986) p. 67.

Chapter 10

1. *Ben Jonson: A Life*, p. 265. For a reading of the 'Execration', see van den Berg, *Ben Jonson's Poetry*, pp. 155–9.
2. See C. J. Sisson, 'Ben Jonson of Gresham College', *Times Literary Supplement*, 21 September 1951, p. 604; and Herford and Simpson, *BJ*, vol. II, pp. 417–35.
3. Ll. 4–5, 119–20. Text is modernised from Phyllis Brooks Bartlett (ed.), *The Poems of George Chapman* (1941; repr. New York, 1962), pp. 374–8.
4. See Herford and Simpson, *BJ*, vol. XI, pp. 593–4. The Simpsons date Chapman's poem in 1634 and link it to Jonson's quarrel with Inigo Jones; see ibid., vol. X, pp. 692–7. This date seems late to me.
5. See *M.P.* X and XI. Browne's work was dedicated to Jonson's patron the Earl of Pembroke; Brooke was a member of the Mermaid and Mitre Tavern groups. For Wither and the Spenserian poets, see Norbrook, *Poetry and Politics*, pp. 195–234; Joan Grundy, *The Spenserian Poets* (London, 1969); and Allan Pritchard, '*Abuses Stript and Whipt* and Wither's Imprisonment', *Review of English Studies*, New Series, XIV (1963) 337–45.
6. *Letters*, ed. MacLure, vol. II, p. 473. For James' proclamation of 24 December 1620 'Against Excess of Lavish and Licentious Speech of Matters of State', see Larkin and Hughes (eds), *Stuart Royal Proclamations*, vol. I, pp. 495–6.

7. See Parry, 'The Politics of the Jacobean Masque', in Mulryne and Shewring (eds), *Theatre and Government*, p. 112; Sara Pearl, 'Sounding to Present Occasions: Jonson's Masques of 1620–5' in David Lindley (ed.) *The Court Masque* (Manchester, 1984) pp. 60–77; and David Norbrook, 'The Reformation of the Masque', ibid., pp. 94–110.

8. See Thomas Cogswell, *The Blessed Revolution: English Politics and the Coming of War, 1621–1624* (Cambridge, 1989).

9. See George Parfitt, 'History and Ambiguity: Jonson's "A Speech according to Horace"', *Studies in English Literature*, XIX (1979) pp. 85–92; Judith K. Gardiner, 'Jonson's Friend Colby', *Notes and Queries*, New Series, XXII (1975) pp. 306–7; Richard C. Newton, '"Goe, quit 'hem all": Ben Jonson and Formal Verse Satire', *Studies in English Literature*, XVI (1976) pp. 105–16; and Thomas Cogswell, 'The Path to Elizium "Lately Discovered": Drayton and the Early Stuart Court', *Huntington Library Quarterly*, LIV (1991) pp. 209–15.

10. See Herford and Simpson, *BJ*, vol. X, p. 213.

11. Reprinted in Herford and Simpson, *BJ*, vol. XI, pp. 385–6.

12. For Jonson's implied allusions to Jones, see Peterson, *Imitation and Praise*, pp. 136–55.

13. For background, see the essays by Gordon and Jordan cited above in ch. 6, n. 23.

14. See Riggs, *Ben Jonson: A Life*, p. 4.

15. For Jonson's sources, see Herford and Simpson, *BJ*, vol. II, pp. 178–84; and Anthony Parr (ed.), *The Staple of News* (Manchester, 1988) pp. 11–20.

16. See Parr, ibid., pp. 22–31.

17. See Pearl, 'Sounding to Present Occasion', in Lindley (ed.), *The Court Masque*, pp. 61–3.

18. 'The Prison-House of the Canon: Allegorical Form and Posterity in Ben Jonson's *The Staple of Newes*', *Medieval and Renaissance Drama in English*, II (1985) p. 262.

19. See Herford and Simpson, *BJ*, vol. IX, p. 251.

20. See Kevin Sharpe, *The Personal Rule of Charles I* (New Haven, Conn., 1992) pp. 209–40.

21. See the theatrical annals in G. E. Bentley, *The Jacobean and Caroline Stage*, 7 vols. (Oxford, 1941–68) vol. VI, pp. 61–77. I see no evidence that Jonson was any more out of favour in this period than other masque writers.

22. See Sharpe, *Personal Rule*, pp. 9–23, 105–30.

23. See Herford and Simpson, *BJ*, vol. I, pp. 236–7, 240–1 and vol. XI, pp. 585–6. King Charles intervened directly in the appointment of the next chronologer, Thomas May; see Bradley and Adams (eds), *Jonson Allusion Book*, p. 199.

24. See Kevin Sharpe, 'The Earl of Arundel, His Circle and the Opposition to the Duke of Buckingham, 1618–1628', in Kevin Sharpe (ed.), *Faction and Parliament: Essays on Early Stuart History* (Oxford, 1978) pp. 209–44; and Conrad Russell, *Parliaments and English Politics 1621–1629* (Oxford, 1979).

25. See Sharpe, *Sir Robert Cotton*, pp. 140–6, 235–40; and David Sandler Berkowitz, *John Selden's Formative Years: Politics and Society in Early Seventeenth-Century England* (London, 1988).
26. Herford and Simpson, *BJ*, vol. XI, pp. 384–5; and Devra Kifer, 'Too Many Cookes: An Addition to the Printed Text of Jonson's *Staple of Newes*', *English Language Notes*, XI (1974) pp. 264–71.
27. Jonson's deposition and the poem are reprinted in Herford and Simpson, *BJ*, vol. I, pp. 242–4.
28. Aubrey, *Brief Lives*, p. 178. Herford and Simpson's suggestion that Jonson had two strokes (see *BJ*, vol. II, p. 191) was later corrected at vol. III, p. 606. His letter to the Earl of Newcastle says explicitly that he was struck with the palsy 'in the year 1628'; see *BJ*, vol. I, p. 213.
29. See Herford and Simpson, *BJ*, vol. I, pp. 244–8.
30. See Herford and Simpson, *BJ*, vol. I, pp. 240–1.
31. Quoted in Aubrey, *Brief Lives*, p. 180. For Jonson's financial circumstances, see Frances Teague, 'Ben Jonson's Poverty', *Biography*, II (1979) pp. 260–5.
32. *Ben Jonson: A Life*, p. 306.
33. See Appendix II, '*The New Inn* and *Love's Pilgrimage*', in Michael Hattaway (ed.), *The New Inn* (Manchester, 1984) pp. 229–30; and Harriet Hawkins, 'The Idea of a Theater in Jonson's *The New Inn*', *Renaissance Drama*, IX (1966) pp. 205–26.
34. The following discussion of Lovel as a version of Jonson and his patrons is indebed to Barton, *Ben Jonson: Dramatist*, pp. 258–84, and L. A. Beaurline, *Jonson and Elizabethan Comedy: Essays in Dramatic Rhetoric* (San Marino, Calif., 1978) pp. 261–72.
35. See Erica Veevers, *Images of Love and Religion: Queen Henrietta Maria and Court Entertainments* (Cambridge, 1989) pp. 14–47.
36. See II.v.77–140 and IV.iii. 4–17. Beaumont and Fletcher make comedy of Don Zanchio's insistence on following the principles of Carranza in *Love's Pilgrimage* V.iv, but since their aristocratic characters all operate by codes of honour, the satiric effect is muted.
37. Compare John Lemly's observation that Jonson's 'late poems often seem personal essays toward a perfect self-containment at odds with the personality of the legendary Ben' ('Masks and Self-Portraits in Jonson's Late Poetry', *English Literary History*, XLIV [1977] p. 263).
38. 'To the Memory,' ll. 64, 68; *Conv.*, l. 45; *Disc.*, ll. 814–18. For Jonson's appropriation of Shakespeare as the model of an Horatian aesthetic, see Peterson, *Imitation and Praise*, pp. 158–94.
39. See John Freehafer, 'Leonard Digges, Ben Jonson, and the Beginning of Shakespeare Idolatry', *Shakespeare Quarterly*, XXI (1970) pp. 63–75.
40. For Brome, see Herford and Simpson, *BJ*, vol. X, pp. 331–2.
41. Replies to Jonson's 'Ode to Himself' are reprinted in Appendix I of Hathaway (ed.), *The New Inn*, pp. 210–28.
42. See Herford and Simpson, *BJ*, vol. XI, p. 416.
43. Reprinted in Herford and Simpson, *BJ*, vol. XI, pp. 390–1, 402–4.
44. See Herford and Simpson, *BJ*, vol. VIII, pp. 653–7 and vol. XI, pp. 294–300. For classical antecedents of the Apollo Room at the shrine at Delphi, see Peterson, *Imitation and Praise*, pp. 113–34.

45. John Buxton, 'The Poet's Hall Called Apollo', *Modern Language Review*, XLVIII (1953) pp. 54–6; for Jonson's convivial laws, see ch. 7 above.
46. 'To His Noble Father', ll. 19–24.
47. Herford & Simpson, *BJ*, vol. XI, pp. 419–20.
48. For criticism, see Ian Donaldson, 'Jonson's Ode to Sir Lucius Cary and Sir H. Morison', *Studies in the Literary Imagination*, VI (1973) pp. 139–52; Peterson, *Imitation and Praise*, pp. 195–232; Mary I. Oates, 'Jonson's "Ode Pindarick" and the Doctrine of Imitation', *Papers on Language and Literature*, XI (1975) pp. 126–48; Suzanne Woods, 'Ben Jonson's Cary-Morison Ode: Some Observations on Structure and Form', *Studies in English Literature*, XVIII (1978) pp. 57–74; Stella P. Revard, 'Pindar and Jonson's Cary-Morison Ode', in Claude J. Summers and Ted-Larry Pebworth (eds), *Classic and Cavalier: Essays on Jonson and the Sons of Ben* (Pittsburg, 1982) pp. 17–30; and W. Scott Blanchard, '*Ut Encyclopedia Poesis*: Ben Jonson's Cary-Morison Ode and the "Spheare" of "Humanitie"', *Studies in Philology*, LXXXVII (1990) pp. 195–220.
49. For Cary's elegy, see Kenneth B. Murdock, 'An Elegy on Sir Henry Morison, by Lucius Cary, Viscount Falkland', *Harvard Studies and Notes in Philology and Literature*, XX (1938) pp. 29–42.
50. See Butler, 'Reform or Reverence? The Politics of the Caroline Masque', in Mulryne and Shewring (eds), *Theatre and Government*, pp. 130–2.
51. See Veevers, *Images of Love and Religion*, pp. 120–30.
52. See R. I. C. Graziani, 'Ben Jonson's *Chloridia*: Fame and Her Attendants', *Review of English Studies*, New Series, VII (1956) pp. 56–8.
53. See Martin Butler, 'Ecclesiastical Censorship of Early Stuart Drama: The Case of Jonson's *The Magnetic Lady*', *Modern Philology*, LXXXIX (1992) pp. 469–81.
54. See Herford and Simpson, *BJ*, vol. X, p. 656, and vol. XI, p. 158.
55. See the articles by Gordon and Jordan cited in ch. 6.
56. Herford and Simpson, *BJ*, vol. XI, p. 419.
57. Sir Henry Herbert's Office Book, quoted in Herford and Simpson, *BJ*, vol. III, p. 3.
58. See Herford and Simpson, *BJ*, vol. IX, pp. 268–75; and Barton, *Ben Jonson: Dramatist*, pp. 300–37.
59. 'Stuart Politics in Jonson's *Tale of a Tub*', *Modern Language Review*, LXXXV (1990) pp. 23 and 28.
60. See John P. Cutts, '"When were the Senses in such order plac'd"', *Comparative Drama*. IV (1970) pp. 52–62.
61. See Herford and Simpson, vol. X, pp. 700 and 706–9.
62. Quoted in Butler, 'Stuart Politics', p. 18; see also Marcus, *Politics of Mirth*, pp. 129–33.
63. See Raymond Urban, 'The Somerset Affair, the Belvoir Witches, and Jonson's Pastoral Comedy', *Harvard Library Bulletin*, XXIII (1975) pp. 295–323. Urban's allegorical reading is undercut by the untenable assumption that a witch named 'Mogibell Overbury' represented Sir Thomas Overbury, not the Countess of Suffolk.
64. Herford and Simpson, *BJ*, vol. I, p. 211. For the 1631 plays and the 1640 Folio, see vol. IX, pp. 85–103.

65. See *Und.* LXXVIII, 'An Epigram to My Muse, the Lady Digby, on Her Husband, Sir Kenelm Digby'. Jonson borrowed from Spenser for the plot of *The Sad Shepherd*, the diction of *The Tale of a Tub* and details of the Cary–Morison ode. See James A. Riddell and Stanley Stewart, 'Jonson Reads "The Ruines of Time"', *Studies in Philology*, LXXXVII (1990) pp. 427–55.
66. For Morley, see Aubrey, *Brief Lives*, p. 180.
67. Herford and Simpson, *BJ*, vol. I, p. 249.
68. Quoted in Wayne H. Phelps, 'The Date of Ben Jonson's Death', *Notes and Queries*, New Series, XXVII (1980) pp. 146–8.
69. See Joseph Quincy Adams, 'The Bones of Ben Jonson', *Studies in Philology*, XVI (1919) pp. 289–302.

Epilogue

1. Herford and Simpson, *BJ*, vol XI, p. 509.
2. 'Brainchildren: Self-representation and Patriarchy in Ben Jonson's Early Works', in Dale B. J. Randall and Joseph A. Porter (eds), *Renaissance Papers: 1986*, (n.p., 1986) p. 59.
3. Reprinted in Herford and Simpson, *BJ*, vol. XI, pp. 429–81. For economy of reference, citations will be to the numbers given the poems by Herford and Simpson, followed by line numbers.
4. T. S. Eliot, *Selected Essays*, New Edition (New York, 1950), p. 127.
5. Renée Hannaford, ' "Express'd by mee": Carew on Donne and Jonson', *Studies in Philology*, LXXXIV (1987) p. 64.
6. See Greene, *The Light in Troy*, pp. 285–6.
7. See Earl Miner, *The Cavalier Mode from Jonson to Cotton* (Princeton, 1971) pp. 43–99; and Martindale, 'The Horace of Ben Jonson and his Heirs', pp. 67–85.
8. *The Light in Troy*, p. 287.
9. See Appendix II of R. J. Kaufmann, *Richard Brome: Caroline Playwright* (New York, 1961) pp. 178–83. For the dramatic works of Jonson's disciples in general, see Joe Lee Davis, *The Sons of Ben: Jonsonian Comedy in Caroline England* (Detroit, 1967).
10. However, for an admiring reading of the play as an image of England in disarray, see Martin Butler, *Theatre and Crisis 1632–1642* (Cambridge, 1984) pp. 151–7.
11. Donald S. McClure (ed.), *A Critical Edition of Richard Brome's 'The Weeding of Covent Garden' and 'The Sparagus Garden'* (New York, 1980) p. 212.

Index

Abbot, George, Archbishop of Canterbury, 119, 139
Academy Royal, The, 152
Aesop, 3, 89
Alabaster, William, 29
alchemy and other pseudo-sciences, 19, 103, 109–11, 139–40
see also astrology
Alexander, Sir William, 156
Alleyn, Edward, 27
Allot, Robert, 40, 182
Anabaptists, *see* Puritans
Anacreontics, 134, 135, 156
Anne, Queen, 65–6, 78–86 *passim*, 115, 128, 130–2, 136, 157
Apollo Club/Room, The, 103, 174–5, 187
Archer, Thomas, 166
Archilochus, 35
Argyle, Earl of, *see* Campbell, Archibald
Aristophanes, 36, 38, 165, 167
Aristotle, 142
Artillery Company of London, The Honourable, 163–4
astrology, 110
Athenaeus, 211n.31
Aubigny, Lady, *see* Stuart, Katherine
Aubigny, Lord, *see* Stuart, Esmé
Aubrey, John, 13, 15, 44, 88, 110, 220n.24
Ayton, Sir Robert, 156

Bacon, Francis, Lord Verulam, 73, 103, 155, 199n.4
Banqueting House, The, 144, 159
Barclay, John, 161
Beale, John, 182
Beaulieu, Jean, 137–8
Beaumont, Francis, viii, 98, 102–3, 106, 185, 187
Bedford, Countess of, *see* Russell, Lucy

Birck, Sixt, 5
Bird, William, 17
Blackfriars (the London district), 94–5, 109, 112
Blackfriars Theatre, 47, 52, 54, 61, 108, 113, 170, 173, 200n.14
Blyenberch, Abraham van, 49, 53
Boccaccio, Giovanni, 150
Bolton, Edmund, 97–8, 152
Bond, John, 100
Bowes, Sir Hierome, 151
Brechtian dialectic, 73
Brent, Nathaniel, 155
Brett, Rebecca (BJ's mother?), 2
Brett, Robert (BJ's step-father?), 1–2, 11, 13, 194n.2, 195n.1
Brett, Thomas, 13, 195n.3
Brett family, 2
Bridling, Saddling and Riding of a Rich Churl in Hampshire, The, 111
Brome, Richard, 173, 187–9, 211n.30
Brooke, Christopher, 100, 162
Browne, Robert, 29–30
Browne, William, 162
Buc, Sir George, 45
Buchanan, George, 65
Buchler, Joannes, 34–5
Buckingham, Duke of, *see* Villiers, George
Bulstrode, Cecelia, 131–2
Burbage, James, 200n.14
Burbage, Richard, 61
Burghley, Lord, *see* Cecil, William
Busino, Orazio, 154
Butcher, Richard, 174
Butter, Nathaniel, 166

C., I. (author of verses on *The New Inn*), 174
Caesar, Julius, 3
Cambridge University, 12–13, 61, 78, 87, 114, 119, 152
St. John's College, 13
Trinity College, 13

227